FAILURE-FREE EDUCATION?

David Reynolds is recognised internationally as one of the founders of the school effectiveness and school improvement movement, and *Failure-Free Education?* brings together for the first time many of his most influential and provocative pieces. Drawing on the author's work from over three decades, these extracts from his seminal books, chapters, papers and articles combine to give a unique overview of how the movement developed, the problems involved in the application of the knowledge and the discipline's potentially glittering future now.

The book also covers the issues raised by, and lessons learned from, his close involvement with English government and educational policy-making from the mid 1990s to date. The book also includes a substantial new 'overview'.

This book is essential reading for those who seek to understand how we can make every school a good school, and what the obstacles may be to achieving that goal.

David Reynolds is Professor of Education at the University of Plymouth, UK.

CONTEXTS OF LEARNING

Series editors: Bert Creemers, David Reynolds,
Janet Hageman Chrispeels

FAILURE-FREE EDUCATION?

THE PAST, PRESENT AND FUTURE OF SCHOOL EFFECTIVENESS AND SCHOOL IMPROVEMENT

David Reynolds

Routledge
Taylor & Francis Group

LONDON AND NEW YORK

First published 2010
by Routledge
2 Park Square, Milton Park, Abingdon, Oxon OX14 4RN

Simultaneously published in the USA and Canada
by Routledge
270 Madison Avenue, New York, NY 10016

Routledge is an imprint of the Taylor & Francis Group, an informa business

First issued in paperback 2011

Typeset in Bembo by Keystroke, Tettenhall, Wolverhampton

British Library Cataloguing in Publication Data
A catalogue record for this book is available from the British Library

Library of Congress Cataloging-in-Publication Data
Reynolds, David.
    Failure-free education? : the past, present, and future of school effectiveness and
school improvement / David Reynolds. — 1st ed.
        p. cm.
    Includes bibliographical references and index.
    1. School improvement programs. 2. Teacher effectiveness. I. Title.
    LB2822.84.G7R49 2010
    371.2'07—dc22   2009034684

ISBN10: 0–415–36783–2 (hbk)
ISBN10: 0–415–61984–X (pbk)
ISBN10: 0–203–02023–5 (ebk)

ISBN13: 978–0–415–36783–7 (hbk)
ISBN13: 978–0–415–61984–4 (pbk)
ISBN13: 978–0–203–02023–4 (ebk)

Contents

Figures and tables

Figures

Tables

Acknowledgements

Materials in this book have the following origins:

Chapter 1 is new material.

Chapter 2 was originally published in M. Hammersley and P. Woods (Ed.) (1976) *The Process of Schooling*. London: Routledge & Kegan Paul.

Chapter 3 was originally published in L. Stoll and K. Myers (Eds.) (1997) *No Quick Fixes: Perspectives on Schools in Difficulties*. Lewes: Falmer Press.

Chapter 4 was originally published in *The Times Educational Supplement*, 7 June 1996.

Chapter 5 was originally published in D. Reynolds, B. P. M. Creemers, S. Stringfield, C. Teddlie and E. Schaffer (2002) *World-Class Schools: International Perspectives in School Effectiveness*. London: RoutledgeFalmer.

Chapter 6 was originally published in BERA, *Research Intelligence* (1998), No. 26.

Chapter 7 was originally published as D. Muijs and D. Reynolds (2000) 'School effectiveness and teacher effectiveness: Some preliminary findings from the evaluation of the Mathematics Enhancement Programme', in *School Effectiveness and School Improvement*, Vol. 11, No. 2.

Chapter 8 was originally published as D. Reynolds, S. Stringfield, and E. Schaffer (2006) 'The High Reliability Schools Project', in A. Harris and J. Chrispeels (Eds) *Improving Schools and Educational Systems*. London: Routledge.

Chapter 9 was originally published as part of Department for Education and Employment (1998) *Numeracy Matters: The Preliminary Report of the Numeracy Task Force*. London: HMSO for DfEE.

Chapter 10 is a heavily edited version of what was originally published as D. Reynolds, D. Hopkins, D. Potter and C. Chapman (2001) *School Improvement for Schools Facing Challenging Circumstances*. London: HMSO for DfES.

Chapter 11 was originally published in National College for School Leadership (2006) *Teaching Texts*. Nottingham: NCSL.

Chapter 12 was published in an extended version by the National College for School Leadership (2007) Nottingham: NCSL.

Chapter 13 was published as D. Reynolds and C. Teddlie (2000) 'The future agenda for school effectiveness research', in C. Teddlie and D. Reynolds (Eds) *The International Handbook of School Effectiveness Research*. London: Falmer Press.

Chapter 14 was originally published in D. Hopkins, D. Reynolds and J. Gray (2005) *School Improvement: Lessons from Research*. London: HMSO for DfES.

Chapter 15 is an unpublished paper presented to the DCSF Seminar on 'Twenty-first century schools: Levers for the future of the schools system' on 27 March 2009. It was written with Paul Clarke and Tony Kelly.

With the exception of Chapters 9, 10 and 12, all other chapters are exactly as originally published.

1

Introduction

School effectiveness and school improvement in
retrospect, 1971–2010, and prospect, 2010
onwards

Introduction

No discipline in the history of modern educational research has risen, and yet
subsequently fallen from view, with greater speed than that of School Effectiveness
and School Improvement (SESI). From a position of total marginality in the 1970s
and 1980s in the educational research communities of only a couple of countries
like the UK and USA, SESI came in the 1990s to be a worldwide phenomenon
and to have a huge intellectual reach and also closely developed links with the
policy-making and, to an extent, practitioner communities in the UK particularly.
Put simply, there were perhaps half a dozen British research articles on SESI-related
topics in the mid 1970s, and maybe a dozen from the United States. By the time
we came to review the world literature for *The International Handbook of School
Effectiveness Research* (Teddlie and Reynolds, 2000), there were over 2,000 references. Now, at the time of writing in 2009, there are probably 3,000 and maybe
more in a still rapidly growing field, from probably 30 or more countries.

But the rapid ascendancy of the discipline, the policy impact in some countries
and the publicity that the work generated set up deep oppositional forces in some
countries that conspired to make the discipline insecure, in professional doubt and
frequently criticised. As fast as doors had opened to it in the 1990s, they closed to
it in the 2000s. Understanding why something so apparently useful in its endeavours
– a simple desire to find out what makes a 'good' school and how to make all
schools 'good' so that all schools could be helped – evoked such hostility is the
subject of our first task in this Introduction.

The medical foundations of the discipline

It is not generally acknowledged nowadays but SESI in the UK had its origins in medical research. The very first findings on school differences came from a team headed by Power (1967, 1972), who were actually working in a Medical Research Council Social Medicine Unit. My own early work came at a time when I was a member of the scientific staff of the Medical Research Council Epidemiology Unit in Cardiff (Reynolds and Murgatroyd, 1974), then headed by Archie Cochrane, who was to become subsequently lionised for his contribution to evaluating medical practice. Indeed, he had tried to apply the same medical research techniques – the randomised controlled trial – to education, in the world's first randomised trial of the effects of corporal punishment upon pupils' misbehaviour, showing a substantial negative effect! I had joined the Unit in 1971 and my own most substantial publication from this time is reproduced as Chapter 2 of this collection.

Work also came from a child psychiatrist, Dennis Gath (1972), who looked at variations in child guidance rates between schools, and of course from Michael Rutter, a child psychologist who co-authored the famous 'Rutter Report', *Fifteen Thousand Hours* (Rutter *et al.*, 1979). Peter Mortimore, who made a major contribution with his 'Rutter for the primary sector' in the book *School Matters* (Mortimore *et al.*, 1988), was a member of the Rutter team. Louise Stoll and Pam Sammons, who both worked with Peter Mortimore, were themselves to make major contributions to the fields of SI and SE respectively.

This medical influence was compounded by the fact that the Association for Child Psychology and Psychiatry funded for over a decade the termly meetings of the School Differences Research Group, which met in London from the mid 1970s and had a mailing list of up to 50 or so SESI researchers, spreading increasingly in its reach to researchers outside the UK through the 1980s.

The criticisms

The medical background was responsible for a number of the characteristics of the discipline, which proved to be both its strength and its weakness. The strong quantitative, positivistic orientation endeared it to politicians and policy-makers, who appreciated the apparent certainties rather than the multiple perspectives beloved of some, but this orientation had been rendered unfashionable by the rise of interpretive, naturalistic and qualitative perspectives from the early 1970s that focused more on school processes than school organisation, and upon the 'culture' of schools more than their structure.

The core value beliefs of SESI – that more children gaining more conventionally defined academic achievement was a 'good' thing that would be associated with societal progress – did not appeal to those who wished to 'problematise' school outcomes, and who argued that other, more non-conventional outcomes were important for the system to aim at also.

The close association between 'New Labour' (as it was subsequently to be described) from the mid 1990s until the early 2000s may have been something that many of us within SESI were proud of, since this perhaps meant that more pupils would do better, but this link generated suspicion amongst many academics in other areas of educational research. It is possible that these close links generated jealousy too. Frequent criticisms that SESI was managerialist in its orientation, allied to a 'technocratic' paradigm and 'singing the policy-makers' tune' were also made.

Nevertheless, SESI persons did sit at the same table as government in a manner that horrified many – Michael Barber headed the Standards and Effectiveness Unit, and was followed by David Hopkins. I chaired the Numeracy Task Force, was on the Literacy Task Force, sat on the boards of government agencies and was a part-time adviser to the DfES (as it was called). This closeness between the leaders of an academic discipline and educational policy was unusual, and was argued by some to be restricting of the conventional role of an academic to critically evaluate ideas from wherever they came, including from government.

There was also one last criticism often made of SESI: that the discipline was inherently a conservative one, inasmuch as celebrating and publicising the schools that often did relatively well *within the existing range of variation* was a conservative act, since it did not study the possibility of alternative, non-current provision being useful or 'excellent'. There was, with SESI, no possibilitarianism, as it were.

A final factor predisposing to academic criticism was that SESI 'cut against the grain', as it were, of the emotional, professional and political characteristics of worldwide educational research communities, particularly that of the UK. Alexander (1996) expressed this view beautifully when he, with rancid intellectual snobbery, talked of some of us in SESI as 'the Essex men and women' of educational research. Alexander's (2000) later tirade against SESI was made in a book which became the AERA Outstanding Book of the Year, suggesting that rancid intellectual snobbery might have become worryingly widespread across the planet!

Drawing on the additional deep academic distrust of the 'applied' in educational research, and the British historical elevation of the pure or the 'blue skies' approach, SESI was – well – just not British in many academic eyes! That not one single scholar from the SESI community, or from the educational administration community, or the educational management discipline, has ever been on any of the Research Assessment Exercise panels from the inception of the assessment process in 1992 – in marked contrast to the positive, inclusive treatment of the largely defunct, irrelevant and small-scale History of Education community – tells its own sad tale of British academic snobbery.

The SESI community and its characteristics

The reaction to SESI from others did not really worry the SESI community. Its members were convinced that their commitments on intellectual and policy matters were helpful to society, teachers and children, and that our close influence with policy was nothing to be ashamed of. Indeed, we were proud of it in the 1990s.

First, we believed that school effectiveness research had convincingly helped to destroy the belief that schools could do nothing to change the society around them, and also helped to destroy the myth that the influence of family background upon children's development was so strong that they were unable to be affected by their schools. In the 1960s there had been a widespread belief that 'schools make no difference' (Bernstein, 1968), which reflected the results of American research (e.g. Coleman *et al.*, 1966; Jencks *et al.*, 1972), and the disappointed hopes that followed from the perceived failure of systemic reform, enhanced expenditure and the other policies of social engineering that constituted the liberal dream of the 1960s (Reynolds and Sullivan, 1981). We believed we were helping to banish this.

The second positive effect of SESI, we believed, was that in addition to destroying assumptions of the impotence of education, SESI took as its defining variables the key factors of school and pupil outcomes, from which it 'back-mapped' to look at the processes which appear to be related to positive outcomes. SESI – and this is very different from many educational research specialities – did not celebrate new policies because they were new or because practitioners liked them, or opposed new policies because they potentially damaged the interests of educational producers. For SESI, the 'touchstone criteria' to be applied to all educational matters concerned whether children learned more or less because of the policy or practice. Fads, fallacies and policy and practice fantasies largely passed SESI by because we tried to form our views of the educational world on a scientific, rigorous basis.

Third, SESI showed teachers to be important determinants of children's educational and social attainments and therefore we believed we had managed to enhance and build professional self-esteem. It was always unclear why teachers accepted responsibility for their individual impact upon individual children, and upon individual classes, but would not accept the importance of their impact upon *groups* of children in schools as *groups* of teachers. SESI hoped that we had enhanced professional self-esteem by emphasising this.

Fourth, and this was the last of our SESI positive contributions, we began the creation of a 'known to be valid' knowledge base which we believed could act as a foundation for training (see the early reviews in Gray, 1990; Mortimore, 1991; Reynolds and Cuttance, 1992; Rutter, 1983; and Scheerens, 1992). With knowledge of school and of teacher effectiveness, the latter of which had unfortunately to be imported from North America until recently because of the historic antipathy towards research in this area in the United Kingdom (see Creemers, 1994), we could avoid the necessity of the endless reinvention of the 'teaching wheel' and could move teachers to an advanced level conceptually and practically, or so we believed!

There was, though, one most unfortunate 'downside', or negative feature, associated with the popularity of school effectiveness research, which was that we were instrumental in creating a quite widespread, popular view that schools did not just make *a* difference, they made *all* the difference. School effectiveness researchers in the UK usually actively sought public attention for their research papers and their books: journal editors and publishers were keen to oblige with this, for their own material reasons. The result was that school quality, the variation in that quality, and the *remedies* for variation in that quality became more extensively discussed topics in the United Kingdom than in most other societies. Politicians of a right-wing persuasion were able to use the climate of opinion that had been partially created by SESI both to attack school standards generally and to propose the improvement of those standards by use of what were clearly non-rational methods, their argument being that the situation was so dire and perilous that urgent action was called for. Indeed, for a long time in the UK the performance measures of schools used in the national performance tables themselves explained all school variation as due to schools, since no non-school background factors were measured.

The UK knowledge base

SESI's rise in the UK was rapid, in terms of the quantity of work and the quality of that work also. Key studies in the 1980s involved:

- 'value-added' comparisons of educational authorities on their academic outcomes (Department of Education and Science, 1983, 1984; Gray et al., 1984; Gray and Jesson, 1987; Willms, 1987; Woodhouse and Goldstein, 1988);
- comparisons of 'selective' school systems with comprehensive or 'all-ability' systems (Gray et al., 1983; Reynolds et al., 1987; Steedman, 1980, 1983);
- work into the scientific properties of school effects, such as their size (Gray, 1981, 1982; Gray et al., 1986), the differential effectiveness of different academic sub-units or departments (Fitz-Gibbon, 1985; Fitz-Gibbon et al., 1989; Willms and Cuttance, 1985), contextual or 'balance' effects (Willms, 1985, 1986, 1987) and the differential effectiveness of schools upon pupils of different background characteristics (Aitkin and Longford, 1986; Nuttall et al., 1989);

Towards the end of the 1980s, two landmark studies appeared concerning school effectiveness in primary schools (Mortimore et al., 1988) and in secondary schools (Smith and Tomlinson, 1989). The Mortimore study was notable for the very wide range of outcomes on which schools were assessed (including mathematics, reading, writing, attendance, behaviour and attitudes to school), for the collection of a wide range of data upon school processes and, for the first time in British school effectiveness research, a focus upon teaching and classroom processes.

The Smith and Tomlinson (1989) study was notable for the large differences shown in academic effectiveness between schools, and for certain groups of pupils a substantial variation in examination results between similar individuals in different subjects, reflecting the influence of different school departments – out of 18 schools, the school that was positioned 'first' on value-added mathematics attainment, for example, was 'fifteenth' in English achievement (after allowance had been made for intake quality).

From 1990 onwards, work in the United Kingdom was even more productive, notably in the areas of:

- stability over time of the effects, positive or negative, of schools (Goldstein *et al.*, 1993; Gray *et al.*, 1995);
- consistency of the effects of schools upon different outcomes – for example, in terms of different subjects or different outcome domains such as cognitive/affective (Goldstein *et al.*, 1993; Sammons *et al.*, 1993);
- differential effects of schools for different groups of students (for example, of different ethnic or socio-economic backgrounds or with different levels of prior attainment) (Jesson and Gray, 1991; Goldstein *et al.*, 1993; Sammons *et al.*, 1993);
- the relative continuity of the effects of different school sectors over time (Goldstein, 1995; Sammons *et al.*, 1995);
- the existence or size of school effects (Daly, 1991; Gray *et al.*, 1990), where there were strong suggestions that primary school effects were greater than those of secondary schools (Sammons *et al.*, 1993, 1995);
- departmental differences in educational effectiveness (Fitz-Gibbon, 1991, 1992; Sammons *et al.*, 1997).

This, then, was the British knowledge base by the mid 1990s. Overall, it had four positive features:

1 High levels of methodological sophistication, in which the utilisation of a cohort design, matched data on individuals at intake and outcome, and multiple-level methodologies were widely agreed as axiomatic. The UK was also in the forefront of the development of multilevel statistical modelling (Goldstein, 1995).

2 The use of multiple measures of pupil outcomes, which included in British work those such as locus of control, attendance, delinquency, behavioural problems, attitudes to school, self-esteem and attitudes to school subjects as well as academic outcomes (see Mortimore *et al.*, 1988; Reynolds and Sullivan, 1981, for example).

3 The use of multiple measures of pupil intakes into school, utilising prior achievement as well as factors such as age, gender, parental socio-economic status, parental education and parental ethnicity or racial background. Cutting-edge research from other countries (e.g. Teddlie and Stringfield, 1993) often utilised either achievement measures or detailed socio-economic data upon background, but rarely both, as in British best practice.

4 The development of advanced conceptualisations and findings about the role of the school level in potentiating or hindering adolescent development, where the early findings within the British sociology of education were usefully built on by the major studies outlined above.

If there were any intellectual 'downsides' to the British SESI tradition in the 1990s they would have lain in the following areas:

- The great majority of British studies that collected data upon school and classroom processes sampled only within socio-economic contexts that were disadvantaged and deprived (e.g. Rutter in a London borough with high levels of social deprivation, and myself in the Welsh mining valleys). This resulted in an inability within the British research community to further investigate the variation in 'what works' by context, which was such an exciting and potentially productive feature of the American school effectiveness research tradition (e.g. Wimpelberg et al., 1989; Hallinger and Murphy, 1986; Teddlie and Stringfield, 1993) that emerged in the 1990s. It was also possible that the near exclusion within British sampling frames of very advantaged catchment areas, of independent schools with intakes from very affluent backgrounds, and of religiously administered schools with intakes of probably above-average achievement levels might have both constrained variance in organisational practices at the school level and also resulted in the generation of accounts of organisational functioning that were not necessarily applicable to all school types.
- The absence of more than a handful of attempts to discern those classroom, or instructional, processes that might have been related to student outcomes, reflecting the absence within a British context of the focus upon classroom learning environments that had been evident within the American research traditions of learning environment research (Good, 1983) and within the Dutch tradition of learning and instruction (Creemers, 1994).

The organisation and internationalisation of SESI

SESI in the UK was helped considerably in its rapid rise by the formation in 1988 of ICSEI, the International Congress for School Effectiveness and Improvement, which held its inaugural meeting in London in January 1988. ICSEI had been the vision of an American, Dale Mann, who convened a small planning meeting of four people in April 1987 at AERA. For the London meeting, which I organised, we had expected about 20 or 30 people, but over 100 turned up, to be billeted in cramped, cold and dusty student accommodation and to be fed at the initial reception with pork pies and cream sherry from a local supermarket, because we had no resources. Thirty people turned up from the Netherlands, when none of us in the UK knew that there were any School Effectiveness and School Improvement researchers in the Netherlands!

Out of the founding of ICSEI came that of the international journal *School Effectiveness and School Improvement (SESI)*, which I co-edited with Bert Creemers, who himself was to make a major contribution to the field in many areas. SESI was in the benchmark American ISI list of journals which were covered by 'Current Contents' by 1996, an extraordinary achievement for a journal in a fledgling field.

ICSEI was of huge importance. Symbolically, it was vital – some annual ICSEI meetings generated a turnout of 500 to 600 researchers, policy-makers and practitioners. Organisationally, it meant that SESI was a truly international field from its beginning, with no need to try to desperately invent an international reach in the 1990s, as was the case with many other educational research specialities in the UK. Researchers particularly were increasingly involved in networks that spread across multiple countries. The interests of the effectiveness 'researchers' and the school 'improvers', who had come from two very different historical paradigms and had brought emotional and practical baggage that might have proven difficult to jettison, were also given an organisational framework in which paradigm building of a new kind could take place. Indeed, many historical school improvers such as David Hopkins – who made a major contribution – became, over time, somewhat similar to the school effectiveness persons they had once criticised.

In the UK and every country, the 'recipe' of the effective school was very similar, and was espoused to practitioners with some force. The effective schools:

- had good leadership provided by the Headteacher, with more effective schools having better Head/Deputy Head relations, and had a management style and structure that involved Heads setting goals, establishing directions and possessing that most popular of 1990s contemporary management terms, a 'mission'. They also had an active involvement of staff in planning the means to achieve school goals through staff involvement in decision making. The effective school had a balance, then, in its management between vertical push and horizontal pull, between laterality or diffusion, and centralisation. Indeed, it possessed a balance between managerialism and collegiality that was ensured by having elements of both present at the same time;
- had academic 'push' or academic 'press', involving high expectations of what pupils could achieve, utilising strategies that ensured large amounts of learning time (such as well-managed lesson transitions), utilising homework to expand learning time and to involve parents, and entering a high proportion of pupils for public examinations to ensure they remained 'hooked' in their final years;
- had parental involvement, both to ensure the participation of significant others in children's lives in the rewarding of achievement and effort, and also to ensure that in cases of difficulty, the parents would, if it was appropriate to do so, support the school against the child;
- had pupil involvement, both in the learning situation within the classroom (though here the involvement needed to be within a firm and organised struc-ture) and within the school in societies, sports teams, leadership positions, representative positions, and the like;
- had organisational control of pupils, which was generated by cohesion, con-stancy and consistency within the school. Organisational cohesion was enhanced by both planning and co-ordination of school activities, and by a degree of ownership of the school by the staff itself, to be generated by a good flow of information and by procedures that involved staff in the school organisation. Organisational consistency across lessons in the same subjects, across different subjects in the same years and across different years in the pupil learning experiences they offered was facilitated by development planning and by those forms of professional development which involved utilising members of staff as 'buddies' to each other, whereby observation of each other's practice ensured

that the range of individual practice was made clearer to organisational members. Organisational constancy was the final requirement to ensure control, which resulted from a limited turnover in the people who passed through the lives of young people.

The UK SESI community was not the only one that went on a steep curve – of reputation, of the quantity of its knowledge and the quality of its insights – in the 1990s. In the USA, major contributions were made by Charles Teddlie, Sam Stringfield and others. In Canada, Michael Fullan and Ken Leithwood both made major contributions. These were paralleled in the Netherlands by Bert Creemers and Jaap Scheerens. As the new millennium dawned in 2000, there were SESI communities in probably 20 countries around the world, and a presence of some kind in 30 or 40.

However, in few of these countries did the discipline take the same central role in educational policy-making as SESI had acquired in the UK, or the same take-up by practitioner communities. In the USA, School Effectiveness had 'boomed and bust' in the 1980s, and interest then moved on to areas such as restructuring. In the Netherlands, SESI had some links with national inspection agencies, but that was all. In Australia, the Federal Government's national School Effectiveness initiative of the early 1990s, which had involved bringing representatives of the SESI community from Europe to propagandise the field, had waned and sociology of education had largely replaced SESI as the discipline that dealt with school processes.

In the UK, by the early 2000s SESI hit what can only be described as troubled times. The Numeracy and Literacy Strategies – filled with content derived from the research and insight of SESI – had initial promising effects, but then national test scores in the UK plateaued in the early 2000s. The teaching profession thought that they had 'done' School Effectiveness when they had been to those whole Local Education Authority Heads' meetings that initially every LEA organised, in the 1990s, and moved on to other things.

Additionally, the SESI discipline in the UK, as internationally, was still largely the group of academics who had established the field in the 1980s and 1990s. There were few new entrants into the group, and precious few 'crossovers' from other fields. SESI was simply growing old! The criticisms had also been intense. The international ICSEI conferences had also increasingly been hijacked by what might be called 'critical perspectives' that criticised SESI's conventional value positions, its policy involvements in places like the UK, and its historical unwillingness to associate itself with international movements of educational and social change. Indeed, the balance of the annual ICSEI conferences became so loaded towards criticism, and so devoid of the 'normal science', that it often seemed like the annual meeting of the International Geographical Association inviting only speakers who thought the Earth was flat!

In the UK, symbolically, the Standards and Effectiveness Unit was closed down at the Department of Education and Skills. Some of us from the SESI community became less involved in the policy-making community in the early 2000s. The enthusiasm for a contribution from Higher Education itself waned in governmental circles – academics were inconvenient, leaked to the *Times Educational Supplement* and had egos the size of houses! National policy became much more centred on the profession actually helping itself, particularly using leading Headteachers, who could be relied upon to be more supportive than academics and who knew how to wear a good suit. 'By schools – for schools' became a national catchphrase coined by the Specialist Schools and Academies Trust (SSAT) – apparently rather little was to be done by SESI any more.

The tragedy is, though, that SESI in the 1990s and 2000s had been generating material that could have provided – and could still provide if used – the transformation of education in the UK, and internationally. Whilst UK policy-makers and practitioners thought they had 'done' SESI, what they had 'done' was use early, simply limited material that came from SESI's first flowerings. We will return to look at these issues in the Conclusions of this chapter.

Now we move to look less at the SESI community but more in detail at what I, as a SESI person, tried to do, tried to say and tried to write over the last 30 years, and at how the national ebb and flow of SESI shows in my own career and material.

First simple stirrings

My own contributions to SESI in the 1970s, 1980s and 1990s and later form a substantial part of this volume, and hopefully show the development of the field over time as very rapid. The chapter on the 'delinquent school' (Chapter 2) shows just how primitive were the early studies of effectiveness – it showed gross empiricism, and minimal attempts to explain what was the precise relationship between the school effectiveness 'correlates' or 'characteristics' and the outcomes being measured. That the more substantial accounts of classroom and school practices now available make this early work seem so simplistic is a measure of how far we have come.

The study was simple in its methodology – it was a cross-sectional study that collected 'input' and 'output' data upon different groups of children, so one could not be sure that any school differences shown were not the result of differences between the groups of children. The data on the intakes was also deficient – it was on the social class of the school catchment areas (not the children) and on the IQ of the pupils, not on more relevant academic data such as their reading attainment. Interestingly, it related to sociological concerns about youth culture, deviancy and school culture more than it did to mainstream educational research, which of course was strongly arguing that 'schools make no difference'. Higher-quality, cohort-based work from Rutter *et al.* (1979), and in the range of studies that were to appear using the 'input, process, output' framework in the 1980s and 1990s (e.g. Mortimore *et al.*, 1988, Smith and Tomlinson, 1989), were to make up for these deficiencies in my work.

But this chapter had considerable reach in the 1970s and 1980s, partly because it was published in a reader for the Open University course 'Schooling and Society', which provided much of the foundations for the British sociology of education as it peaked in its popularity and professional relevance in the 1970s. Additionally, the chapter was linked to three Open University television programmes based in the Rhondda Valley, programmes that were redolent with themes of fragmented communities, disappointed ideals and disappointed hopes of social and economic change. These gave the research – done as it was on the Rhondda Valley – a considerable airing. Perhaps it was this high visibility that brought both praise and criticism in equal measures, with one critic rather tartly noting that the work was 'widely applauded but highly implausible'!

Between the mid 1970s and the early 1990s, when ICSEI and the SESI journal began to spread and develop the discipline, many of us in the British school effectiveness research community became heavily – and exhaustedly – involved in the dissemination of the knowledge base to teachers, schools and local authorities. There cannot have been an English or Welsh LEA (as was) that I did not lecture in – sometimes in groups of two or three a day, nearly always travelling by car. I can still fully remember one day starting off by car from Cardiff at 4.00 am, lecturing in Newcastle at 11.00 am, going across to Carlisle for another lecture and then going on to Manchester for an evening teachers' meeting. Other researchers had a similar commitment to these activities, which took out large swathes of our time.

In my own case, the 1980s saw the publication (late, of course, which was to become a habit) of *The Comprehensive Experiment* (Reynolds *et al.*, 1987), our study of a naturally occurring experiment where half a community switched to comprehensive education and half of it stayed selective. The selective sector considerably outperformed the comprehensive, a performance which we somewhat lamely explained as reflecting on the fact that the comprehensives were not truly comprehensive.

It was in the 1990s that I made what was probably my most sustained attempt to push out the SESI boundaries, almost totally the result of the friendships and contacts made internationally through ICSEI and SESI. We noted earlier in this chapter that the entire community was making progress and that we were becoming cleverer as a discipline. I tried to do the same.

Ineffective schools

The third chapter of this book shows what happened when I was provided with an opportunity to further develop ideas that I had always had about the social, relational and emotional characteristics of schools, through speculation about what a school that was defective in all these areas might look like. And my own history of researching 'bottom of the barrel' secondary modern schools in a South Wales Valley had accustomed me to educational pathologies. There was a flurry of interest in the UK in this topic in the 1990s, which was not sustained. Had SESI made more attempts to look at the 'sick' schools and to intervene with them in programmes of planned school improvement, then a number of benefits would have ensued. SESI would have been a more integrated enterprise of SE and SI, and there would have been no 'back-mapping' of the characteristics of the effective schools as what the ineffective schools needed. There would instead have been an ongoing, practical study of 'what works' seen from an experimental situation.

That SESI did not study the 'sick', and spent nearly all of its time finding out why the 'well' were 'well', was to handicap the discipline greatly, but politically and pragmatically it would not have been possible to focus research and practice only on the schools that were performing poorly, since that would have identified the discipline as being concerned with 'failure', an altogether more difficult concept to get space for. Additionally, problems of access to schools for research purposes would have been intensified if access to schools for researchers was being sought on behalf of any 'school failure' brigade.

However, the chapter shows the beginning of my own involvement into trying to work out the usefulness of SESI for real live schools and teachers that was to become a near obsession by the 2000s. Already, I was speculating about other bodies of knowledge in addition to the conventional SESI studies that I thought were needed to improve education. I was reflecting on:

- international comparative work about 'what worked' in other countries;
- the utility of work from organisations that were not allowed to fail, the so-called 'High Reliability Organisations';
- the 'technologies of practice', as I was to call teacher effectiveness.

In a number of publications (Reynolds, 1994), I began to speculate about reaching out into these three new areas, probably unaware of the historic blocks within British educational research on looking this far outside normal disciplinary boundaries.

Comparative education

It was my comparative education work that probably had the highest public and professional visibility in the 1990s, and a whole series of different research events suddenly coalesced to further my interest in this area. In the early 1990s I had visited Taiwan with colleagues, as part of the preparatory work for the international comparative study that was then only a gleam in our eyes, which eventually was to become the International School Effectiveness Research Project (ISERP). We planned the process of setting up the study totally scientifically, and the initial phase was to be a literature review of SESI from all countries around the world, so that we would be able to plan our new study on the foundations of what already existed. We therefore reviewed the literature, speculated about appropriate methodology, and began to consider the desirable instrumentation for what was going to be, in our view, the best international effectiveness study yet conducted. This reviewing generated an in-house book published by our hosts in Taiwan (Reynolds *et al.*,

1991), which in turn was expanded into what became a SESI industry standard textbook later (Reynolds *et al.*, 1994).

Personally, the genie of international work was out of the bottle. Visiting Taiwan showed me an educational system that did not tolerate failure and which believed all children could learn – exactly the tenets of the school effectiveness movement as articulated by Edmonds (1979) in the early years, but this time at a whole community level. Teaching methods in Taiwan were based upon the teacher actively taking curriculum content to the whole class of children, not on the highly individualised methods whereby children worked on their own that were prevalent in the United Kingdom. Whole classes would stop until the last child grasped the lesson content before moving on – what a difference this was from the UK classes, where our differentiated work threw the children back onto their own resources and the more able children moved on rapidly. And yet Taiwan's educational system was not 'right wing', as its critics might claim. The children elected their own representatives to the school councils, which had the power to criticise all aspects of the school, including individual teachers if necessary. Besides, a Taiwanese system that generated excellence for all was, if anything, socialist rather than reactionary.

Then serendipity happened, although of course serendipity always favours the prepared mind! The BBC television programme *Panorama* was planning to cover the visit of a Pacific Rim politician by some, probably hostile, attempt to get behind the social, economic, educational and political structure of the 'Asian Tigers', as those booming countries were being called. When they phoned to ask for ideas I was, in spring 1996, already reviewing the literature on international achievement comparisons for OFSTED, mentioned this to the programme team and in general discussion we then formulated the idea of a programme to explore the reasons for the high educational standards and processes of the Pacific Rim societies. This was to be based upon the literature review and upon the experience of one successful Pacific Rim country – of course, it was Taiwan.

The programme involved considerable footage of Taiwanese educational methods – whole-class interactive teaching – with additional material upon the UK Barking and Dagenham schools that were trialling originally similar Swiss methods, in which children in the classroom sat in a 'U' shape and were taught as a whole class with the aid of high-quality OHPs for over 90 per cent of the time. The programme also featured an interview with Chris Woodhead, the then English Chief Inspector of Schools.

The programme was controversial, to say the least. Apparently, there were thousands of phone calls to the BBC afterwards – mostly from teachers who wanted to know more about the Taiwanese methods. Not one letter of criticism appeared in the Letters page of the *Times Educational Supplement*, because not one had been sent in, despite the fact that the story was the front-page lead and was also featured as the lead 'Opinion' article (reprinted here as Chapter 4). My telephone at the University of Newcastle, where I had been working as a Professor since 1993, rang solidly for one and a half days, the calls coming from press, television, schools, friends and genuinely interested teachers, not to mention the genuinely interested members of the public.

However, what had seemed self-evident to me – that we from the UK education system should look with an open mind at other countries and their practices in the same way as we encouraged our children to behave intellectually open-mindedly – was clearly not self-evident to all (especially to those academics who had closed their minds many years before). The publication by OFSTED of the 'Worlds Apart' pamphlet in July caused even further publicity, and the associated espousal of 'whole-class teaching' by Chris Woodhead unfortunately painted the thesis in many professional minds as 'right wing'.

At the same time as this literature review, ISERP was collecting its student- and classroom-level data from 1992 to 1994, with further school- and country-level data being collected for some years afterwards as we struggled to make some sense of our findings. ISERP had all the right research ideas, but operated on a financial shoestring, which constrained our progress. Because the countries involved – the UK, the USA, the Netherlands, Taiwan, Australia, Hong Kong, Ireland and Canada – had been selected on various pragmatic grounds (like knowing someone in the country), there was correspondingly a huge variation between the countries in the international research team in their practices as SESI researchers.

Also, because the core group of organisers – myself, Creemers, Teddlie and Stringfield – were clearly what could be portrayed as white Anglo-Saxon males from countries with a sad history of economic and cultural imperialism, we hesitated to impose any agreed standards on the study, rather leaving it to operate as an uncoordinated methodological and practical democracy. We also did not have the financial resources to train the teams of colleagues from all countries adequately. What ensued was a highly variable, unreliable implementation of the research design.

The conceptualisation had been leading-edge – children aged seven were chosen, in cohorts, moving through their schools of different effectiveness levels, to see if the same things 'worked' in differently effective schools and classrooms in different countries, with particularly intensive data being collected on the children's days in their classrooms and their experiences of their teachers' methods. The study appeared in conference presentations in the UK and internationally, in book chapters and in my general SESI writing from 1994, but we were unable to fully publish it until 2002, a full decade after data began to be collected.

The final chapter of the ISERP book on the study is published in Chapter 5 of this volume, but there were a number of findings of international importance that we somehow failed to convey in the launching of the book. They were:

- Our sample of countries 'played in position' (Pacific Rim doing better than elsewhere), which was further support for the existing findings of comparative research.
- Most of the key classroom/teacher effectiveness 'correlates' 'played in position' in terms of what one would have expected from our SESI knowledge base. The factors that discriminated between differentially effective teachers across the world were the *same* as SESI had put forward – clarity, questions, high expect-ations, a commitment to academic achievement goals and structured lessons, for example.

- Many of the factors which had become axiomatic in the *school* effectiveness literature also discriminated between schools in our different countries – the leadership of the principal or headteacher, the nature of the school's expectations of students and the way in which the 'level' of the school was used to potentiate the quality of the classroom learning experience. But while *conceptually* the same school factors travelled, at school level the precise operationalisation of what the effective principal/headteacher *did* varied according to the cultural context of the particular country.

We emerged out of the ISERP work considerably more confident as a group of scholars – not only did the teacher effectiveness and school effectiveness factors 'work' within countries like the UK and USA, but they also 'worked' around the planet. We also thought we had made considerable methodological advances which we published separately (Reynolds *et al.*, 2002), involving our mixed methods, and our use of the innovative 'whole school day' approach in which the experience of the individual (median) child in a class was charted in terms of the quality of their learning experience over a full school day, to see how their education was experienced in different settings (rather than concentrating upon how education was seen only theoretically or in policy terms). Our 'inter-visitation' techniques, whereby some of the ISERP team visited and brought a common 'lens' to the schools, classrooms and policies of very different societies – and often recognised with a clarity that shocked them why their own countries' methods might be failing – we also regarded as a valuable methodological advance.

We also generated what we believed were 'universals' that were necessary for any effective educational system, anywhere, to possess. We argued:

- that world-class schools needed strong systems to create them, not any reliance on the unusual people or 'Superheads' that some countries' educational policies elevated, since there would never be enough of those unusuals to resource an entire system;
- that they need a 'taken for granted' attitude from society to enable them to function cohesively, without which they would be as fragmented as the society that created them;
- that they needed 'technologies of practice', rather than individual teachers variably self-inventing their methods;
- that they needed educationalists to 'think the unthinkable', and rapidly change classroom/school educational methodologies in accordance with new societal demands and needs.

I find it a salutary experience to consider now – many years later – whether as a UK society we have paid any attention to these reflections. Assuming, of course, that they are accurate, it is profoundly worrying that we haven't.

Teacher effectiveness

The experience of reviewing the literatures of many diverse countries, and of becoming familiar with the intellectual communities of educational researchers in these countries, led directly into the second area in which I became involved from the 1990s – that of teacher, or as the Americans call it, instructional effectiveness. When we reviewed the world's educational effectiveness knowledge bases for ISERP, it was clear that most countries – except the UK – had much more work conducted upon what makes a 'good teacher' than what makes a 'good school'. In the United States, for example, in the 1990s their *teacher* effectiveness studies were in the thousands, many more than their school effectiveness studies, which were only in their scores. If one took a simple factor such as 'wait time' – the time that a teacher should take between asking a class a question and waiting for an answer – the USA had probably several dozen studies on this topic. In the UK, this number would have been only one.

In the ISERP countries too, it was clear that the educational policy discourse in virtually all of them was about *teaching*, rather than about the Anglo-Saxon discourse of *schooling*. When these countries had educational debates about what could be done to improve standards, it was to teachers and teaching that they turned. But in the UK, partly as a response to New Labour's suspicion of teachers and its concerns about the quality of the teaching profession, our discourse was about pulling the policy lever of the '*school*', which was safer for politicians and policy-makers to become involved with.

This focus – some would say obsessive focus – at policy level upon the school was in retrospect bound to disappoint. The learning – or classroom – level explains much more variance than the school, when multivariate analysis is done. The teacher in the classroom is closer to the children. It is the teachers themselves who are responsible for producing their outcomes – much more so than their school. Teachers are smaller units than their schools.

Whilst my own interests in the teacher effectiveness area were burgeoning, an invitation arrived from the Teacher Training Agency (TTA) to present their Annual Lecture for 1997. The themes I wanted to address were obvious to me – the importance of teaching, the absence of a body of scientific knowledge about it, and the costs of this in terms of how this might be harming our children. I began the lecture – and I remember until this day the emotional tone in the lecture theatre – with the observation that if a Martian were to arrive on our planet, what would surprise him or her is that we had no applied science of teaching, that we had no plans to generate one and that many people were happy with this situation! The audience probably comprised those who thought that teaching was an 'art', not a science, because there was a somewhat muted response!

The lecture (Chapter 6 of this book) was followed by a period of research on teacher and school effectiveness, based upon the large-scale studies that I initiated, funded by the Gatsby Charitable Trust, in over 30 primary schools from 1998 for the next five years. These studies were well resourced, with high-quality data being collected on the performance of thousands of pupils at the beginning of each school year and at the end of the year. The generous funding (a credit to the organisation) made it possible to collect a large volume of data – on teachers' classroom behaviours, their beliefs about their methods, their education and their pupils' backgrounds and attributes – that began to appear in conference presentations and journal articles from 2000 onwards. Much of this reflects the major contribution of Daniel Muijs, whose own subsequent research in collaboration with a number of other scholars has continued the progression of the 'teacher'-level work. One of our joint publications is included in this volume as Chapter 7.

Why the effective teacher wasn't studied

For a while in the late 1990s, it seemed possible that a new focus upon 'the teacher' rather than 'the Headteacher', and upon 'the classroom' rather than 'the school', might have developed. All the conditions were in place – a recognition that pulling the school-level policy 'lever' may not have delivered, the multi-level analyses that showed the 'variance' explained by the classroom to be much greater than for the school and a recognition that the teaching profession might be more interested in teaching, and therefore discussion about its core concerns, rather than the school-level managerialism that bored all but the ambitious.

But although there was some limited British work, and of course our own work too, fatal mistakes had been made by government and their advisers. First, even though the databases existed that would have permitted national, multi-school research into the 'teacher effectiveness' factors that might exist in different contexts derived from the NFER evaluation of the Numeracy and Literacy Project Pilots from 1996 to 1998, government could not be persuaded to find the money for this kind of research. Second, in spite of this, the evaluation of the National Literacy and Numeracy Strategies could have given us the key, still largely missing, 'teachers and teaching' knowledge base, but it was decided to evaluate these initiatives not as micro-level pedagogical interventions but as a macro-level policy strategy, with Michael Fullan and his team employed to do this. Their reports delivered insights about macro-level educational reform, which we didn't need, but no advances at all in the area of teacher effectiveness, which we did. In fairness, there were a number of us who argued strenuously against both these decisions on the Literacy and Numeracy Strategy Group, from 1997 to 2000, but we lost, and often lost badly. Interestingly, the Group was terminated in 2000.

The decision to award the contract for design and specification of the national teacher 'Threshold' system to Hay McBer, on the basis of apparently good work they had done in Australia, was the final nail in the teaching coffin. Hay McBer brought to the research their own conceptualisation of effective practice, taken from commercial and industrial settings, not classrooms. It was aimed at exploring the 'deep' motivational areas that (in their language) were the 'nine tenths of the iceberg' below the water, rather than the teaching *behaviours* that were the one tenth above. But children, of course, saw the tenth above the water. They saw behaviours, and responded to them. It was the wrong choice of research team.

Hay McBer drew a sample of 'unusually effective teachers', and others, and then gathered data upon the teacher attributes, although not their methods. I was drawn into looking at the correlation between these characteristics and the value added progress of the children of the different teachers (which came in at the low side of 0.4, positive). The academic research community was enraged that people who apparently knew little about teaching, and even less about research, were doing the work. The publication of the material was a damp squib. The greatest hole in UK SESI work – 'what is a good teacher' – remained, and still remains, tragically unfilled.

High Reliability Schools

At the same time as many of us were becoming more sure of the *validity* of our knowledge on 'what works', a delivery mechanism to ensure that the knowledge was put in place was clearly becoming a necessary option. We had, we were sure, validity – what we needed was *reliable* systems ensuring that all children received the 'it'.

The comparative investigations had shown us that some societies routinely ensured reliability through their teacher education, their inculcation in all teachers of an agreed teaching practice and their refusal to permit unreliable self-invention – Taiwan amongst them.

Now – again serendipitously – I became dimly aware of systems, not just countries, which could apparently transfer to all the valid knowledge bases that we were creating. These organisations were known as High Reliability Organisations (HROs) and they existed in many societies of the world. They were organisations within which any failure of a system would have such dire consequences that it had to be 'designed' and 'organised' out. In short, these organisations were 'failure free', in a phrase which resonated through British education for some years after Michael Barber had picked up some of the HRS thinking and developed it in his Greenwich *Times Educational Supplement* Lecture in 1995 (Barber, 1995).

That 'reliability' has been the key to understanding effective educational policies was suggested by a number of analyses of the American Special Strategies programmes which suggested that whether a reform attempt was followed *reliably* by a school staff was more important in determining results than the precise programme that was being adopted. Also, in the Teddlie and Stringfield (1993) Louisiana School Effectiveness Studies, the more effective schools had, in their lovely phrase, 'an intolerance of large negatives' and tried to knock the bottom of their distribution of teachers into the middle, or to truncate it. Their ineffective schools were less consistent and stable, classroom to classroom, and year to year. They simply had less reliable delivery mechanisms, even though they all possessed pockets of good practice. They had not made their best practice their universal practice.

Two events – one in the USA and one in the UK – resulted in the High Reliability ideas being tested out in schools. Sam Stringfield, in the USA, was sitting on a plane travelling to the West Coast when over a Bourbon or two he started chatting to the passenger at his side, as it turned out a former employee of the nuclear power industry. 'Incidents' (this person said) had been substantially reduced when the industry started focusing on HRO principles, which was clearly good news for those who lived in the neighbourhoods of the plants.

Stringfield began to dig into this literature, and told me of his new interest. In the UK on one hot, lazy summer's afternoon, whilst presenting an 'in service' Friday session in the West Country, I had just delivered my 'stock' school effectiveness session and was becoming bored, as was the audience of Headteachers. 'Have you heard of this crazy guy Stringfield and his material on HROs?' I asked, desperate to promote interest. A few asides on HROs then turned into a 40-minute discussion, which then developed into a programme that was to take ten years of our professional lives. We piloted the programme, based upon the principle that our volunteer schools from the meeting would co-construct with us how to make schools reliable delivery mechanisms, in three different areas of the UK. Areas 1 and 2 were disappointing, although Area 2 has since taken off in achievement terms, but Area 3 – the Welsh authority of Neath Port Talbot – created with us what is the most effective secondary school improvement programme in the world, which showed improvement on the 'core' outcome indicator of five or more A* to C GCSEs at more than double the rate of Wales as a whole. This improvement outcome ran for a decade, and is still in the 2009 figures, and is continuing, even though we as a research team have not been near the schools since 2000. Indeed, the schools have been improving more without us than with us! This material is reproduced as Chapter 8 of this volume.

The early floating of High Reliability Schools (HRS) ideas in the UK had sometimes used the exemplars of air traffic controllers as the classic failure-free reliability mechanism, to some mirth, magnified when the *Times Educational Supplement* carried a cartoon attached to a story about HRS, which showed books flying around an air traffic control tower! As results have come in over the years, some HRO concepts (failure-free, Standard Operating Procedures, data richness) have entered the educational lexicon and influenced the educational zeitgeist of the UK.

Interestingly, the success of HRS followed a dire, stuttering start. Other very powerful programmes had similarly poor starts, such as Slavin's (1996) Success For All. Maybe it is that the very big effects in life don't come quickly – that elephants don't run very often, as it were. Maybe, if you have powerful medicine – and HRS is *very* powerful medicine – then it can do damage too, as well as good.

From research to policy: making policy

By the late 1990s I had begun to become impatient, personally and professionally, with what I saw as the slow recognition within the UK educational systems of what we now had to offer in the SESI community. Some of the first criticisms of SESI from the 'liberal' wing of the educational researchers irritated me (e.g. Elliott,

1996), and I replied to them, with Pam Sammons, for one of the few times in my life (later work on dyslexia in a different field evoked replies too).

Because of the furore surrounding my comparative education work, the British educational research community was not necessarily a totally hospitable environment. Invitations from Michael Barber and David Blunkett, then in 1995 the Labour Shadow Education Spokesperson, to become involved on the Literacy Task Force and to chair the Numeracy Task Force therefore provided a number of things – a group of like-minded people to work with, an affirmation that the UK educational research community did not give, and most importantly, the opportunity of taking SESI into government to the potential benefit of students and teachers.

The Numeracy Task Force, which was established in 1997 and reported in 1998, took the insights of the findings of SESI into every classroom. We were evidence-based – no substantive discussions took place until six months after we had started, because we didn't permit ourselves to start discussing our remedies before we researched issues. We had an international reach. We wanted to be evolutionary and avoid the frequent changes and root-and-branch destruction of existing practice that had marked UK education policies historically. And we espoused what we were to call 'whole-class interactive teaching', a far from fashionable method in the UK in the 1990s, although one supported in the literature on teacher effectiveness in mathematics. Chapter 9 of this volume contains our detailed philosophy about how we worked.

We were also made up entirely of educationalists, since a firm proposal to me from New Labour advisers that we have Carol Vorderman as a member I could not agree with. I strongly argued that we would be seen, with her on board, as a New Labour 'stunt'. I won the argument, but it was made crystal clear that by doing things my own way, I would bear total responsibility were things to go wrong. And wrong they nearly did go.

There were some extraordinary stressful moments. One week when I was in the USA trying to write up ISERP, two Task Force members – one from the traditionalist wing and one from the liberal wing – both phoned me and resigned, uncoordinated with each other, on the same evening. They later relented. At our very last meeting, one member of the Task Force, who was opposed to the emphasis on whole-class interactive instruction, brought out a two-foot-high pile of academic papers which, they said, showed that whole-class interactive teaching was *not* effective, and said that they would resign rather than sign up to the final draft as it stood.

For about five seconds, I did nothing and sat in silence looking down at the desk in front of me, as I did not know what to do. The silence was broken by another member of the Task Force arguing for 'whole-class interactive', as we called it, to be followed by all the others. The membership of the group did what I could not have done – kept the one person on board, and itself together. They also saved me.

There were also the unpleasant aspects of involvement at the interface between educational research and politics. The government leaked to a Sunday newspaper on the weekend before our publication that we were going to totally ban calculators, which of course was untrue. We, naturally, denied this and stood our ground, which did not make us popular. Then there was the later Numeracy Summit, at which a number of us, plus assorted academics, Headteachers and others, assembled in 10 Downing Street with all Education Ministers present, at a meeting chaired by Tony Blair.

Blair had a colour-coded seating chart in front of him, with every participant being coloured in a certain way, presumably an indication of the individual's background and/or ideology. Every person who spoke, or made a point, was answered courteously by Blair, except for the Headteacher of a Welsh language school who made a passionate speech about how her school was a community-based comprehensive. She was the only person that Blair said nothing to – he just sat and looked.

At coffee afterwards, the same Headteacher said to Blair that she was the Head of a 'Welsh medium' school. 'Ah,' said Blair, 'so you're a middle school?' So much for the domain knowledge of our former leader! At coffee, I asked a senior political adviser what would happen because of the summit. 'Nothing,' he said. Apparently its purpose had been only to acquire some space in newspapers, which it did. In the case of the *Daily Telegraph*, this meant an embarrassing front-page picture of me and some others. The summit was merely to give the appearance of action – it was not 'real', a distinction that has become repetitive in my experience over the last decade.

From research to policy: advising on policy

Numeracy was considered by most commentators to have been a great success – in the eyes of many, a helpful antidote to the obsessively detailed Literacy Strategy, and something which was widely seen as having the right 'emotional tone'. Test scores on the national Maths SATs indicators rose rapidly, but had plateaued by 2001, and there was no further supplementation possible with more sensitive, powerful and relevant methods because the knowledge base in teacher effectiveness that could have provided this supplementation was not forthcoming, as we noted earlier.

Political opinion also turned against what was regarded as 'prescription', and a new philosophy of 'specification' that was related to generating an 'informed professionalism' was espoused by Estelle Morris when she succeeded Blunkett in 2002. More recently, the 'centre' which used to ensure that the educational system received knowledge about good practice – from without itself, from HE or from abroad – has been slimmed down. A new ideology of the system helping itself, of 'by school for school', has grown up, and linked with it has been a shift away from academics as the useful servants of the policy community to using Headteachers, who appear to be more collaborative, leak less, don't argue in public and wear better suits.

The years since 2001 did, though, see my involvement with policy-making continue unabated. The Hay McBer work mentioned above was followed by a

year working with the City Academy Support Service, a salutary experience since there was then – and to great extent now – no definition of what 'Academyness' was, other than its being about brand-new buildings. School after school I visited had Heads who much preferred to be among their contractors and building sites rather than their classrooms and their teachers. Many wore the yellow, contractor hard hats as a mark of pride even away from the building site. And the pedagogic rationale for Academies – that they would provide new, inspirational learning experiences – were forgotten in the celebrations on their openings, at which politicians with cheesy grins posed before brightly polished nameplates attached to schools that had great buildings but no educational soul.

In these years, I kept up the attempted delivery of SESI insights to the profession in the usual way. A national programme for those Schools Facing Challenging Circumstances involved reviewing the literature on how to improve schools – that review (Chapter 10 here) went out to over 400 secondary schools in five regional meetings, and was also adapted for academic audiences. This programme was the forerunner of the present National Challenge and Coasting Schools Programmes, which interestingly have nothing comparable by way of provision of knowledge. Now, it is the profession which apparently improves itself, a mark of how much SESI has been marginalised in the 2000s.

Another example of my attempt to bring SESI to the teaching profession was work that I did for the National College for School Leadership on the implications of the teacher effectiveness research for practice (Chapter 11 of this volume). Even the most cursory reading of the material shows that it is simple, and many would say simplistic. The list of areas where we needed to know more – contextual variation, variation by school subject and the teaching of affective or non-academic outcomes – amounted to a list of pretty much everything there was to know! This is sad because education in the UK will be changed when our teachers change what they do – not before. Trying to change the 'teacher supply' is slow-working and may be impossible. Changing teachers' classroom behaviours is fast-acting and definitely possible. But there is still not the knowledge base to resource it.

The material in Chapter 12 – on within-school variation – is not so much an attempt to review existing knowledge as an attempt to deliver the promise of a new era of potential policy importance. Since the mid 1970s, when Carol Fitz-Gibbon (1985) reported on differences between mathematics departments in secondary schools, little attempt has been made to explore the potential importance of this issue. Within-school differences are much bigger than differences from school to school – schools are aggregates of different subjects and departments, after all – so the policy 'lever' may be more powerful than that of the whole school.

The chapter reported on pilot work that was conducted on how to learn from schools' own best practices to make them 'standard' practices. A technology of how to do this – involving attention to the creation of data systems, focusing on middle management training, committing to work upon teaching and learning, utilising student voice as a check on organisational quality and introducing Standard Operating Procedures to improve reliability – now exists and is being further refined in ongoing work in association with the Training and Development Agency for Schools (TDA) and the National College for School Leadership (NCSL).

The promise is enormous. No need for schools to wait for the arrival of help from outside themselves – which often comes late, and in the form of the giant egos of the 'Superheads' who became something of a New Labour obsession. Every school can become, in this new form of school improvement, an engine of its own development. And the emotional tone is so much more helpful than historically – improvement can be within every school, based upon their own best people.

Chapter 12 is the last in this volume that summarises what I have said in the past, about the past. The final three chapters all in their own different ways look forward, hopefully to a new dawn in which governmental policy in the UK and elsewhere attempts to become more informed by what SESI knows and can do for its students. The first of them, Chapter 13, attempts to chart what it is that SE and SI might do to improve the knowledge base and maximise the chances of purposive educational change. It argues that we need to move beyond simple organisational characteristics, when we describe and attempt to change schools, by looking at them as complex sets of human and social relationships too. It also looks at our need to fully explore the age-old and enduring problem of educational policy – the tendency for poorer children to attend schools that are less effective. It also looks at neglected areas that need our urgent attention – the curriculum in terms of its content, the new kinds of outcomes that public policies are bringing to us, and the need to link together our findings in the form of theories that make them better able to be understood by practitioners and policy makers. And we need to generate theories. Historically we maybe have seemed to be what the critics have alleged we are – purveyors of goods that are lists of school attributes which do not cohere into theoretical science. Those in practice and in policy may have seen us as 'grubby empiricists'.

The final two chapters of my work take up this theme of how we can maximise the SESI impact upon policies, to make them more rational. These chapters were both generated by invitations from the DfES (as was) and the DCSF (as is), to speculate about the needed contents and trajectory of education policies. The facts do not need repeating at length again – outcomes of the educational system have only increased incrementally, whereas what is needed is transformational change, or 'step change', to use the New Labour phrase. Policies have been more 'reliably' or obsessively enforced, but outcomes still disappoint, leading to the beginnings of doubt in policy circles as to whether the policy paradigms being utilised are adequate for the task.

And the policies that SESI – with its now thirty-year history – would suggest we employ in schools? In both chapters they are clear – a focus on the teaching and learning level, rather than the endless focus upon a 'school' set of policies that pull less powerful levers, would be of primary importance. A willingness to explore how the range of variation within schools can be utilised as a building block, as we noted above. And a commitment to maximising the attempts to simultaneously combat the effects of social disadvantage and of poor schooling upon children.

But it is at national policy level that SESI has perhaps its biggest implications. Policies in the UK have systematically attempted to be 'tight' on the precise organisational factors that are thought to be important in affecting the quality of education, through the OFSTED inspection check-lists and through the general State focus upon the Headteacher and the global 'effectiveness' characteristics that are in the public domain.

But SESI has changed in its core findings since its first flowerings made it 'the policy-makers' friend' in the 1990s. There is abundant evidence that 'what works' may be variable in terms of what is necessitated by the socio-economic composition of a school's catchment area, its effectiveness status, its improvement trajectory, its culture and the personalities of its educational players. Even at classroom level, there are some hints of the ways in which effective teaching needs to be implemented differently in different circumstances.

Increasingly, SESI is telling policy-makers that it may not be necessary to be tight on *what is done* – that may be suitably and necessarily variable in accordance with local circumstances. The most important thing to be tight on may be *how it is done*, in the sense of requiring schools to be systematic in how they set in place systems to improve themselves, and in what the characteristics of these systems are.

Such an approach, if it were to be adopted more enthusiastically than in the present OFSTED regime, would transform educational life. Instead of a world in which educational professionals are increasingly dumbed down into persons whose role is to faithfully implement the processes they are told are important by others, they would generate knowledge of what is 'effective' in their own schools. They would be rational, empirical problem solvers, not apprentices sitting at the feet of governments or leading Headteachers who tell them what to do. They would be able to determine their future based upon the great knowledge bases of the world, and upon systems which would enable them to build better. It is a great pity that national British educational policies contrive to be so non-rational in their continued concentration upon enforcing not systems to determine processes, but processes.

There is one final challenge for SESI to address, and one discipline that is even younger than itself which it needs to learn from – cognitive neuroscience, which is already having a worldwide impact. In the second of these last two invitational papers we look at the evidence on this that suggests there are implications for SESI in a number of areas. Research suggests that the cerebellum is the 'organiser' of cognitive activity in the sense of making learned skills automatic, but cerebellar development is not potentiated in the same way as the 'thinking brain' is. For cerebellar development schools need to focus upon exercise, upon diet, upon water supply and upon resourcing the brain to permit cognitive development to take place, with arguably a very different kind of school needed to that of the simple 'effectiveness' models that we have had.

The promising experiments in 'distributed practice' or what is called 'spaced learning' – in which teaching is focused in much shorter bursts of activity interspersed with gaps to enable the brain to make new connections and delete existing ones that are no longer appropriate – point to a future in which education

in general and SESI in particular will need to rapidly change its concerns and the
levers that it recommends to policy and practice, if development is to be optimised.

Conclusions: the future of school effectiveness and improvement

It is clear from what happened to SESI that whilst in the 1990s it was pushing hard
to gain recognition at what was an open door, in the 2000s it is more of an outsider
in the practitioner and policy-making communities, where doors, if not shut, are
certainly ajar. Partly this is because educational research in general, and educational
researchers in particular, have fallen out of favour with government, due to their
propensity to ask the difficult-to-answer questions about whether New Labour
educational policies have worked and their propensity to ask them publicly in ways
that have subsequently frequently been taken up by what has become New Labour's
obsession, the media.

SESI has been particularly excluded. Its association with the prescription of the
years 1997 to 2000, the volume of criticism of it, the departure of some high-
profile SESI researchers from educational policy-making (as with Michael Barber's
move to the Downing Street Delivery Unit) and the absence of much disciplinary
progress in the last few years of the 1990s to excite and gain interest, all had the
effect of making the discipline less visible.

In practice, schools thought that they had 'done' SESI and interest moved
towards more transformational, indeed sometimes semi-Messianic, accounts of
improvement.

However, it is as well to remind ourselves of the considerable knowledge base
that now exists in major areas of interest for practitioners and policy-makers, in the
following areas of SESI:

- the characteristics of those schools which 'add value' to their pupils, and those
  that might be adding rather less value in challenging circumstances;
- the characteristics, behaviours and values of those effective classroom teachers;
- the outcomes in academic, social, affective and related areas that can be measured
  in schools;
- the extent to which 'what works' is different in schools/classrooms of different
  socio-economic backgrounds, different effectiveness levels, different improvement trajectories and different cultures;
- the ways in which theories can link together those patterns of factors at
  classroom, school, district/local authority and national level;
- the ways in which professional practice in schools and classrooms can be
  improved in deliberate and programmatic ways.

It is as well to remind ourselves also that the historical mission of SE is as true
and necessary today as it ever was – the generation of students with their cognitive
and social skills developed in ways that make them able to understand the society
around them, to relate to it and to each other, and by so doing, change it.

There is no doubt that the volume of criticism of SE historically must have had effects in denting the self-confidence of its proponents – many of the criticisms were so vicious, so personal and so laden with emotion that it would have been hard to ignore them. But most of the critics have now retired, or left the country to go to other societies to criticise them, or have found other targets, or are dead. Lots of them were criticising because at the time they were going out of the door of the educational room, and were afraid of SE inheriting their positions.

But if SE can recapture its self-confidence and increase its research outputs in terms of the quality and the quantity of studies and insights, there is no doubt that the social, economic and educational situation that it finds itself in is probably the most favourable for its development since the heady days of the 1990s when it first arrived on the scene globally.

The first factor that makes societies again receptive to SE is the social, political and economic situation brought on by the international economic situation generated by the banking crisis. The sheer scale of borrowings necessary within many advanced industrial societies means that public expenditure will be under pressure in all areas of State welfare for probably the next decade. Doing 'more with less' consequent upon the inevitable expenditure cuts or restrictions in expenditure in the schools sector will become the watchword. Ensuring that the *quality* of education is optimised even though there are fewer *quantities* of resources available will be increasingly axiomatic, replacing much of the historic 'improvement through additional spend' paradigm that dominated the last decade. SE is ideally placed to resource – intellectually and practically – the new policies.

The second factor that makes the situation one of immense opportunities for SE is the arrival of many societies in the world at precisely the time that is ripe for them to embrace the discipline. Societies such as China, India and those of Latin America such as Brazil have been showing explosive rates of growth largely on the back of the simple factors of rapid urbanisation, and the application of limited amounts of capital in their industrialisation. Extra resources have been allocated to education systems in terms of new buildings, more teachers, more technology and more time at schools for students, yet across these societies there is a dissatisfaction with the results of these policies, not unsurprising because it is clear from all the SE evidence that these policy levers are weak.

There is some evidence of increased awareness within these societies' educational systems of the existence of SE – China, for example, has its own national association for school effectiveness, with considerable links to the other SE research communities of the world. Given that these societies are at 'lift off' in their search for educational quality, SE research might become a viral force in these societies as it has been in those where it is better established. There are 22 million teachers in China. They serve 400 million children. Were it to 'root', it would be a seismic event.

The third factor that is generating a favourable situation for SE to re-emerge is the clear evidence of limited outcomes from the other groups that have tried to address the issues of school quality.

In the UK, governmental enthusiasm has been for use of unusually effective Headteachers to advise on policy, serve on quangos and be a general repository of wisdom. But it is increasingly clear that many of these people are unusual creatures and may not necessarily be those whom an educational system should be modelled on. They are often the 'edge of the circle' innovators – truly, with some of them, 'the ego has landed'. Using them has brought considerable advantages – they wear a good suit, are charismatic, practical and have added usefulness in that they have actually done the business of running schools, rather than talking about it or researching those who do, which is the more academic role.

But their unusual characteristics are increasingly seen as posing problems for governments. They have used methods which may not be useful for all. They are a very small sample on which to base the practice of school change and transformation. In short, the academic research may be by those at one step removed from practice, with all that means, but at least SE academics use large samples, more representative persons and they try to separate out the 'personal' from the 'organisational' in the search for 'what works'. I suspect this is increasingly being recognised.

Fourth, the reactions against the historic influence of research – and of SE – have produced a situation where the need for 'thought leadership' has never been stronger. This plays to SE's strengths. SE, after all, thought itself from the margins of academic life to be the central educational research discipline of the age.

The problem has been that 'thought leadership' has been seen as threatening, especially to those who can't think. The Department for Children, Schools and Families has seen most of its original thinkers leave, happy to leave in most cases a situation in which they have been marginalised by a managerial, corporate culture. New Labour's paradigm shifts over the 2000s ended up in a focus on improving the reliability of delivery, rather than original thought about the validity of the delivery model or the processes being delivered themselves.

The practice of using Headteachers and others from the educational system has also generated a restrictive educational culture, in which 'by schools for schools' has become not the liberation from the irrelevance of academic work and policy-maker excesses, but a restrictive culture in which only what the system thinks is regarded as worthy of use. Thought leadership is badly needed, as is increasingly recognised. SE can provide it.

Lastly, SE is in a fortunate position, because whilst many other disciplines would be hard put to find much evidence of progress in their insights over the last years, SE can show much progress. If we were to take those areas of research where there has customarily been the evidence of large 'effect sizes', assessment for learning approaches seem to be rather similar, in conceptualisation and practice, to the findings of a decade ago. Comparative education still seems to be a collection of individual scholars sending home their picture postcards from overseas trips. Approaches that combat learning defects seem to have changed little. Whils is much 'noise' in issues to do with school transformation, whether there is a substantive body of practice and theory seems in some doubt.

By comparison, look at SE. Progress in its 'core' areas of school effects, teacher effects, context effects and improvement effects. And, unique recognition of the needs to generate theories of learning on its own and in its relationship with cognitive neuroscience.

For SE, then, the situation could not be more positive and alive with potential. With its head in the 'pure' theoretical clouds and its heart resting on the applied ground of practice in schools, and with – now having been tested – the emotional, social and intellectual equipment to hold that academic head and heart together, there should be no limit to what SE can do. The failure-free school, where all children have the birthright beloved of reformers for hundreds of years of a right to the best that it is known, and to the approaches that can create better. It *is* achievable now. The only question is whether we will try.

2

The delinquent school

Sociologists, criminologists and educational researchers have expended an enormous amount of time and money in their search for the causes of youthful problems like juvenile delinquency. In this search for what is almost the criminological equivalent of the 'Holy Grail', these researchers have lavished attention on delinquents' families, their physical type, their IQ, their personality and even on the sanitary amenities of their homes – they have concentrated on explaining deviance and delinquency as a consequence of individual, familial, cultural or neighbourhood pathology.

One societal institution which has escaped much of the attention that criminologists have lavished upon children and upon their families is the institution of the school. Certainly some notice has been taken of the way in which the educational system may impose certain stresses and strains on large numbers of its working-class children. The blocked goal attainment hypotheses of Cohen (1955) and Cloward and Ohlin (1961) suggest that the educational system and the middle-class teachers that staff it may, because of their middle-class assumptions as to what constitutes a 'good pupil', deny working-class pupils status within the schools because these pupils have not been socialised to fulfil the status requirements of middle-class society. Delinquency outside the school may thus be a working-class child's solution to his problem of status frustration within the school, a solution that, as work by Hargreaves (1967) suggests, may be made even more likely by specific school practices such as streaming by ability.

However, the interest which sub-cultural theorists have shown in the educational system as a 'generator' of delinquency has yet to be marked by any rigorous analysis of exactly how it is that the educational system actually manages to produce the problems that it is said to produce. C. M. Phillipson, writing on the same theme, argues that '[t]hroughout the literature the reference is to the school rather than to particular schools; sociologists seem to be operating with highly abstract models of the school which rest on their intuitive hunches about what schools are really like' (1971, p. 239).

Even the recent emergence of the 'interactionist' school, with their insistence on the importance of studying the social interaction between rule breakers and those who label them, has – with the exceptions of the work of Werthman (1967) and that of Cicourel and Kitsuse (1963) – generally neglected to study the key social problem defining agency of the school. Ritual mention is often made of the 'importance' of the school in the lives of delinquents, yet such mentions are rarely followed by anything more than informed gossip about the nature of within school social life and within school social interaction. The result of our general ignorance as to exactly how the process of within school interaction is producing the problems that it is said to be producing is that we are still operating with the implicit assumption that all schools of a particular type are the same in the type and quality of this interaction and therefore in their effects – as Phillipson (1971, p. 239) notes:

> The implicit suggestion is that all schools are sufficiently alike to produce a standardised response from their pupils. The idea that there may be considerable differences between overtly similar schools, that some schools may facilitate and others hinder the drift into delinquency does not seem to have occurred to writers on delinquency.

Since children spend much of their time in schools and since few sociologists would dare to talk of 'the family' as if all families were the same, yet regularly talk of 'the school' as if all schools were the same, it is worthwhile trying to discover why there has been so little examination by researchers as to whether different schools may have the effect of producing or generating pupils with different rates of deviance.

The principal reason for this neglect appears to be the general societal conviction that education – by definition – exerts at best a worthwhile influence and at worst a neutral influence on the young people that undergo the process, a belief which tends to defy qualification and rejection. Whilst such a belief as to the value of education may be understandable amongst elite groups who have profited from the educational system – one government report argued that problems like delinquency 'may arise not because boys are at school but because they are not at school enough' (Central Advisory Council for Education, Crowther Report, 1959, para. 63) – many social researchers have simply taken the school regime as something given. They have individualised the explanation of institutional problems by concentrating on the family background, ability and personality of the deviant child without ever looking at the nature, quality and operation of the school regimes from which he or she is held to deviate.

A good example of how educational research often takes for granted the institutions and explains their problems as resulting from the pathologies of their children, is provided by some research into truancy. One study (Tyerman, 1958) compared a group of truants and so-called 'normal' children and concluded:

> Few of the truants had a happy and secure home influence. Most of them came from broken homes or homes where there was open disharmony. In general, the parents set poor examples and were unsatisfactory characters. They neglected their children, were ineffective in their supervision and took little interest in their welfare. The view of many writers that the truant is born in an inferior environment seemed to be confirmed.

Even where some of the truants gave reasons connected with school – such as fear of the teachers – as the explanation for their behaviour, the author comments (p. 220):

> These reasons may to some extent be valid but it is unwise to accept truants' excuses at their face value. The limits of self deception are wide and it is easier to blame other people than oneself. Parents and children look for scapegoats and teachers are often chosen.

An alternative view of truancy, delinquency and rebellion at school is to see them as a form of rational rebellion against a system which the children feel has little to offer them. Working-class children may thus see the school as an alien institution whose middle-class teachers deny them status, and may therefore rebel against their schools by exhibiting what to the schools is problematic behaviour. Rather than discounting the reasons and motivations given by the problem children and truants for their own actions as the products of 'abnormal' personalities, it may be worthwhile to pay some regard to the reasons that lie behind these deviant acts, since the problem behaviour may simply be a reaction to what the children see as unsatisfying environments within some of their schools.

While one can understand the reasons for the existence of this normative belief as to the value of the education our society provides, the effects of this belief have been, in general, to stultify the asking of critical questions about the nature of our educational processes.

The second reason for this basic lack of research into secondary school regimes and their possible effects in producing deviance and delinquency amongst their pupils is that the organisations which control research works' access to the schools have seen this type of evaluative research as a great threat. Local education committees have been worried that any variability in the quality of the service they run may be exposed to public view and teacher unions have been concerned that evaluative research of this sort smacks of the hated 'payment by results' philosophy of the nineteenth century. Michael Power's work into differences in delinquency rates amongst Tower Hamlets secondary schools, called by some reviewers the most important work on delinquency for decades, was in fact stopped by London teachers and by the Inner London Education Authority. Certainly some organisations like the Schools Council have found it easy to secure access to schools for the purposes of doing research, yet this type of research – usually in the area of curriculum development – has been marked by its generally unquestioning approach to the organisation of schooling. Quite simply, there is very little work on the organisational effectiveness of different schools because very little work has ever been allowed (Power, 1967).

A third reason for the lack of evaluative research is the severe practical and methodological problems that are encountered when undertaking the research. Much of the information that is needed – school delinquency rates for example – requires a laborious effort to obtain. The demise of the standardised eleven plus exam and its replacement by teachers' estimates; and the increasing use of internally moderated school leaving exams means that schools' data on academic input and output are not of use since they are not strictly comparable from school to school.

Such research into school factors is furthermore very broad ranging – if we find that school A in the suburbs has a low delinquency rate and school B in the slums a much higher rate, then we need to find out whether these schools are receiving similar children from similar neighbourhoods before we can ever presume that we need to investigate what is happening in their schools. Research into school factors and differences, then, is simply unscientific without comparable research into family factors, neighbourhood factors and pupil factors.

Research into within school interaction is also invariably difficult research because of the absence of any substantial body of knowledge or satisfactory theoretical basis to inform the research. Certainly recent years have seen a growing interest by educational researchers in the processes whereby pupil success and pupil failure is produced within schools and within classrooms (Hargreaves, 1972; and for a recent review of developments see Chanan and Delamont, 1975). There are certainly valuable insights to be found in this type of work which emphasises how the quality of pupil/teacher interaction and teachers' definitions of their pupils may affect the success and failure of individual pupils and perhaps of whole classes. But the literature within this area tends to be rather more satisfactory in generating hypotheses than in testing them and, as one authoritative review of the sociology of school learning concludes, 'We are still in the conjecturing stage as far as identifying the aspects of in school experience and the kinds of in school interaction which contribute most to academic success' (Boocock, 1972).

Research into differences between schools as learning environments is therefore both difficult and wide ranging in its scope. Because educational researchers have looked at the easiest areas of their discipline first, no substantive sociology of the school exists to guide and help research into school variation. The result of this is that we probably know more about the relationship between the absence of internal toilets and children's reading ability than we do about the sort of school experience that may inhibit or promote pupil delinquency and other problem behaviour.

The fourth – and most important – reason for the absence of much research into this topic is that the educational research that has been undertaken suggests that the individual school is only a weak influence on pupils' behaviour, attainment and attitudes when compared to the strong influences of family social class and neighbourhood environment. The summary of recent research in Jencks's *Inequality* all agrees that different schools do not have greatly different effects on their pupils' academic development, whatever the variation in their quality. In fact, Jencks's conclusion was unequivocal (1972, p. 256):

> the character of a school's output depends largely on a single input, namely the character of its entering children. Everything else – the school budget, its policies, the characteristics of the teachers – is either secondary or completely irrelevant.

School differences, in other words, make no great difference.

However, these studies such as Coleman and Plowden are subject to important criticisms (Dyer, 1968; Corwin, 1974). They tend to include in their analyses very few school variables by comparison with the number of family variables and those that they do include are usually simple resource-based indicators, such as the age of the school buildings, size of the playground or the number of books in the school library. Pupil/teacher relationships, teacher character or headteacher competence do not figure prominently as possible school 'factors'. Furthermore, the studies use only measure of output – cognitive ability on non-verbal or verbal tests – on which children's performance is likely to be substantially determined by home background and family social class. Whether or not schools affect pupils' self-conception, self-esteem, deviance rates, attendance rates or vandalism rates does not appear to be a question that these researchers have ever posed.

So far, it has been argued that research into those factors that generate delinquency has concentrated on children's family background, neighbourhood and character as their explanatory variables. Researchers have mentioned 'the educational system' as having delinquency-producing potential but do not examine if there are variations in this potential within the system. This neglect reflects the ideology that education solves, not creates, problems; the difficulty of ensuring access to the schools; the practical and methodological problems of doing the research and the absence of any body of theory to guide enquiry into this highly complex field. This neglect is further explained by the ready and uncritical acceptance of the view that the individual school has, in any case, little independent effect of its own upon its pupils' development.

However, over the past few years a small but increasing body of knowledge has gathered, which suggests that our neglect to develop any sociology of the school has greatly limited our understanding of the process of adolescent social and educational development. Michael Power's work already referred to showed wide variations – from 0.8 to 17.0 per cent per annum – in the incidence of delinquency (defined by a guilty court appearance) in the secondary modern schools of Tower Hamlets; variations that he could not explain by simple factors such as school size or the age of school buildings. Furthermore, Power suggested (1972) that the school rates were largely independent of neighbourhood characteristics and that, therefore, the school itself was an important influence on whether pupils drifted towards delinquency.

Recent work by Rutter in the primary schools of South London also suggests the existence of substantial 'school effects' and that there is something about certain schools in themselves which is associated with low rates of educational attainment and high rates of behavioural deviance among their children, a conclusion that is echoed by Gath, whose researches have revealed large differences between schools in their delinquency rates and child guidance referral rates (Gath, 1972; Rutter, 1973). Further research from the United States has also suggested that the academic climate of high schools is an important influence on pupils' scholastic attainment. Not surprisingly, students have been found to make better progress where teachers and fellow students place a high value on achievement (McDill and Rigsby, 1973). Although we can therefore conclude that the individual school may have an important independent influence on its pupils' attainments and behaviour, the size of this influence and the precise features of the schools that may make their pupils different are, as yet, unknown.

Over the past three years work has been going on in our research community to see if, in fact, some schools are managing to prevent – and others promote – the growth of deviancy amongst their pupils and to see what it is about the successful schools that may help them excel. The particular community itself has two great advantages for this type of research, concerned as it is to sort out the relative effect of family, school and neighbourhood factors upon pupils' development. It is, firstly, a relatively homogeneous former mining community, with very small differences in the social class composition of the people who live in the catchment areas of the different schools. Any differences between the schools of the area in the sort of pupils they are producing are therefore more likely to reflect differences in the effects of their schools and less likely to reflect initial differences in the type of children the schools are receiving.[1]

The second advantage of this community is, quite simply, that the headteachers, staffs and education committee concerned agreed to allow the research in the first place. At a time when sociologists often emphasise the reluctance of official bodies to allow research into 'sensitive' areas such as the organisational effectiveness of aspects of the social services, it says much for the schools of the area that they should grant a researcher virtually unrestricted freedom to ask whatever questions he wants and also write what he wants about them and their schools.

Although this action may surprise some of their critics of the 'school as hell' or 'teacher as imperialist' variety, the teachers of this community, at least, appear keen to know how they can help – and how they may hinder – the development of their children.

Our work has concentrated so far on a group of secondary modern schools and on boys only within these schools. We have found large differences between the schools in the characteristics of their output of pupils, assessed in terms of rates of attendance, academic attainment (going on to the local technical college after leaving school) and delinquency (being found guilty before a court or officially cautioned by the age of fifteen). As Table 2.1 shows, the school with the top attendance rate averaged 89.1 per cent attendance over the years and the bottom school only 77.2 per cent. One school gets over half its pupils into the local

Table 2.1 Secondary modern school performance, academic years 1966/7 to 1972/3 (per cent)

School	Delinquency (first offenders per annum)	Attendance	Academic attainment
A	10.5	79.9	34.8
B	8.6	78.3	26.5
C	8.3	84.3	21.5
D	8.1	77.2	8.4
E	7.4	89.1	30.4
F	7.2	81.3	18.5
G	5.2	87.0	37.9
H	4.5	88.5	52.7
I	3.8	83.6	36.5

technical college – which is regarded locally as the key to obtaining an apprenticeship or craft – and another manages to get only 8.4 per cent. The school with the highest delinquency rate has 10.5 per cent of its boys recorded as officially delinquent each year and the school with the bottom rate only 3.8 per cent per year. All the schools also exhibit a remarkable consistency in their relative performance over the years – the Kendall coefficient of concordance for the nine schools' attendance rates over seven academic years is 0.85 and that for academic attainment is 0.56. Even with national social change, local population movements and with seven different intakes of pupils, the relative performance of the schools remains substantially unchanged over time. As Table 2.2 shows for the attendance figures, year after year the 'effective' schools retain their effectiveness. The school differences are furthermore remarkably consistent with each other – schools high on delinquency are low on academic attainment ($r = -0.526$) and low on attendance ($r = -0.579$). The nine schools are therefore producing children who appear to be very different, to be consistently different over time and to be consistently different on three separate indicators.

It is possible that these officially generated statistics may reflect not just differences in behaviour between groups of pupils at the different schools but also variations in the administrative methods and definitions which are used to produce the statistics (Kitsuse and Cicourel, 1963), yet it is difficult to explain the differences in this way. The attendance registers were collected in the same way in all the nine schools and all of them used an identical system of 'processing' of their truants by means of Educational Welfare Officers. Further work also shows that the differences between schools are not explicable by variations in the size of their catchment areas or by differences in the amount of illness amongst the pupils at the different schools. The academic attainment figures of numbers carrying on with their education at the local technical college, the entry to which is dependent on four passes in the local School Leaving Certificate, are of course dependent on the numbers of children that the individual schools enter for the various exams. Although it is possible that differences between schools may reflect not real differences in the academic performance of their pupils but simply the fact that some schools enter a higher proportion of their pupils for the exams than other schools which enter only their most able children, this does not explain these findings. If the entry policy of the school were the determinant of its results, we would expect schools entering only the most able of their children to have higher pass rates than those entering a greater proportion of their ability range. This does not happen – school D, whose total fourth year of 65 pupils were entered only for 60 different exams in the 1972 School Leaving Certificate, achieved an overall pass rate of 47 per cent, whereas school H, whose fourth year of only 27 pupils were entered for no less than 130 exams, achieved an 85 per cent pass rate. Since schools entering a small proportion of their pupils achieve the greatest failure rates of all, it is unlikely that the differences between the schools represent anything other than the fact that some schools are producing pupils who cannot – or more likely will not – show much academic ability.

Table 2.2 Attendance rates for boys at secondary modern schools by year and school, academic years 1966/7 to 1972/3 (per cent)

School	1966/7	1967/8	1968/9	1969/70	1970/1	1971/2	1972/3
E	88.5	89.7	90.9	90.6	90.0	87.5	87.2
	1[a]	1	2	1	2	2	2
H	88.0	87.3	91.6	88.9	90.1	88.2	85.7
	2	3	1	2	1	1	3
G	87.1	84.4	86.5	88.4	87.6	86.2	88.2
	3	5	3	3	3	3	1
I	86.3	87.9	84.2	84.6	83.0	80.0	80.0
	4	2	5	4	5	5	5
C	85.0	85.9	84.5	82.0	83.2	83.5	85.2
	5	4	4	7	4	4	4
F	83.9	82.8	83.5	82.5	80.6	77.3	79.0
	6	7	7	6	6	8	7
A	83.2	83.3	84.0	82.6.	77.6	75.4	75.1
	7	6	6	5	8	9	9
B	82.7	75.4	81.3	77.5	73.0	79.0	79.3
	8	8	8	9	9	6	6
D	74.9	74.8	77.7	79.7	78.2	78.5	76.5
	9	9	9	8	7	7	8
Annual average attendance for all nine schools	83.8	82.3	84.1	83.1	81.1	80.7	80.9

Notes
Kendall coefficient of concordance = 0.85 ($P < 0.001$ significant)
a Ranking of school in each year

The statistics of delinquency are perhaps those most open to doubt, since these rates may reflect variations in the processing of offenders by the local police force (Cicourel, 1968). It is easy to see how a school with a high delinquency rate may get a bad name with the local police, who may in turn patrol its catchment area more intensively and be more likely to 'book' offenders in that area rather than use their powers of discretion to warn them. Differences between schools may therefore be exaggerated by the results of differential police action. We know that area police based in the catchment areas of two of the schools have, in fact, been proceeding informally with offenders from those two schools – school A and school F – by taking them to their school for punishment, rather than by taking them through the formal legal processes, yet both these schools already have official delinquency rates that are above average. Since it is possible that other sources of bias might also be operating, we are currently studying the patterns of police patrolling to see if certain areas are 'over patrolled' relative to other areas and are also giving self-report studies of delinquent behaviour to samples of pupils in the schools as a check on the validity of the official records as indicators of the total amount of delinquency committed by their pupils.

Accepting that these statistics reflect real differences in the relative performance of the schools, further large differences in the pupils' performance are also in evidence even after they have left their schools. Table 2.3 shows the pupil unemployment rate for the various schools, compared to an overall ranking order for the schools, which has been calculated by simply averaging each school's relative position obtained on the tables of the three measures of output. The clear indication is that those schools which have the lowest relative success rates with their pupils

Table 2.3 Pupil unemployment rate and overall school performance

Overall rank	School	Pupil unemployment rate (per cent)[a]
1[b]	H	1.4
2	G	0.0
3	I	1.9
4	E	1.3
5	C	1.0
6	F	2.6
7	A	5.4
8	B	7.0
9	D	no information

Notes

a Pupil unemployment rate is the proportion of all leavers (boys and girls) in summer 1972 who had not found employment by the beginning of January 1973.

b In this and following tables, rank number 1 represents the most successful school.

also tend to have the highest rates of unemployment among their school-leavers ($r = -0.714$). Whether this is due to the fact that – because of their poor academic performance – some schools' pupils cannot get jobs, or whether this is due to the fact that some schools' pupils do not wish to find jobs in any case, we cannot be sure. All we can say is that – given the link between unemployment, low income and the generation of other social problems – some schools are sending out into life pupils whose life chances appear disturbingly poor.

The crucial factor is, of course, whether these large, consistent and associated differences between the schools in their success rates simply reflect the fact that some schools are getting a more 'problem-prone' intake of children. Since the nine schools draw their pupils from geographically separate areas of the community and since they take a fixed two-thirds of the full ability range on each case, it has been possible to assess the social characteristics on the individual wards from which the nine schools take their pupils. Table 2.4 shows the overall school performance ranking, compared to the proportion of the employed population in each catchment area who are semi- or unskilled manual workers. Although a high proportion in these latter social groups could be the explanation for some schools' inferior performance, since the correlation between overall school performance and the proportion of the catchment area who are of low social class is low ($r = -0.134$), we can conclude that our schools' outputs vary virtually independently of the social background of their catchment area.

Further evidence to support our hypothesis as to the independent effects of the secondary school regimes comes from an analysis of the academic quality of the intake to the nine schools. Table 2.5 shows the mean raw score[2] on Raven's Standard Progressive Matrices test of non-verbal intelligence (Raven, 1960) obtained by the boys of the autumn 1974 intake that went to the secondary modern schools. Since there appears to be no suggestion that the more successful schools were receiving academically more able children,[3] we must conclude also that the reasons for some schools' evident success and other schools' manifest failure can hardly lie in the relative ability of their pupil intakes.

Table 2.4 Social class of catchment area and overall school performance

Overall rank	School	Proportion of population in social classes 4 and 5 (per cent)
1	H	37.5
2	G	42.5
3	I	42.9
4	E	42.2
5	C	43.9
6	F	43.4
7	A	44.8
8	B	38.1
9	D	38.9

Table 2.5 Academic quality of pupil intake and overall school performance

Overall rank	School	Mean raw IQ score of intake (1974)
1	H	34.3
2	G	33.1
3	I	34.0
4	E	35.4
5	C	34.7
6	F	34.5
7	A	33.2
8	B	35.5
9	D	no information

Since it appears that the schools of our area do have an independent effect of their own, do we know what it is about the school that can so dramatically affect the social and academic development of its pupils? Over the past three years, a programme of research has been undertaken in eight of the nine schools in an attempt to find out what it is about these schools that makes a difference for their children and what it may be about some schools that may make their children different and deviant. Apart from the collection of routine data on the resources, rules and organisation of each school, this work has included interviews with headteachers and staffs, and assessments of the social climate of the schools, the system of rewards and punishments used, the quality of the teaching, and the type of pupil (and teacher) sub-culture to be found in each regime. Further important insights into the school regimes' operation have come from the observation of the day-to-day functioning of the different schools conducted over two years by the writer and by a specially trained participant observer. This observer – who was not told the relative success rates of each school – spent a considerable time in each school taking lessons, talking to staff and pupils and assessing the nature of each school's educational and social ethos.

The first set of clues to explaining the relative success and failure of the schools is provided by analysis of the simple demographic data on school size, class size, adequacy and age of buildings and staff turnover. As Table 2.6 shows, there is evidence that the more successful schools tended to be smaller ($r = 0.634$), a suggestion which fits well with the available literature on the relationship between the size of educational institutions and their capacity to mobilise their pupils towards acceptance of the schools' educational and social goals (Boocock, 1972). The explanation for this finding is not altogether clear – teachers in the small schools tend to say that their school size means that they can know more pupils as individuals than is possible in the larger schools. If this is true, then it is likely that the close primary relationships possible in the small schools may lead to greater identification of the child with the teacher and perhaps to greater knowledge of their children's problems by the teachers.

Table 2.6 School characteristics and overall school performance

Overall rank	School	Number of pupils (1974)	Mean class size (1973)	Staff turnover (1973/4) (per cent)	Age of main building	Adequacy of facilities or buildings
1	H	136	22.5	0.0	1904	poor
2	G	263	28.8	18.2	1906	poor
3	I	176	23.3	22.2	1905	fair
4	E	201	26.1	25.0	1903	poor
5	C	182	29.1	0.0	1903	fair
6	F	355	30.2	37.5	1914	poor
7	A	299	26.5	12.5	1912	poor
8	B	233	23.9	10.0	1937	good
9	D	264	31.7	42.9	1966	good

As Table 2.6 also shows, staff turnover tends to be higher in the least successful schools ($r = -0.549$), although whether this finding indicates that the staff turnover was causing some schools' lack of success or whether the lack of success was causing the teacher turnover, we cannot be sure. It is likely, though, that high staff turnover functions to produce an adverse pupil response to their schools by its adverse effects on their level of identification with the teaching staff – as Phillipson notes (1971, p. 247):

> A high staff turnover means that pupils are regularly faced with different authority figures who make different and often conflicting demands upon them; the lack of steady, stable relationships will tend to result in a confusion among pupils about how to respond in similar situations to a constant flow of different teachers. A regular turnover of teachers provides a setting for the growth of cynicism among pupils about the worth of their school; one result may be a steady decline in the evaluation by pupils both of the school and of themselves.

Whereas these findings on school size and teacher turnover rates are – in view of existing research findings – to be expected, our findings on the relationship between class size, the quality and age of school buildings and the overall success rate of the schools are more surprising. Although a reduction in class sizes has been a priority of governmental policy for years and although teacher unions strongly support such a policy, research has tended to suggest that class size is not a crucial variable in terms of influencing pupil success and failure. In fact, several studies have shown children in large classes to make better than average scholastic progress (Little et al., 1971; Davie et al., 1972). Our data show that successful schools tend to have smaller class sizes ($r = -0.549$); interestingly, class size appears also to have the most marked effect on the academic attainment of pupils ($r = -0.78$), rather than on attendance ($r = -0.34$) or delinquency ($r = +0.38$). Whilst it might appear that this finding would support recent evidence on the importance of the resources available to each school as crucial determinants of pupil success rates (Byrne and Williamson, 1975), the differences in class sizes among these schools at least tend to reflect the fact that some schools cannot get staff to come and teach in them, not simply that they have less staff posts available in the first place. Once some schools have posts they cannot fill and therefore have also above average class sizes, it seems likely that this will affect the overall level of success of the school, making it more and more likely that the school, because of its reputation and lack of success, will continue to be able to utilise less resources per pupil than others. A school with problems, then, will tend – by this cyclical process – to remain a school with problems, because rising class sizes will perpetuate its lack of success.

Our findings on the influence of the age and adequacy of school buildings are also somewhat surprising. Certainly findings from Britain (Plowden, DES, 1967), America (Coleman et al., 1966) and Michael Power's Tower Hamlets study (1972) all suggest that the age, state of repair, adequacy and amenities of school buildings are of negligible importance in determining pupil success or failure, but in fact our findings suggest that the best schools tended to have older buildings and to be – according to the Director of Education's ratings as given in Table 2.6 – in less adequate accommodation. Although it is best to be wary of the importance of findings such as this (the implication is, in fact, that making buildings less adequate will make schools more successful!), it is perhaps worth saying that educational policies which assume that the provision of ever more luxurious buildings will necessarily result in greater pupil success are – according to these findings – in urgent need of critical analysis.

So far, then, it is clear that basic data on the schools suggest that the more successful schools tended to be smaller, have lower staff turnover, smaller class sizes and to be situated in older and less adequate buildings. Further work is in progress to establish both the relative importance of each of these factors and also the precise ways in which these factors appear to have their effects.

Analysis of both the organisational properties of the schools and the nature of the educational and social ethos that may explain their relative success rates is currently only in its early stages. This analysis is of course fraught with difficulty, not only because of the obvious complexity of studying the institution of the school and the practical problems of observer bias that are inherent in the use of the technique of participant observation, but also because the schools appear, at first analysis, to be very similar regimes. All had very similar curricula, because preparation for the exams their pupils sat imposed very similar demands on their teachers. Only one of the schools – the relatively successful school E – had what can be remotely described as a parent–teacher association, and this was merely a hesitant and intermittent experiment rather than a manifestation of a radically different school–teacher ideology. None of the schools had school counsellors – all used the traditional form master as their mechanism of pastoral care. All the schools used corporal punishment, all had formalised morning assemblies. In fact, the nine schools appear – as they are – rather 'unprogressive', traditional working-class secondary modern schools, closely modelled on the grammar schools that have had such high prestige within the educational system of Wales.

In most of the school rules that they attempted to enforce, too, the schools appeared very similar. All the schools banned swearing in class, cheeking teachers, going out of the school grounds without permission, and fighting in school buildings. All of them tried to stop their girls from wearing jewellery and all of them encouraged their girls to play separately from their boys at break and lunch times. Yet in spite of the apparent similarities in much of what the headteachers and staffs enforced, close observation of the schools has revealed subtle, qualitative differences in some areas of school interaction that can begin to enable us to account for the quantitative differences in the rates of deviancy and pupil problems that each school is producing.

As Table 2.7 shows, the schools differ widely in the strategies that they use to orientate their pupils towards their goals. Successful schools appear to be more likely to use prefect systems, although precisely how this may make for a school's success is not clear. Part of this method's effectiveness may be due to its pervasiveness as a form of social control within the school, since the presumably pro-school prefects will be in informal interaction with both their peers — and also younger children at many times when staff authority may be absent — in school G, for example, two prefects from the fifth year stopped some younger children from the second year smashing school windows. In addition to splitting the pupil sub-culture of the fifth year by the creation of a generally more pro-school prefect faction, these pupil authority systems are believed by the schools to be effective as methods of 'rescuing' deviant children — school G, for example, makes 11 or 12 prefects a year out of a year of 40 and usually attempts to make at least half of these appointments from the 'B' stream. The aim, as the headmaster put it, is 'To try to sort out the difficult ones'. All the evidence from these schools would suggest that the

Table 2.7 Aspects of school regimes and overall school performance (participant observer's 'blind' ratings)

Overall rank	School	Uniform years 1, 2 and 3	Uniform years 4 and 5	Prefect system	Enforcement of no chewing gum rule	Enforcement of no smoking rule	Institutional control	Corporal punishment
1	H	yes	yes	yes	low	low	low	very low
2	G	yes	no	yes	medium	low	very low	very low
3	I	no	no	no	low	medium	medium	medium
4	E	yes	no	yes	low	low	low	low
5	C	yes	no	no	low	low	low	low
6	F	no	no	no	high	high	high	high
7	A	no	no	no	high	high	high	very high
8	B	no	no	no	high	high	very high	very high
9	D	no information available						

prefect system also acts as an unrivalled form of social control over those elevated to the position.

The occupants of the role appear to derive some personal pride from it and also some status within the more pro-school peer group of the 'A' stream – the usual green 'Prefect' badges are invariably worn. To be a prefect is also widely thought to confer advantages, in terms of a better reference and recommendation, upon individual pupils. Thus the pupils' commitment to this 'leadership' role gives the school a further symbolic sanction – the remove from office – that it can use to ensure the good behaviour of its pupils. One prefect in school H, for example, who was found to have written various slogans on the school walls and in the toilets, was simply stripped of his prefectship, an action which – being committed to the role – deeply hurt him and embarrassed his parents.

A prefect system, then, acts as a means of social control for the school in general and for the prefects in particular, since being given responsibility for the administration of part of a social structure leads people to shift in their attitudes towards an increasing adoption of the values of that formal system.

A further method that the successful schools tend to use to try to orientate their pupils to identify with their schools is the wearing of school uniform. In the schools that enforce this rule, it is seen as a method of promoting pride in the school and an identification with it, although, as Table 2.7 shows, only one of these schools really tries to enforce this rule with its fourth and fifth year pupils. School G, which enforces a school blazer, regulation-colour pullover and trousers with its first three years, attempts to enforce a school tie only with the fifth year boys and girls. By enforcing a uniform on years 1, 2 and 3 and then not really attempting to continue to fight battles over uniform that they cannot win with their fourth and fifth years, the successful schools believe that they are gaining what they see as the benefits of this enforcement with little of the trouble that is often assumed to accompany it.

While the successful schools appear to be characterised by their use of school uniform and school prefect systems, they are remarkable because of the relatively high degree of autonomy that they give their pupils in other areas of school life. Elsewhere (Reynolds, 1976b) I have argued that a 'truce' between teachers and taught appears to operate in the successful regimes, a truce which lays down boundaries beyond which the participants in the schools will not carry their conflict. This truce is in the nature of an unofficial arrangement for the mutual convenience of both sides of the school, made between working class pupils of low aspirations who seek a stress-free time within their schools and teachers who realise that many of the rules and regulations which should, in theory, govern the interaction between them and their pupils would, if applied, only make their task as teachers more difficult.

The acceptance of the 'truce' situation by the staff is usually manifest in decisions about how hard to enforce three crucial rules – those against smoking, chewing gum and outside school behaviour – which are concerned to limit the autonomy of their pupils, and particularly of their senior pupils. Schools where the truce exists tend not to put great store on the enforcement of 'no chewing gum' rules – at school G, less than a quarter of the staff ever bother to observe this rule at all, whereas at school B it is universally observed. The punishments meted out for its use also reflect the different orientations of the staff – the punishment at school G is simply putting the gum in the bin, whereas at school B the usual punishment is to be hit round the head or arms and then be told to put it in the bin.

In their attitude towards pupil smoking, too, the schools differ in the autonomy they allow their pupils. Some – like schools A and B – try to stop this deviant behaviour and use special smoking patrols by the staff at break and at lunchtimes to root out the 'smokers' corner' which usually assembles round the playground wall or in the boys' toilets. School B has a quite remarkable ritual in which two members of staff go out round the playground wall following the customary group of smokers and lookouts, who go themselves from corner to corner, keeping a hundred yards between them and their enemy. As could be expected, the importance which the schools attach to their pupils not smoking is reflected in the punishments meted out if they do – school G merely confiscates the cigarettes of its caught smokers, whereas the staff of schools A and B usually hit or cane them, as well as confiscate their cigarettes. Since the schools where there is a rigorously enforced no smoking rule are those where there is the highest rate of smoking by the pupils and since the pupils at the schools appear to have very similar rates of smoking outside of school it seems likely that making an issue of whether the pupils smoke may only serve to increase the numbers who do. Quite simply, the more that a school seeks to restrict the within school autonomy of its senior pupils in this way, the more that these pupils may decide to commit the acts that the school has defined as deviant.

The unsuccessful schools, who do not appear to be motivating their pupils to conform and who are restricting some of their autonomy within school, are likely to be faced with increased cohorts of children whose opinion of their teachers and their school environment is unfavourable. In the absence of much normative commitment to the institution's demands that can ensure obedience, these unsuccessful schools appear subsequently forced to apply a much higher level of organisational control in the attempt to reach their goals and maintain commitment. Table 2.7 shows that 'institutional control', which includes factors as the degree to which silence rules are enforced in lessons, and the existence of various restrictions on movement and activity, is higher in the more problem-prone schools. Schools B and F, for example, force their pupils to line up in silence in the playgrounds. In school B the pupils, having been distanced from each other by putting their arms out to their side, are then marched in single file through the corridors of the school, where members of staff wait to try and ensure that no-one talks and to hit anyone if they do. The same school's lessons are rigorously repressed – little more than copying out of books is ever attempted because of the fear that a more 'informal' or 'relaxed' classroom atmosphere may weaken the control that the staff believe to be so tenuous. In the lessons of school G, though, there is likely to be more noise, even more pupil misbehaviour such as talking to another pupil in the next desk, yet there is also likely to be more teacher participation in the lesson and also greater pupil acquisition of knowledge. In school G, as is to be expected, there is no ritualised lining up after breaks and before morning and afternoon school begins and there are no rules that pupils should walk on one side of the corridor when entering or leaving school buildings.

The conflict between staff and pupils in the schools where there is no truce and no easing up on the enforcement of some rules by teachers, is continually fuelled by the attempt of the staff to exercise control in areas of the pupils' lives where they expect autonomy, such as in their behaviour outside school. One boy from school B described what this means:

> If they see you smoking in the night or in the pictures they get you when you come back to school. I remember one incident when me and my friends went to the pictures on a Saturday night and we had all been drinking before we went, and as the ice-cream woman came around we all got up to buy ice-cream, and as we were buying it one of the teachers in our school came over and asked to smell my breath and he smelt my breath and he said he will see me Monday morning. So I went home that night and told my mother what happened she gave me a scolding for drinking with the boys but she said it's nothing to do with the teachers. If we had more time I think I could go on for ages writing about the things about our school.

The acceptance of the truce by the staffs of the successful schools, on the other hand, means that the teachers accept that their authority does not extend outside the school gates or outside school hours. Drinking in a pub under age will be ignored by the teachers in schools such as school G, as will smoking going to and from school and various petty misbehaviours such as fighting in the street.

It is worth saying quite simply that the evidence from these schools suggests that the more a school seeks high control over its more senior pupils by increasing organisational compulsion and decreasing pupil autonomy, the more these pupils may regard their schools as maladjusted to their needs. Rebellion within and delinquency without will be the result of the failure of the pupils and their teachers to declare a truce.

The unsuccessful schools' problems in the control of their pupils which led them to attempt high organisational control in the first place are also in evidence if we consider the type of punishments that they use and the frequency with which they use them. Whereas in the successful regimes, with their more pro-school peer groups, a simple telling-off by the teacher or the occasional clip on the head may be enough to punish deviants and ensure pupil conformity, the unsuccessful schools cannot use these strategies successfully because they do not have the same type of normative commitment from their pupils. In fact, in some of these schools, to be told off by the teacher is likely to have the effect only of increasing the status of the deviant in his peer group. Where teachers cannot use verbal sanctions because they are not effective, these schools tend to use physical punishment to try to control their pupils. As Table 2.8 shows, there is a consistent tendency for the unsuccessful schools to use physical punishment as their normal punishment for rule-breaking – punishment which may include formal canings by the headmaster, informal canings by the staff or informal hitting of children around the head or on the arms. As we would expect, then, and as Table 2.7 shows, physical punishment of children of a formal and informal nature is highest in the least successful school regimes. It is possible, of course, that this association of physical punishment with high rates of 'problem pupils' reflects nothing more than the fact that some schools, having more problem-prone pupils on entry, are forced to use physical punishment to control them. But since the intakes of the schools appear so similar in terms of their ability and social class background, a more likely interpretation of these findings is that high rates of physical punishment may actually generate or cause an adverse response to their school regimes from the pupils in these schools. Such findings, which agree with other surveys (Clegg and Megson, 1968), would suggest that '[c]orporal punishment is likely to delay, rather than promote, the growth of self-discipline and it is humiliating for staff and pupils' (Newsom Report, quoted in Berg, 1968). Quite how high rates of physical punishment may have this adverse effect is not clear – maybe the extensive use of violence as a means of control may set an example of dealing with problems by means of aggression to the children. Perhaps high rates of physical punishment affect children's sense of self-worth or

Table 2.8 Typical punishments for breaking school rules and overall school performance

School overall rank (top most successful)	Rules		
	No smoking	*No fighting in school*	*Swearing aloud in class*
H	cigarettes taken and told off	told off	told off
G	cigarettes taken and told off	told off	told off – rarely caned
I	cigarettes taken and told off	told off and occasionally caned	told off
E	cigarettes taken and told off	told off and occasionally caned	told off – sometimes caned
C	cigarettes taken and told off	told off	told off
F	cigarettes taken, hit and caned	told off and hit	told off and caned
A	cigarettes taken, hit and caned	told off, hit and caned	told off and caned
B	cigarettes taken, hit and caned	told off, hit and caned	told off and caned
D	no information available		

self-esteem. Whatever the reason, the successful school does not appear – or does not need – to use high levels of corporal punishment with children.

To summarise and conclude the analysis so far, we can take an example of a regime that is relatively unsuccessful – school B – and see how the various aspects of pupils' school experience in this regime are inter-related. School B has no prefects to diffuse the authority system and no school uniform to promote an identification with the school in the pupils' early years. There is no 'truce' in the school and social relations between teachers and pupils are characterised by hostility and by the low regard in which pupils hold their teachers.

> I want teachers which associate with us pupils. The teachers like – can't take a joke or have a laugh.

> Mr —, he's hard. He's more of an assassin than a teacher. I want teachers who can take a joke and understand you.

Because of their lack of commitment to the teachers and their unwillingness to see them as 'significant others' in their lives, the teachers need to apply increased coercion to ensure their control.

> They hit you around like you were dirt here. Billy goes mad with you – he grabs your hair, pulls down your head and knees you in the stomach.

The increased coercion is likely to produce lower commitment to the school on the part of the pupils and – as a consequence – lower expectations of the pupils on the part of the teachers.

> I don't like a few of our teachers. Some if you don't know what to do they don't help you and if you go out to ask them they just say why aren't you working why don't they help us? I think that's because we are in B that they haven't any time for us B boys.

> Some teachers just tell you what to do and if you ask a question says 'Work it out yourselves' and calls you a lout.

> Only two or three teachers teach us our work properly. Others just write things on the board for us to copy. That way we don't learn anything for ourselves.

The conflict between pupils and teachers is continually fuelled by the attempt of the staff to exercise control in areas of the pupils' lives where they expect autonomy, such as in their behaviour outside the school, and in some aspects of their behaviour inside it. In the schools like this one that have no truce, there are many pupils who wish for one.

> The rules that I don't agree with are no smoking and no talking in class. The rule of no smoking in the school is pathetic as if they stop us smoking in

school we will only smoke outside or behind the teachers' backs so is it worth punishing boys that do smoke as there are plenty more behind their backs.

And if they stop you talking in class – it's a load of rubbish. All boys will talk in class so is it worth bothering to keep this rule? Besides, they can never stop you talking. You are punished for asking the boy you sit by what page is next in maths.

Where there is this sort of conflict in a school such as school B, there will invariably be vandalism within it, truanting from it and delinquency outside it. Such a reaction from the pupils of these schools is likely to reflect a weakening of the 'moral bind' which ties the child to conventional adult life and institutions and indicates that where the initiation of the child into the accepted ways of life of the adult community that the school undertakes is perverse, then so too will be the child's response. An initiation that the pupils are likely to regard as perverse is produced by the attempt of the teachers to exercise control over the pupils in areas of their life where they feel they should have autonomy. The attempt by the school to exercise control in this area is likely to set in motion a circular process of deviancy amplification – the pupils will regard the teachers as using illegitimate authority and will be less likely to defer to their wishes in other areas of school life. Teachers, perceiving increased opposition, may intensify their efforts to ensure compliance with their rules, which will invariably mean the increased use of coercion, as the teachers are less likely to receive the normative commitment of their pupils. Such coercion is unlikely to reduce the total amount of misbehaviour exhibited by the pupils, and may only increase it, since informal social status within an increasingly alienated student body will increasingly depend upon pupils doing things which are wrong in the eyes of the school.

The successful school, on the other hand, does not fight battles over chewing gum, smoking and out of school behaviour that it knows it cannot win, and does not even attempt to enforce the wearing of school uniform when that enforcement becomes problematic. It does not use high rates of physical punishment and is not harshly authoritarian in its mode of control. The school that produces conformity in its pupils, like the family that produces conformity in its children, is small and diffuses responsibility among its members. This type of school is not non-directive or permissive in the classical sense of the term, since it is clearly directive about some things. The important thing about these schools is not whether or not they are directive, but is rather in which areas of pupils' lives they attempt to direct and how they attempt to do so.

Conclusions

The outline above, based upon our participant observer's ratings of the schools, is of course only tentative and poses almost as many questions as it answers. We need to know why the teachers at the different schools are using different methods and the ideological underpinnings and rationale that they may have for their use. We need to know about the process of within school and within lesson interaction whereby the beliefs and expectations of the teachers are mediated to their children. Most important of all, we need to know why the children appear to be so different at the various schools and why the children at some schools appear to be so 'deviant'. Are the self-perceptions of the cohorts of children at the different schools different, as they should be if some of the schools have encouraged the growth of a delinquent or deviant self-identity among their children? Further work to answer these questions is in progress.

But even though we are still discovering what it may be about the individual school that has the effect of promoting deviance or conformity to societal norms, we know from this study and from the other studies mentioned earlier, that the individual school does have a substantial effect on the sort of young people that its children turn out to be. What, then, are the implications of these findings?

The first important implication concerns the practice of educational research and the areas of their subject matter which educational researchers have viewed as worthwhile areas of investigation. When faced with the need to explain pupil problems, researchers have sought their causal explanation in the nature of the pupils' home and neighbourhood culture, but rarely in the nature of their schools, so that discussion of school deviants is rarely based on any examination of the institutions from which the deviants deviate. As a consequence, much educational research of recent years (Davie et al., 1972) tells us only what we knew to be the case already – namely, that certain children from 'disadvantaged' homes are at higher risk of educational failure. The type of regime that may exacerbate, or help, the process is rarely discussed because it is a question that is never explored.

In recent years the emergence of the interactionist approach in the sociology of education has meant that increased attention has been given to the 'micro' level of the school and to the generation of classroom success and failure. Far more than before, the attempt is being made to understand why certain children should fail and others succeed, an attempt that is based upon an analysis of the teachers' own beliefs as to what constitutes 'educable' or 'ineducable' children. It is this whole neglected area of school life – the sociology of schooling – that needs further development if we are to advance our knowledge of the process whereby adolescent self-perception and identity are socially formed. In brief, then, it is perhaps time that more educational researchers brought schools back into their work.

Second, if the school is – as I believe – an important influence upon its own pupils' levels of truancy, delinquency and educational failure, we should perhaps consider the direction of some of our current educational policies. When confronted by social problems like truancy, delinquency or so-called 'behavioural disorders', our automatic tendency has been, and still is, to appoint more educational psychologists, employ more advisers and introduce more school-based social workers. A veritable army of members of the 'helping' professions now exists to 'help' – or rather, force – the child to adjust to the reality of his school existence, irrespective of whether the reality is worth adjusting to.

Instead of continually merely treating the deviant and delinquent children, we should perhaps begin to look and see if the reason for their rebellion lies squarely in the nature, process and operation of some of the schools that we offer them. If the reason does lie there, then perhaps we ought to seek changes in some of our delinquents' schools.

Notes

1 The schools all take from defined areas of the community, as there is no system of parental choice of school or any overlap of school catchment areas.
2 Raw scores are used, rather than age-adjusted scores, because the age distribution of the pupil intakes of the different schools was very similar.
3 In fact, the correlation between overall school position and ability of intake is slightly negative ($r = -0.454$), suggesting that the more successful schools tended to have lower ability intakes than the unsuccessful. Further tests given to the intake have been concerned with verbal and mathematical ability, and analysis is proceeding to see if these tests indicate the same rather surprising results.

Acknowledgement

First published as Reynolds, D. 'The delinquent school' in M. Hammersley and P. Woods (Ed.) (1976) *The Process of Schooling*, pp. 217–219. London: Routledge & Kegan Paul. Reprinted here with permission from Taylor & Francis.

3

The study and remediation of ineffective schools
Some further reflections

Introduction

The study of school failure, 'ineffective' schools or 'failing' schools has not been an activity that has interested many within the British educational research community historically. With exceptions (e.g. Barber, 1995; Reynolds, 1991, 1996a; Stoll, Myers and Reynolds, 1996) and with the notable exception of the contributors to this book, researchers have preferred to study effective school institutions and assume that this study will help us understand and potentially remediate the ineffective ones (see reviews of this tradition in Reynolds, Bollen, Creemers, Hopkins, Stoll and Lagerweij, 1996; Reynolds, Creemers, Stringfield, Teddlie, Schaffer and Nesselrodt, 1994). Why has this been the case?

First, the early seminal work of Coleman, Campbell, Hobson, McPartland, Mood, Weinfeld and York (1966) and Jencks, Smith, Ackland, Bane, Cohen, Gintis, Heyns and Michelson (1972) generated in the mid-1960s and 1970s a widespread dissatisfaction with education and a widespread professional and public belief that 'schools make no difference'. Researchers were therefore unwilling to study *failure* and consequently studied *success* because they felt that the study of failure might have further contributed to the overwhelming sense of pessimism about the condition of education.

Second, the association of many in the educational research community with the professional development of teachers on in-service and pre-service courses has historically made researchers unwilling potentially to damage inter-professional relationships by studying professional failure. The needs of the Departments of

Education within the higher education sector to market themselves in years of declining enrolments and the related more general need not to upset our 'partners' involved with us in teacher education has made researchers reluctant potentially to wound professional self-confidence. This is shown particularly in the case of the absence of research on teacher effectiveness, where the British context shows considerable variability in teacher quality (Reynolds and Farrell, 1996) but a virtually total absence of the teacher effectiveness knowledge base that is a common feature of educational discourse and research in the United States, the Netherlands and Australia (see Creemers, 1994, for a review).

Third, we have been held back in our understanding of school ineffectiveness by our difficulty in actually attracting 'ineffective' or 'failing' schools into our research studies and the consequent impoverishment of our knowledge. Virtually all the major British and American school effectiveness research studies have suffered from sample attrition and although it is obviously difficult to get reliable information on this matter, one's impressionistic assessment is that the schools that have dropped out were performing more unfavourably on student outcomes, and were in more difficult socio-economic circumstances, than those schools that permitted the research to take place. In the original Reynolds (1976a) school effectiveness studies, for example, the one school to drop out of the sample of nine schools was widely seen within its community as ineffective.

In school improvement, too, the samples of schools providing our knowledge base appear to be highly unrepresentative of all schools. Many schools come into improvement projects precisely because of the location of their senior personnel on school improvement or school effectiveness courses – schools sending people on such courses are highly unlikely to be representative of all schools. Many improvement projects, for example the innovatory 'Improving the Quality of Education' project from Cambridge described by Hopkins and colleagues (1994), are additionally based upon 'volunteer' schools that are unlikely to be typical of all schools.

Fourth, since we have lacked for a variety of reasons detailed information about the ineffective schools, and since we have been anxious to celebrate effective schools, we have therefore tended to do a number of things involving the 'back mapping' of the effective schools' correlates or characteristics into the ineffective schools as the proposed solution to the ineffective schools' problems (see descriptions of such ideas and related projects in Reynolds, Bollen, Creemers, Hopkins, Stoll and Lagerweij, 1996). However, these 'effectiveness factors' are of course the processes and structures that have come from studies of schools that have already become effective – such studies do not tell us the school characteristics needed to reach the status of 'effective'. Furthermore, by mentally planning our research to focus upon the sites of effective schools and then operating with a kind of 'school effectiveness deficit model', we may miss those factors (such as poor staff/staff relations, for example) that are present and exist in the ineffective schools but not in the effective schools. Particularly, we may simply look to see the quantity of the 'success' or 'effectiveness' characteristics the ineffective schools may or may not have, without looking to see whether there are separate 'failure' characteristics that exist in the ineffective schools that require different conceptualisation, operationalisation and measurement (see also Myers and Goldstein in Stoll and Myers, 1998).

The existing knowledge base reviewed

In other publications, we have outlined what the characteristics of ineffective schools seem to be, based upon the experience of our attempted interventions in them over a number of years (Reynolds, 1991, 1996a; Reynolds and Packer, 1992). It has been argued that they possess numerous characteristics that may not permit easy improvement, in particular:

- the widespread belief that change is for other people;
- the belief amongst staff that the school should stick to its past methods of operation;
- the reluctance of individual staff to stand out from the prevailing group culture;
- the reluctance of many staff to attempt new things, fearing that they may fail;
- the blaming of factors external to the school by the staff for the failure of the school;
- the absence of any understanding among the majority of the staff about possible alternative policies;
- the belief among the staff that outsiders have little to contribute to turning the school around;
- the presence of numerous personality clashes, feuds and cliques within the staff group, in a setting of generally grossly dysfunctional relationships;
- the unwillingness or inability of staff in the school to see that its 'presenting' problems of failure mask the 'real' problems of the institution.

Others have usefully contributed to our knowledge in this area. Rosenholtz (1989) studied the social organisation of a sample of schools in Tennessee and generated a typology of types of school, the one called 'moving' or learning enriched, and the other 'stuck' or learning impoverished. Teddlie and Stringfield (1993) note that in their 'outlier' ineffective schools, selected on the basis of poor levels of value-added academic achievement over time, expectations of pupils' achievements were lower and principals were more involved in activities peripheral to the attainment of the major academic goals. Myers (1994 and 1996) has also speculated upon the 'deep culture' of ineffective schools and usefully explored the importance of their collected myths, which are seen as very pervasive and additionally very destructive and disempowering of change. Stoll, Myers and Reynolds (1996) have also surveyed the various perspectives – and policy remedies – that have been applied to this sector of education, and Barber (1995) has also related the problems of ineffective schools within their local and national policy contexts.

Some further evidence on ineffective schools

The picture of the schools that one has viewed in the existing literature is not, then, a particularly hopeful one for those expecting it to be an easy task to turn such schools around. The organisational problems of the school (an absence of 'effectiveness' characteristics and the presence of 'failure generating' characteristics) combine with the culture of the school (fatalism, pessimism and a hostility to those outside school factors that might be helpful for change in positive directions) and the relational patterns of staff (cliques, fractiousness) to generate a three-dimensional block upon the possibilities of change.

My more recent experience of ineffective schools in the late 1990s suggests, though, that the above picture may have been a somewhat partial and overly pessimistic one. This experience, derived in part from being a member of the governing body of two schools that have been in receipt of 'special measures' as determined by OFSTED and in part from undertaking consultancy and in-service work with schools, other than those in Wales that had formerly formed the totality of my experience, suggests that there are a number of other factors in the organisation, culture and ethos of ineffective schools that are of relevance.

One of these factors makes the difficulties of an ineffective school probably even more severe and probably even longer lasting. This is the likelihood that the schools possess governing bodies that have historically both moulded, and subsequently reflect, the 'ineffective' cultural characteristics of the school itself. Both the governing bodies of my experience possessed considerable passivity, a considerable knowledge deficiency about what to do to improve matters, and a very fractured set of interpersonal relations, with these being based upon racial lines in one of the schools studied. In this particular school, the racial balance of the pupils in the school had reached the crucial 'threshold' of comprising 35–40 per cent Asian, Oriental and Afro-Caribbean children, the level at which 'white' children often become somewhat threatened and accordingly indulge in racist attacks, racial abuse and the like. The numerous racial incidents in this school became paralleled by considerable racial conflicts between 'Asian' and 'white' governors, which meant that the governors were unable to give a unified response when the school needed leadership to deal with the 'special measures' routine of OFSTED and the associated involvement of local education authority inspectors.

There are, however, a number of features of ineffective schools that may also make their problems more remediable than we have argued hitherto. First, all the available evidence from studies both of 'effective' and 'ineffective' schools suggests that ineffective schools are not merely possessed of a low 'mean' or average of the teacher behaviours linked to effectiveness, they are also possessed of a much greater 'range' or variation in these behaviours. The work of Teddlie and Stringfield (1993), for example, shows this wider range of teaching behaviours in their ineffective schools and Murphy (1992) has rather nicely noted the symbolic, organisational and cultural 'tightness' that prevails by contrast in effective schools.

It is of course easy to see how ineffective schools may generate this wide range, since they are less likely to have possessed the leadership and management that could generate coherence and cohesion in school organisational response to pupil needs. It is also easy to see how the student academic and social outcomes from these ineffective schools may also be affected by a large within-school range: inconsistency of teachers' standards and behaviours makes the possibility of socialisation of young people into 'core' standards and values thoroughly problematic (Reynolds, 1996b).

However, the existence of this range also has the potential for *facilitating* the improvement of ineffective schools, since it means that even within such schools there will be *relatively* good practice. Given that the range of variation by department *within* schools is probably three or four times greater than the average variation *between* schools (Reynolds and Cuttance, 1992), then it is likely that the typical ineffective secondary school will have some departments which have relatively good practice *when compared with all schools of all levels of effectiveness*. It is of course highly likely that there will be problems within the ineffective schools in actually making purposive use of their variation by utilising the experience and excellence of their effective departments. But the existence of such effectiveness is a potential resource that few have considered to date.

Second, it is important to note that the 'movement' in effectiveness status that can be obtained from ineffective schools may be considerably greater than might have been predicted from earlier analyses. Precisely because ineffective schools are highly likely to have been in an unstable, stressed and 'unsteady' state, they may be amenable to rapid improvement in the same way as some of them have been amenable to rapid dissolution and decline. One of the two schools we have recently been involved with was to a considerable degree turned around within three months of the appointment of a new headteacher, whose initial diagnosis of the school's problems was that the school needed, above all, 'order' in the playground and in its corridors so that there was a predisposition to order in the classrooms. This gave teachers who had spent historically much of their within lesson time in simple 'fire-fighting' as behavioural problems occurred, the chance both to teach academic material again and to rediscover the enjoyment of their 'craft' of teaching. The power of external reinforcers such as market-based competition, the publicity given to schools that have failed and the strong community pressure upon both of the schools to improve were all factors which in both schools made their 'turnaround' a more rapid process than might have been expected from the existing literature.

Third, not all the staff to be found in ineffective schools are the tired, defeated 'old lags' or 'rump of poor practice' that have been so prevalent in past descriptions of the schools. In recent years, the pressures upon teachers in general and in the ineffective schools in particular have encouraged the premature retirement of many of the disillusioned, less competent 'trailing edge' of poor practice that might have comprised maybe up to two-thirds or three-quarters of the total of the staff in some of the more ineffective schools. Whilst many of these posts have been permanently lost because of the need to cut school budgets, some limited staff replacements have arrived in these schools: staff who are invariably young and invariably ambitious to show that they can survive in difficult circumstances. Indeed, the lack of competent applicants for posts such as that of head of department within such schools invariably means that quite youthful teachers are often given very considerable responsibilities by comparison with what teachers of similar ages would have been given elsewhere in other schools.

In one respect, the arrival of those who are sometimes called the 'Young Turks', or who are sometimes called in American inner-city schools the 'Young Guns', may pose the ineffective schools problems, since the remaining 'rump' of older, more weary and more fatalistic staff may well not react positively to 'new blood', particularly since many of the 'rump' will themselves have been trying for promotion within these schools for some considerable time without success. Already fragmented staff relations may be made more difficult by such staff changes.

However, the presence in the ineffective schools of some youthful enthusiasm, and some energy allied with some ambition, may generate a rather more positive environment for change than might have been expected from some earlier accounts of this sector.

Do we have the technologies to turn ineffective schools around successfully?

A generally more optimistic assessment of the prospects of the ineffective schools' 'setting' being improved should lead us naturally to assess those interventions in the lives of such schools that may have positive effects. In past publications, we have simply posed some questions as to what may be appropriate forms of 'remediation' or 'intervention' or 'treatments' in such schools without explaining the knowledge base and experience that led to such questions in the first place. Here, we attempt to flesh out in more detail exactly what the content of successful interventions with ineffective schools might be, utilising examples of strategies and interventions that have been successfully used in ineffective schools in the last few years.

First, it is likely that ineffective schools need information on how to improve themselves that they haven't got, but all attempts to reach ineffective schools with this information have faced problems because the school organisations themselves are likely to reject the information that they need if it comes in the form of interventions in the life of the school by outsiders, particularly if it were to be through 'university so-called experts'. One successful method has proved to be the 'Trojan horse' technique of reaching schools, whereby the knowledge the schools need in the fields of school effectiveness, teacher effectiveness and departmental effectiveness is brought to the schools in the form of one of their own members, who is given the knowledge outside school by the 'university so-called experts'. In the Cardiff Change Agents project (Reynolds, Davie and Phillips, 1989), senior personnel from schools, which in many cases were ineffective schools, were admitted to a course which involved one day a week attendance at the local university. These individuals were given bodies of knowledge concerning effective practices and also a wide variety of knowledge bases concerning useful and appropriate interventions in the lives of schools, including psychotherapeutic techniques, group work techniques and behavioural approaches to school management. The teachers themselves took the knowledge bases back to their schools, and found a much more ready acceptance of the knowledge bases amongst their colleagues than would have been the case had the knowledge bases gone to schools through direct university transmission of knowledge to individual schools.

Second, it is highly likely that within ineffective schools are a set of damaged interpersonal relationships, and we have noted above that the ineffective school is likely to possess a large number of cliques, warring factions and fragmented relationships which make coherent organisational responses to its problems very difficult. Staff meetings and general disclosure may well show individuals 'playing the person' rather than 'playing the ball' and individuals agreeing or disagreeing with statements and policy proposals not because of the inherent value of the proposal but because of the origin of the proposals in terms of the person or persons that they came from within the school.

In such a setting, the rebuilding of interpersonal relationships is clearly of great importance. One technique is to generate greater unity amongst the staff by using those who are outsiders to a school to provide a common source of hatred: the so-called 'cognitive dissonance' approach whereby individuals are believed to like each other more if they have a common enemy to dislike. One example of the use of this approach is in the role of external persons to a school giving in-service presentations that are calculated to generate a unified response from staff. Arranging for university people to give in-service sessions in hotels, involving provocative lectures after a dinner in which large quantities of alcohol were served to fuel anger with the outsider, would be a classic method of rebuilding relationships by generating a degree of 'fellow feeling' among staff.

Third, the attempt to turn around ineffective schools clearly needs as many reinforcers as possible, given that many of the patterns within such schools may well have been in existence for considerable periods of time. The staff group, although there may be young staff keener on change than their fellow members, may well not provide a very powerful lever for change. The catchment area outside the school may not be heavily involved with the school. In such circumstances, the attempt to turn around such schools needs to find alternative sources of power to use to change the staff as a whole and particularly to change those members of staff who may be particularly ineffective. In these circumstances, pupils and parents have been used to try and improve their schools: in one case, the use of pupil questionnaires for Years 10 and 11 concerning their opinions of their teachers was introduced into an ineffective school under the guise of encouraging consumer response and evaluating consumer opinions, reasons with which it was hard for staff to argue. Another example from another school was the use of parent questionnaires in which parents were asked to give their opinions on the school in *general*, which of course very often turned into the giving of both global descriptions of things that parents liked or didn't like about the school and very highly *particular* and personalised descriptions of staff they liked and staff that they didn't like within the school. Again, it is virtually impossible for the 'rump' of staff to stop parental surveys, given both the rhetoric and reality of consumerism that pervades educational discussion currently and the clear need for any school (in particular an ineffective school which may well be losing pupil numbers) to protect its intake and therefore protect teachers' jobs.

Fourth, it is highly likely that turning around ineffective schools requires the exercise of a large number of micro-political skills (see also Stoll and Fink in Stoll and Myers, 1998). In many areas of education it is clear that coalition building, micro-politics and management of power are key components of school improvement, although of course such techniques receive very little attention either within the discipline of educational management and administration or within school effectiveness currently. If the 'playing of politics' is so crucial in determining the organisation of all schools, it is likely to need to play an even greater role within those schools where, for whatever reason, the school has developed an abnormal cultural and organisational response to pupil needs. One way of 'playing politics' is clearly to attempt to bring on, and give enhanced influence to, effective teachers within the school and to increase the proportion of these competent staff by progressively chipping away at the numbers that comprise the 'rump' of poor practice. This rump may comprise two-thirds or three-quarters of the total staff of some ineffective schools but can very easily be reduced in numbers and in importance by working with its more competent members and giving them enhanced responsibilities. Such responsibilities can be generated through formal promotion or, in the absence of promoted posts or responsibility allowances to give, can be achieved through giving such people informal status by organising improvement committees or such like.

The playing of politics can be taken further, however. In one school, which improved rapidly over time, the newly arrived headteacher decided to 'play politics' with his staff immediately on arrival at the beginning of the academic year. The usual 'beginning of the year' staff meeting was held, at which all staff expected the new headteacher to make clear his intentions about what was to happen to the school. They expected a mission statement and a clear blueprint about what it was that the new person wanted. The new headteacher, though, decided that the best thing he could do was to 'audit' the staff and audit the school's organisational responses, in order to understand enough of what the problems of the school were to propose sensible solutions. The first staff meeting of the year, therefore, was simply an administrative exercise with no clear guidance given about the direction of the mission or the content of change. The headteacher subsequently announced that he was very happy to talk to any members of staff individually about the future direction of the school and said that his door would be open for members of staff to come in and talk to him about what they thought should happen within the school.

Members of staff then, as individuals, began to slip in to see the headteacher, with the first group going in being the 'Young Turks' who were ambitious and who wished for preferment from the new regime. As the old lags saw the 'Young Turks' going in, many of the old lags became somewhat insecure, thinking that the Young Turks would be closeted with the headteacher and communicating what they thought about themselves and their deficiencies. The old lags then started going in to see the headteacher themselves, with the result that by the end of the autumn term virtually every member of staff had been in at least once to see the headteacher and had, to use the headteacher's expression, 'thrown their cards away' by telling the headteacher the background of the school, things about themselves and what the internal processes of the school had been. The headteacher, therefore, was playing a complicated micro-political game, in which he had revealed none of his own beliefs but was waiting for individuals to make clear their own situations and beliefs before telling both individuals and the staff as a whole what his plans were.

Fifth, it is important for coalition building and for gaining a sense of momentum within ineffective schools that goals are chosen that are both easily achievable and achievable in a short time period. Choice of such targets as 'a litter-free environment' or 'a graffiti-free school', or a focus upon the school attendance rate or suspension rate (where rapid improvements can be made by altering the behaviour of only a small number of pupils), will work much better than choice of 'medium-' or 'long-term' goals such as the school's level of academic achievement, which may take two or three years to influence. With successful attainment of 'low level' targets, competence will be established, confidence will rise and the atmosphere within the school will become more favourable for the major structural and cultural changes that are needed.

Sixth, it is essential that ineffective schools are given the truth about their situations, otherwise known as 'brute sanity' (Fullan, 1991). The need to do this, but the equally important necessity of not alienating the school staff to the situation where they will not respond at all through doing it, is one of the most difficult things to handle within the ineffective school. Successful use of external consultants to *diagnose* with the aid of the specialist expertise, rather than as providers of information about what to *prescribe* on the basis of the diagnosis, is likely to be productive (see Learmonth and Lowers, and MacBeath in Stoll and Myers, 1998). Such persons can bring in 'value-added' analyses that will show incontrovertibly that a school's performance is not simply due to the quality of the catchment area or the intake but is in reality due to the quality of the school's organisation.

Such 'brute sanity' often has a further function apart from truth telling, in that it often flushes out from the 'rump' of staff the views that need to be contradicted and corrected in order for school improvement to occur. On one occasion in an ineffective school, the statement that the school was 'well below the line' in terms of what was being predicted in academic achievement relative to its intake evoked an aggressive protest from one of the leaders of the school 'rump', who complained that the catchment area was so severely deprived that the school had no chance of achieving any more than its present level of GCSE results. The interaction between the outside consultant from higher education and the rump's spokesperson then became so antagonistic that the headteacher had to insist that the discussion was broken off.

The importance of this symbolic 'showdown' as the 'brute reality' of the diagnosis from outside met the different diagnosis from inside the school was considerable. The representative of the rump had clearly lost the argument, and the school staff had been made aware of the school's own role in the generation of failure, but the headteacher could still try to be the leader of *all* the teachers in the school because the diagnosis and truth had been told by someone else other than he. Indeed, as the outside consultant left the meeting of staff at morning breaktime, the headteacher could be heard saying to the staff, 'Whilst I wouldn't agree with everything that Professor X has said, you have to admit that there's something to it, and that the school does need to improve!'

Further broadening our perspectives on ineffectiveness

The above somewhat revised, and somewhat more optimistic, picture of ineffectiveness that more recent experiences with schools suggest, together with what one would regard as the beginning of a technology of 'treatments' that may work in their specific contexts, is clearly of potential importance in broadening the way in which the schools have been seen away from the conventional 'pathology' model that has predominated historically.

Further broadening and enlightening of our perspectives can take place through the further reorientations that are associated with appreciation of two additional bodies of knowledge on:

- the study of other countries' educational philosophies, and their systemic technologies of education;
- the use of experience and analogies from other non-educational disciplines, such as applied science and medicine.

To take the comparative educational dimension first, it is clear that not all societies have the range of variation in school quality that is so marked in most accounts of the British experience. Data from the International School Effectiveness Research Project (ISERP) shows that while the school/classroom level explains approximately 20 per cent of pupil variation in the United States, and 12 per cent of variation in the UK, in Taiwan it explains only 1–2 per cent (Reynolds and Farrell, 1996). The latter society, and other Pacific Rim societies also, is committed to utilising a strong 'technology' of education in which teachers are taught in pre-service education to utilise a small number of teaching and schooling strategies which are repetitively and thoroughly taught to all. Likewise, the ways of organising schooling are heavily standardised, involving central government provision of children's textbooks, centrally determined assessment methods and content, and central determination of such factors as school goals and 'mission' (see Reynolds and Teddlie, 1996; Creemers and Reynolds, 1996 for further exploration of this theme).

By contrast, British methods of both teacher development and school organisation have traditionally been much more concerned with a voluntary approach, in which the technologies of education are chosen by individual teachers and headteachers from a range of strategies, some of which may be teacher- or school-generated or 'invented'. Whilst the generation of their own individual methods may be responsible for the 'artistry' of the leading edge of British teachers and schools that has historically been much commented upon, it is possible that it may also be responsible for the 'trailing edge' of British practice also seen in the ineffective schools. Methods utilised in other societies whereby good practices in teaching and in schooling are discovered, codified and routinely transmitted as part of the routine procedures of professional education, may have positive effects, therefore, on our educational variation in general and upon our ineffective schools in particular.

The second body of knowledge that might be useful to us in understanding and remedying ineffective schooling is that derived from the experience and interventions of both applied science and the applied science of medicine. Applied science, for example, attaches enormous importance to the investigation of any failure in its technology, such as bridge failure or the failure of machinery of any kind. Medicine studies sickness and ill health, wishing to examine in detail the characteristics of the problem, its epidemiology, and the possible remediation of the condition (in marked contrast to conventional school effectiveness research which has studied the 'well' or effective schools and assumed that the way to improve the 'sick' or ineffective schools is to give them health-producing characteristics, rather than study and remedy their illness).

Whilst it is clear that it is possible to establish cause and effect relationships within the physical sciences that have eluded us so far in the study of education, the insights that other disciplines' strategies of 'problem identification' and 'problem remediation' might give us are potentially useful as we seek to advance the study of school ineffectiveness from its early somewhat simplistic base (see Hargreaves, 1997, for speculations on this theme).

Conclusions

Whilst we noted earlier that the study of 'ineffective' schools has not been central within the educational research community, there are increasing signs of interest in the sector. Some of the earlier, more pessimistic approaches to the schools need to be complemented by a recognition that the schools have potential for improvement, and that we may have a 'technology' of improvement of use to them.

It is clearly crucial that our knowledge of the sector increases further. The present wide range of schools in 'special measures', and the large number of researchers involved in attempts to help such schools, constitute an experiment of a nature where the effects of such interventions on school processes, outcomes and functioning could be measured and codified. It is therefore vitally important that the current wave of policy interventions contribute directly to knowledge as well as to practice.

Acknowledgement

First published as Reynolds, D. (1998) 'The study and remediation of ineffective schools: some further reflections' in L. Stoll and K. Myers (Eds) *No Quick Fixes: Perspectives on Schools in Difficulties*. Lewes: Falmer Press. Reprinted here with permission from Taylor & Francis.

4

The truth, the whole-class truth

We live in a shrinking world. The information revolution has ensured no part of the globe can remain immune to the ideas and experiences of other parts. The downside of this process is global homogeneity. The upside is the capacity to learn from the achievements – and the mistakes – of others.

In education, we have been far too slow to realise the advantages of looking beyond the white cliffs of Dover. Other countries have processes in their schools and classrooms which we do not have and have different traditions and different ways of organising themselves to generate high-quality outcomes. They also have different economic, social and cultural structures that should make us wary of any direct transplants of practices.

Our own research in the International School Effectiveness Research Project (ISERP) and the review of the international literature on educational achievement reported in part on *Panorama* this week suggest that English performance at all ages except 16 to 19 is rather poor by comparison with that of other societies, particularly those from the Pacific Rim. While there are numerous problems concerning the validity of the surveys, at the very least they give cause for concern.

Some of the reasons for the success of other societies are undoubtedly not educational. There is no doubt that the stress upon hard work in Pacific Rim societies, teachers' status, the ambitions of parents and the survival of extended family and community networks that routinely transmit respectable attitudes are all factors implicated in their performance.

But it is clear that the educational system also has considerable effects – how else can an excellent performance from older British children be explained? If in Britain the same culture and social structure generates both a poor and an excellent set of results for children of different ages, the explanation must lie in the educational system.

So, looking at the education of other societies may be useful to help us improve. In the Pacific Rim, it is clear that the educational system has a limited number of clear goals. There is a widespread belief that all children can learn, and that the role of early-years education is to ensure all children have the basic skills on which later learning depends.

Within schools, teacher collaboration is made possible by having a fifth of time as 'frees'. Mixed-ability classes, in which more able children help slower learners, only move on from a topic when all children have grasped it. Frequent testing makes it possible for teachers to know where children have got to.

Within classes no 'trailing edge' of children is permitted, extra work in lesson breaks and lunchtimes being the remedy. Lessons are of high-quality direct instruction from the teacher, facilitated by work from common textbooks and workbooks.

Looking at other countries that may be more educationally successful than we are can generate, then, ideas for us to use. Given the differences in context, though, between the Pacific Rim and Britain, it would be unacceptable to propose anything other than initial experiment with some of the most important factors. High-quality interactive whole-class instruction and additional work with the trailing edge would seem to be obvious candidates.

Looking at other countries can give us even more. One can use the lens of their systems and experiences to look back at our own culture and system with profit. Seen from this perspective, the continued problems in Britain with key stage 2 and ages 7 to 11 may be understandable. Where have we gone wrong?

First, when faced with a range of achievement on entry to primary school it is possible that our fondness for differentiation in such areas as mathematics has increased the range of achievement. Other countries act directly to reduce the range – by extra work in Taiwan, or holding pupils down in countries like Switzerland and Germany. We, by contrast, systematically vary our pupils' opportunities for learning.

Second, in Britain we have systematically reduced the constant of the teacher to maybe 20 per cent of total lesson time, and shifted the burden of learning to children and their achievement-differentiated groups. It is not surprising then that children may both receive less knowledge and show a greater range.

High-quality whole-class interactive teaching – not the whole-class teaching that is the mantra of some – gives children their teacher. We give children mostly themselves.

Looking at other countries does more than make one doubt the wisdom of some of our practices. It makes one doubt the value of conventional discussions of 'progressive' and 'traditional' as used within the current anodyne wrangle that has characterised British discussions of primary education.

Taiwan, for example, holds back the clever until the less able are ready to move on, believes that all children from all backgrounds can learn and gives all children a similar opportunity to learn. Yet Taiwan is called 'traditional' and Britain, which leaves children more to work on their own, streams the able within lessons, and systematically withholds knowledge from some children, is called 'progressive' or 'trendy'. Labels like these simply no longer accord with any reality, save only the mental strait-jackets and limitations of their proponents.

It should be no surprise, then, that I believe that studies of other nations can do considerable good. They can alert us to practices that appear to work in other contexts, for us to try in our own. They can help us understand our own problems. They can indeed help us be aware of ethnocentricity and labels which are long past their shelf life.

At their best, they can help us in the task of generating new sets of policies that are not so much philosophically as practically based. Through looking at the best of our own and other countries' practices, we can envisage synergistic blends of practice, for example of whole-class interactive teaching when there is knowledge to inculcate, and group/individual work when there is knowledge to access. By so doing we can create primary schools that may not be pure in terms of educational philosophy but may be more potent in terms of achievement.

Blending elements together in these ways is under discussion in many societies. The tragedy for Britain is that one will hear more of this in other societies than in ours.

Acknowledgement

First published as Reynolds, D. (1996). 'The truth, the whole-class truth', *Times Educational Supplement*, 7 June, p. 2. Reprinted here with permission from the *Times Educational Supplement*.

5

Creating world-class schools

What have we learned?

Introduction: our research strategy reviewed

We ranged in this book across nine countries and four continents in our search to understand issues to do with 'what works'. One of our goals has also been to attempt to answer questions as to 'why' certain things may work. When we began this study, the education debate was becoming internationalised with the possibility being increasingly realised that other countries' schooling practices might be useful in educational reform in different countries. We also noted that the school effectiveness discipline had recently neglected to further research its core, namely 'what works' in promoting positive pupil achievement and whether 'what works' needs to be quantitatively and qualitatively different in different social settings. We also noted the criticisms of school effectiveness research and the need for the discipline therefore to move forward.

We outlined our quantitative data on school outcomes and processes both at pupil and classroom level, and studied in detail the more effective and the less effective schools we have found in the different social contexts within different societies. In Chapter 13 we summarised our findings about the classroom and school factors that appeared to be affecting multi-year outcomes. We found a large number of variables that apparently were universal and important in all countries, and some others that were specific to certain countries, and then speculated about the explanations for these findings.

In this final chapter, we move on to the question of what the educational lessons for diverse countries may be, based on the data we have gathered and analysed.

In some places in this chapter, we consciously go beyond what our inevitably sometimes partial data can tell us. However, our speculations and hypotheses are not offered without support – we have, as a team, a combined experience of over 80 'person years' as school effectiveness researchers. We also, as a team, have spent some years wrestling with the themes that we now take up. Although we may go *beyond* our data, we are not *light* on data or on the *experience* involved in interpreting it.

We noted in the first two chapters the details of our research strategy and why we were adopting it. We took a cohort of pupils who moved through their schools over two years, and collected a range of data upon them, their classrooms, their schools, and the societies that provided the context for their education. We explicitly reflected a mixed methodology tradition, and utilised both quantitative and qualitative data pragmatically, choosing to use the particular methods that we found appropriate for the research task in question. We developed a range of instruments that were novel in this research field, including pupil attitude questionnaires, observation systems of classrooms and measures for obtaining data on the child's actual experience of education across an entire school day. We developed an innovative intervisitation system to chart the variation between societies in their contexts and cultures and the 'taken for granted' that might have gone unintentionally unreported by members of country teams. We also collected rich, intensive and high quality data from contrasting schools of different levels of effectiveness in every one of our nine countries, with each school being described and contrasted on a common set of parameters covering their organisation, leadership, staffing, expectations and related factors that, together, represent probably all the dimensions that have historically been utilised in effectiveness research internationally (Teddlie and Reynolds, 2000).

We are confident that ISERP stands among the most conceptually advanced and methodologically sophisticated studies in our field. The multiple levels of the data collection, the multiple methods of study, the multiple outcomes on which data was collected over three cycles and two school years, and the range brought to the study by the choice of countries and contrasting schools within countries, all mark out the study design as of high quality. However, it should be clear from our discussion in this volume that the high quality of the study design was not always marked by high quality implementation of that design. There were never the resources available to fully train and monitor country teams into fully implementing the agreed methodology in exchange for resources, and there were never the resources to closely monitor how each of the nine country teams was progressing. Like most studies in the area of international effectiveness, our study needs a health warning attached to it in several respects, although for the teams involved our studies have a considerable amount of 'face validity'.

Our confidence in our findings is confirmed by the fact that although we were not even sampled to be a 'country versus country' study of achievement differences, such as the TIMSS project, the relative position of our nine countries on the mathematics tests utilised was quite similar to the position shown by those countries in TIMSS and in most of the international surveys to date (see Reynolds and

Farrell, 1996, for a review). We note, in particular, that the comparable fourth grade TIMSS mathematics results showed students from Hong Kong scoring, on average, above those from the United States and Canada, who in turn had higher scores than those of England, Norway, and Ireland, just as our results do. Findings on the influence of the social class of background of pupils in English speaking societies also parallel the findings from a wide range of studies in this area, as do the findings on the positive relationship between pupils' attitudes and their academic achievement (see Mortimore *et al.*, 1988 for comparable findings). Although there were inevitable flaws in the implementation of the research strategy, there are enough areas of strength to draw on, enough consistency of findings with other studies and enough overlapping 'intervisitation' experience to make one certain that the results that constitute what is being reported here are not simply an artefact of variation between research teams.

Our findings reviewed

We summarise our findings as follows:

- Whatever the problems we had encountered as our research design was implemented internationally, it is clear that the great majority of schools 'played in position' in all countries, with lower social class schools getting lower initial maths achievement scores than middle social class schools, and less effective schools getting lower scores than typical or more effective schools.
- Pupils' increasing time in school weakens the relationship between pupils' achievements and their parental ethnic, educational and social class backgrounds, in all our countries where we have usable data. These findings indicate the power of schooling to combat disadvantage. They tell us, as have many other effectiveness research studies (Teddlie and Reynolds, 2000), that schools clearly *can* make a difference.
- It is clear that there are interesting variations between countries in the reliability of their education systems, with some evidencing 'low variance' and some, predominantly Anglo-Saxon societies, showing larger between classroom and school variability. We speculate later in this chapter on how this may reflect on a 'weak' system of education, one where individual headteachers and teachers of Anglo-Saxon societies are the building blocks of schools, rather than schools being formed by 'strong' systems.
- It is clear that there is variation across the country contexts in the extent that the social background of pupils influences their progress at school, with the two Pacific Rim countries of Taiwan and Hong Kong showing the lowest background effects in two different analyses that we undertook on this issue (one from each analysis, we should make clear). Whilst it is unclear the extent to which this reflects the presence in all social strata of these countries of values derived from historic religious and cultural traditions, this finding may also reflect the extent to which strong technologies of practice exist that are applied

deliberately to the education of all children, a theme we return to later in this chapter.

- It is clear that many of the factors that have formed the intellectual backbone of the teacher effectiveness research and practice movement internationally, to do with the quality of teachers' classroom management, their instruction and their classroom climate, do explain variation in pupils' achievement gain in many diverse countries across the world. Indeed, at the level of the discrete behaviours exhibited by teachers, it is factors such as clarity, questioning, high expectations, a commitment to academic achievement and lesson structuring that have formed the core constructs of the teacher effectiveness tradition that partially explain why the less effective schools of the world differ from the typical and the more effective. These amount to the *universals* that we wished our study to test out the existence of. Indeed, as one reads through the case studies of classrooms that are reported in the school case studies under the heading 'A Day in the Life of a Child', one is struck by how similar is the experience of children in the classrooms of effective schools across the world in terms of the teachers and teacher behaviours they are encountering.
- It is also clear that many of the concepts that have formed the intellectual backbone of the school effectiveness research and practice movement internationally, concerning the quality of the headteacher/principal, the nature of school expectations and the extent to which the school level potentiates the quality of the classroom experience, do travel in explaining why some schools are effective in a wide variety of different country contexts. They also travel in explaining variation between schools in their effectiveness in different socioeconomic status contexts. The factors that do not travel so well (school resources, school image and school relationship with local authorities) are exactly what one would expect from this literature.

However, it is clear from the case studies reported that whilst *conceptually* a factor such as 'the quality of the principal' is a universal factor determining the level of a school's effectiveness in all the various countries of the world we worked in, the precise *operationalisation* of the effective principal differed according to the cultural context of individual societies. In the United States or the United Kingdom, a 'top down' orientation was the precise method that was associated with effectiveness – in the Netherlands, it would be a more 'lateral' or collaborative orientation to one's colleagues. In marked contrast to the classroom level, where the universals are the same conceptually *and* behaviourally, the school case studies show that the precise ways in which effective school factors showed themselves were somewhat different across international contexts, much more different than the teacher behaviours.

We cannot stress this too highly – *many factors that make for good schools are conceptually quite similar in countries that have widely different cultural, social and economic contexts.* The factors hold true at school level, but the detail of how school-level concepts play out within countries is different between countries. At the classroom level, the powerful elements of expectation, management, clarity and instructional quality transcend culture.

The implications of the findings for policy-makers

We noted at the beginning of this book that policy-makers have begun to look across the globe in search of practices that might improve their schools. Reasons for this worldwide search may range from simple curiosity to, perhaps, near desperation for further increments in school quality. Much of the search may also be due to the genuine realisation that societies other than one's own may have useful educational practices, initiatives, policies, and processes that might be worthy 'try outs' in policy-makers' own societies. Trying to 'cast a broad net' while seeking solutions to specific, country-level, vexing problems seems to be a generally laudable policy for policy-makers to follow.

Whatever the reason for the enhanced policy internationalisation, policy-makers should be reassured by the findings of our study, since it is clear that 'what is necessary for schools to work' is a conceptually very similar range of things in different countries. The classroom, the principal and the other factors that make schools 'more effective' or 'less effective' across the globe appear to be an established set of findings that should be drawn on without fear of irrelevance, or contextual irrelevance, by policy-makers.

However, policy-makers' ability to use studies such as ours with the confidence that the same school-level concepts discriminate between good and less good practice internationally should not be confused with the simple borrowing of the *detail* of these concepts and school practices. As an example, although the principal appears as a key factor in determining what are effective schools virtually across the globe, the precise way in which a principal is more effective in a Taiwanese context (by being rather vertical in leadership orientation) and in a Norwegian context (by often being quite horizontal or lateral) are somewhat different.

In the classroom, teaching and instructional area, by contrast, it seems that not only do the same *concepts* explain which classrooms and schools 'work', but that the precise *details* of the effective factors themselves often look identical in different country settings. As an example, questioning techniques, giving opportunities to review and practise, and the 'learning level' factors we talked about in Chapter 13 are micro-level behaviours which appear to be identical in the classrooms of effective schools in all countries.

All this suggests that policy-makers may therefore find it useful to see which interesting practices from countries other than their own might be a useful focus for experimentation and trial in their own country. One should, of course, always be aware of the dangers in 'cherry picking' teaching and schooling practices and then proposing that they should be translated into the practices of other societies. Nevertheless, policy-makers should also be made aware that effective practices do not necessarily cease to exist past the limits of their own geographic boundaries. As an illustration here are some examples of potentially useful practices as seen by the United States researchers in the ISERP team that would be available to any policy-maker that would be able to visit the same countries that we did:

- A great deal of discussion has focused on increasing teacher collaboration and *community building*. Countries as diverse as Norway, Taiwan, and Hong Kong provide examples of how to make this happen on a stable, ongoing basis. Existing US systems default to a teacher with her desk in a classroom, 15–35 students with that teacher for 4.5–6 hours per day, with a few minutes of planning time before and after school, and perhaps two additional planning periods per week, often at her desk in her classroom. If one wanted to create a system immune to all change, one probably could not have done better.

- The non-English speaking countries in particular had two very substantial differences in the organisation of teachers' time and space: (a) shared planning space and time, and (b) attractive teachers' work space. Teachers' desks in Hong Kong and Taiwan were not located in classrooms. Rather, they were located in central teachers' offices. The effect was that when teachers had planning periods, they were already among their peers. Seeing excellent instruction in an Asian context, one can appreciate the lesson, but also understand that the lesson did not arrive magically. It was planned, often in conjunction with an entire grade-level team (or, for a first year teacher, with a master teacher) in the teachers' shared office and work area.

- If one wants more collaboration among teachers, and if one wants the development of more thoughtful lesson-provision to our students, Asia provides a cost-achievable method for getting there. They have done this by having a substantial number of specialist teachers working with classes daily (physical education, art, music, etc.). The net effect is that even primary grade teachers often spend less than half of their paid hours instructing. Rather, they are planning, often in teams, or grading students' papers, or meeting with parents or other adults.

- The trade-off that is made for more out-of-class time is that when teachers are teaching, they often are doing so with larger numbers of students. As an example of how this trade might work in the US, consider a school that currently has six first and second grade teachers, each teaching 22 students virtually all day (132 students total), with little planning time. Such a group might want to consider having four groups of 33, with two specialist teachers in maths, science, physical education, or other areas moving among the classes so that the four remaining first and second grade home room teachers all get two extra shared planning periods per day. They would have their desks in a common teachers' office that includes all of their desks, telephones, and no students. The office would have a materials storage and preparation room next door. The two office and materials rooms would be former classrooms.

- The second issue to do with physical space for collaboration was made obvious in our visit to Norwegian primary schools. To visit a teachers' area in Norway was, in our experience, to visit a space with many of the comforts of home. The chairs, couches, and amenities were comfortable, modern, and inviting since it is obvious that the most expensive component of a school is the paid adults. A pleasant lounge would logically make those people feel more appreciated and more professional. It can also serve as a space in which collaboration is facilitated. In Norway, Taiwan, and Hong Kong, we never saw a teacher's work space or lounge that included a television. The first theme in this observation is that if one wants more thoughtful, more collaborative instruction, we need to structure our schools so that teachers have the time and a place to plan, share, and think.

- The second suggestion in this area is that if we are to upgrade the status of teachers and teaching, we need to upgrade the quality of the environment in which they interact. Teachers' lounges should be upgraded. We were also impressed with how much the Taiwanese students seemed to take *pride in and ownership of their schools*. In the poorest neighbourhoods, we didn't see graffiti on school walls, or vandalised areas within school compounds. At first this was confusing and we thought it was simply a cultural factor that we could never match in the US. Then one morning we were observing in maths classes when the lesson ended. Vivaldi's *Four Seasons* came on the entire school's intercom, and students moved to diverse 'cleaning up' tasks. Our (language and educational) translator explained to us that this was a standard ten-minute feature of all of Taiwan's primary schools. We looked around the rooms. Every child had a job. Some put all the chairs on top of the desks, others were sweeping, others mopping, others washed windows or sills or blackboards. Some children went out and cleaned their classes' designated sections of the hallways. Students from older grades cleaned exterior walkways, and efficiently swept the paved playground. Some of the students from the highest grade went to the special education classes and helped those students with their tasks. The entire student body was organised to spend ten minutes per day looking after their own school. This taught students responsibility and respect. It gave them physical activity which their young bodies needed, it provided a very clean school at a very reasonable price, and it freed maintenance people to keep up with major repairs. These schools were teaching socially desirable traits (responsibility, cleanliness, and respect) while obtaining spotlessly clean schools at low cost. All countries could learn something here.

- In debriefing in Hong Kong, it became clear that in other countries we simply didn't have the sort of consistent institutionalised homework and classwork assignment books that Hong Kong's and Taiwan's students took home. These books provide a daily update on each student's work, a place for a teacher's note home to parents (Asian teachers have several hours of prep time every day), and for parents' notes back. In countries like the US, there was no equivalent of the Asian administrators' regular check of all students' assignment work. In these regular exercises a 'dean' (assistant principal) or principal looks at every child's *actual products* in a certain subject. Where is the equivalent quality control in the United States, for although there has been some discussion of 'portfolios' of students' best work in the US, there is rarely anything like the type of student accountability for all of their work, and parent and teacher accountability for being sure that all of the work is completed and corrected, that exists in Asia. If we want all children to learn, we are going to have to have measures of all children's work and progress that are much more proximate than annual achievement tests.

- Observations and interviews in *small schools* in Norway and the Netherlands left us with few doubts that smaller schools can be more 'home like'. They can be very personal and humane. They can reduce the number of students having to get on a bus or be driven by their parents to school each day. Smaller schools can help build stronger relationships between parents and teachers, the school and the community.

- At the same time, we must report that the Taipei, Taiwan schools we visited had between 3,000 and 6,000 elementary grade students, and produced a level of achievement and civility that would be the envy of most US schools. Our conclusion is that the issue isn't so much school size per se, as the posing of the question, which surrounds this entire study, of 'what does the society want?' This relates back to and refines one of the overall themes above: among the things that have to be taken for granted are a focused number of goals. Most days those goals can be implied, but at some point they must be specific. Our sense is that the US generally, and US educators in particular, are vexingly unable to come to a finite set of goals and say, 'these things must come first'. No one can improve everything first. We need finite priorities. School size is just one very visible representation of this unstated compromise.

- As a separate, perhaps quite important, example of the above general rule, we were quite impressed with the extent to which our Norwegian schools focused on teaching *democratic values* to their students. Because our Norwegian peers had talked so much about this dimension, we discussed diverse situations with these young people. They often answered with examples of responses to potential values conflicts that focused on the importance of each of their peers' self concept and dignity, whether an old friend or a new member of the community. As with the Taiwanese ten-minute clean-up lesson in shared responsibility, these weren't schools passively waiting for some abstracted cultural values to assert themselves. These were schools actively teaching a specific way of thinking about dilemmas and values. Democratic values are learned, and can be taught and modelled.

- Moving on to *employment policies* the Australian 'Outback' is a rural, dry, often desolate part of the world. Some of it is in Queensland, the state from which our Australian sample of schools was drawn. While our sample was in greater Brisbane, the effect of the Outback could be seen even there. Virtually every teacher in those largely urban/suburban schools had, in the first years of their professional work, taught for two years in the Outback. This was almost never by choice. Rather, the two years of service were a state-mandated condition for long-term employment for any teacher.

- Rural and inner-city school districts in the US often have a hard time obtaining adequate numbers of teachers. Australia made us wonder if states couldn't make two years of service in rural or urban areas a condition of long-term employment in, for example, Montgomery County or Baltimore County, Maryland, or suburban Jefferson Parish, Louisiana.

- In *school architecture*, form should follow function. Moving around schools from Norway to Taiwan, we were struck with the extent to which facilities largely reflected the realities of their contexts, and with how often US urban and suburban elementary schools do not. Urban schools in Hong Kong and Taiwan included a brick or concrete wall surrounding the entire school and playground. The only unlocked entrances to these latter schools were inviting entryways that went directly past the school office. All persons, both desired and undesired, had to enter and exit directly past the school secretary and principal. Further, young children could not accidentally kick a ball into the street or be easily drawn into casual commerce with a drug dealer. These schools were designed for modern realities, and addressed those unfortunate elements in a way that allowed for maximum student safety while retaining space for students' physical activity.

- Urban/suburban America moves by car and truck. It contains far too many highly entrepreneurial drug dealers and such. To continue building schools that have large outdoor spaces and inadequate barriers between children and streets (with their fast-moving cars and street-entrepreneurs) places our children and our schools at perpetual risk. There are many urban elementary schools in the US where the principal has cancelled all outdoor recess because her experience is that she cannot keep the students safely removed from the problems of the surrounding community. Hong Kong has architecturally removed that entire range of challenges to student safety. The solution saves money (e.g. the schools don't have to hire full-time police), and allows young people the safe, physical activity they need and crave.

- Several nations (e.g. Norway, Hong Kong) guarantee *schools funding* in advance. The effect is to allow rational school-level planning. Entirely too many urban schools in the US have had the experience of having their discretionary budgets 'frozen' (e.g. removed) sometime after Christmas of a school year, due completely to a central administrator's inability to successfully manage budgets. If we really want 'rational' site-based management, we need to provide opportunities for rational site-based budget control, with budgets protected once in place.

- There were a variety of '*little things*' in the countries' classrooms that the team suspects had a positive cumulative effect. Here are two examples from Taiwan: instead of having the speaker system sound a shrill 'bell' at the end of periods, have it sound the 'Westminster chimes' or movements from Vivaldi's *Four Seasons*. The message to students and teachers is the same (class is over), but the latter eliminates unnecessary jarring of nerves several times a day. First-grade classrooms in Taiwan have a one-step 'stage' in front of the front blackboards. The effect is that when (inherently short) young students write on the board, their peers can see the work. The Taiwanese don't ask their six-year-olds, who are just learning to write, to write far above their heads when they are in front of their classes. Little things. They appeared to add up to something bigger.

The implications of the findings for researchers

For researchers, the ISERP study has validated for those of us involved in it the value of comparative study, for three reasons. Firstly, we have simply seen in other societies a variety of educational practices at classroom and school levels that would not have been seen had the core research team stayed within their own societies. In Pacific Rim societies for example, the majority of lesson time is filled with what has been called 'whole-class interactive' instruction, in which relatively short lessons of 40 minutes are filled with fast, emotionally intense presentations from teachers, with accompanying very high levels of involvement with pupils. This model of teaching, which is also found within a European context in societies such as Switzerland, is now the subject of considerable debate within United Kingdom schools.

In Norway, as a contrast, there is no formal assessment of children through the entire phase of their elementary/primary education from the age of seven, a marked contrast to the English language nations' practice of formal assessment and associated publication of results. In Pacific Rim societies again, one can see micro-level educational practices such as teachers teaching from a stage at the front of the class some six inches high (to help those at the back of the class to see), pupils marching to assembly through corridors in which loudspeakers play pleasant music (to ensure a relaxed attitude), and pupils starting the afternoon session of school with a 'sleeping' lesson (to deal with the fatigue brought about by the frantic pace of the school and the heat/humidity of the climate). Put simply, comparative investigation shows an enhanced range of what is educationally possible.

The benefits from comparative investigation are more than simply a knowledge of educational factors that might be utilised in programmes of experimentation in one's own country. They are, secondly, that one is made aware of educational philosophies that are radically different from one's own, or those of the government of one's own country. In Norway, for example, there is a strong commitment to the child as an 'active citizen', and to what are called 'democratic values' that have no British or American equivalents. In Pacific Rim societies, there is a philosophy that the role of the school is to ensure that all children learn, and that a strong 'technology' of practice should be employed to ensure that children are not dependent on their family background. Such societies are very concerned about the use of practices to improve the achievement of their trailing edge of pupils, therefore, and are therefore rather less concerned with the education of the 'gifted and talented' that appears to be the obsession of the United Kingdom and United States.

A third reason for comparative investigation is probably even more important than the two above, concerning the possibility that within the right kind of comparative framework one can move beyond looking at the practices of other societies and actually so empathise with other societies that one can look back at one's own society with the benefit of their perspective. Such 'acculturation' is what happened to many of us in ISERP when we were confronted with, and may have identified with, Pacific Rim educational systems. Looking back at the British and other systems through their 'lens', one wonders at the utility of the combination of the very complex technology of practice that has been evidenced in British primary practice, for example, with methods of teacher education that have been premised on the importance of teachers 'discovering', or at the least playing an active role in learning about, the appropriate methods to use. To a Taiwanese educationalist, this celebrates the desires of teachers for their long term developmental needs above the needs of children to receive a reliable, consistent, predictable, and competently provided experience as they pass through their schools.

The use of another culture's 'lens' adopted through the intervisitation programme to better understand the limitations and strengths of one's own educational practice also applies at the level of educational philosophy as well as educational practice. As an example, those of us involved in the British ISERP team would have historically viewed our primary education practice as loosely 'progressive' and indeed would have thought that in many senses it was the envy of the world. The encouragement of children to learn on their own rather than simply being instructed, the new sets of social outcomes that the system is widely argued to concentrate upon, and the reduced emphasis upon the testing of knowledge acquisition have been widely argued to be the hallmarks of progressive practice in the British system.

Seen from a Pacific Rim perspective, however, the characteristics of the British system would be seen as regressive, not progressive. Transferring the burden of learning to pupils would be seen as maximising both social class influences and variation between pupils within Taiwanese educational culture, since pupils' learning gains would depend on what they brought to the learning situation in terms of achievement levels and backgrounds. Removing the 'constant' of the teacher would be seen as further maximising individual variation in knowledge gain. Avoiding the testing of basic skills could be seen as maximising the chances of children who have missed acquiring particular knowledge bases being left without them, through the absence of short term feedback loops that alert school authorities that certain children have not learned.

For all these reasons, it remains a great pity that comparative education in general, and the international achievement surveys in particular, have not shown consistent improvement in the quality of the data gathered, and in the insights derived from that data, over the last 20 years. In the absence of an intellectually vibrant comparative education community, the increasing tendency of educational research to be cross-national or international in focus will not be resourced, and the sub-disciplines of education may make the kind of intellectual and practical errors that comparative education could have warned them about.

Within comparative education, the large scale cross-national achievement surveys retain high public and professional interest. These surveys are well known by educational researchers and policy-makers, and command attention because of the themes they address. For all their faults, they have a common dependent variable and therefore, in theory, can handle the explanation of the effects of different patterns of independent variables. They include material on the focal concerns of educational research – schools and, to a more limited extent, classrooms. From our own experience, the quality of this work would improve if it:

- utilised multiple methodologies and strategies of data collection;
- focused upon classrooms more, utilising observation of teachers and children's whole school days;

- adopted multiple outcomes;
- was sensitive to the variation between countries in their basic educational discourses;
- ensured that the factors studied were representative of the likely causal factors across all countries;
- utilised cohort studies that kept researchers in touch with the same children over time;
- utilised intervisitations across countries by qualitative researchers to understand educational phenomena better.

Current research needs to move in two directions. First, the field needs a large number of small studies in which investigations focus upon the interactions between individuals, classes, schools, and countries in a wide range of different locations. These may well show us the complicated nature of any search for good practice, but may, if the ISERP experience is a valid one, also show us universals that appear to matter in explaining the effectiveness of schools and teachers in different contexts. These conceptual universals may also lead to elucidation of interesting practices that might work outside the contexts that they are now found in.

Second, the effectiveness of these factors could be tested in programmes of planned intervention in different countries, in which the effects of the interventions are studied. Some of these interventions will have positive effects on pupil outcomes and no doubt a few will have negative effects, but this study of effectiveness in varying contexts both between and within countries will add inestimably to our knowledge. As interventions 'ripple through' to affect outcomes or are blocked by within-system, or perhaps without-system, factors we will learn much more about the complexity of the class/school/society interaction, and about the complexities of the schools and the classrooms themselves. The way to understand something is clearly to try to change it!

Some critical views

Whilst it is clear to us now that the largest single inhibitor to the evolution of truly world-class schooling in any or in all nations is our international inability to look outwards to other schools and contexts broadly, and then to have the self-confidence both to integrate and to amalgamate what we see with what we currently do, there are many who argue that one should be wary of exactly the kind of experimentation with the methods of other countries that we advocate here. Teacher behaviours and ways of administering school are, for these persons, not universals but have to be chosen specifically with the characteristics of the culture receiving the experimentation in mind. Seen from this perspective, 'what works' is not reducible to a set of behaviours or organisational processes readily transferable.

The kind of international trawl for potentially useful teaching and schooling factors, that can then be trialled in countries different from those that generated them, that we outline here is therefore not something that appeals to all comparativists or researchers alive to international educational comparison. In the United States, Stigler and Hiebert (1999) have shown in fascinating detail the very different patterns of classroom teaching exhibited by teachers in Japan, Germany and the United States, yet view these things as part of the broader cultural views of education, schools and children possessed by different country cultures. Teaching is 'cultural', they argue, and 'the widely shared cultural beliefs and expectations that underlie teaching are so fully integrated into teachers' world-views that they fail to see them as mutable' (p. 100). Stigler and Hiebert continue to argue that it is not the behavioural *practices* of teachers in educationally successful countries that need to be universalised, since 'what works in one classroom might not work in another' (p. 134), but that it is the methods of professional development of countries like Japan which are classroom-focused that should be 'borrowed'.

In the United Kingdom the recent attacks upon the school effectiveness paradigm from numerous sources (see the Special Issue of *School Effectiveness and School Improvement*, Volume 12, Number One) have extended to attacks upon the ISERP study and the thinking behind it. Alexander (2000), for example, criticises the focus of international school effectiveness work on teaching behaviours and school organisational forms, arguing that conceptually teaching cannot be isolated from the complex cultural, social and economic processes that it is embedded in. Launder (2000) also criticises any 'policy importation' as potentially violating the complex interaction between 'culture' and 'educational processes'.

These arguments, which appear to encompass a range of persons from those who believe that effective teaching/schooling practice is culturally specific to those who believe that culture needs to be more understood, appear to be frankly nonrational to a marked degree. Firstly, there is an already extensive body of research which shows substantially reproducible findings across cultures in the 'correlates' of school effectiveness generally (Teddlie and Reynolds, 2000). If we were to look at the teacher effectiveness level, then there is substantial international agreement on the importance of such factors as expectations, high quality review and opportunities to practise (Muijs and Reynolds, 2001). For specific subject areas like mathematics, virtually all the international literature shows a positive effect of whole-class teaching, time management, pupil engagement and a negative effect of a high proportion of time for individuals working on their own (see Reynolds and Muijs, 1999a).

Second, as well as the literature on effectiveness factors showing *agreement* cross-culturally there are specific programmes that are apparently effective in widely different cultures, such as Success for All (Slavin, 1996).

Third, there are the results of this research itself which suggest a slightly more complicated position in the field than previously, but that at the teacher level, a large number of the international teacher effectiveness behaviours still discriminate when schools of differing levels of effectiveness are compared. For countries as diverse as Hong Kong and the United Kingdom, when schools are grouped by effectiveness status, many of the teacher effectiveness factors discriminate as predicted. At school level, many conceptual characteristics are the same across countries, although the precise organisational features associated with these are different in different contexts, as the case studies showed earlier.

Quite why the critics of studies, like ISERP, in the international effectiveness tradition appear so doubtful about the possibility of creating new blends of behaviours and organisational features independent of particular cultures is unclear. Throughout their writing is an intellectual temerity and doubt about 'what works' that probably reflects simple ignorance of the literature. Additionally, their rampant context specificity may reflect their historical ideological commitment to teacher education and professional development that is primarily based upon loosely guided self discovery of 'what works', a position that is conceptually and practically threatened by the existence of any universals, which should of course imply a need for countries to ensure 'core' activities independent of context. Perhaps the critics are simply taking refuge in 'context specificity' rather than face an intellectual challenge of determining the universality and specificity of educational factors that is simply beyond them.

However, if attention is paid to them, the critics may, wittingly or unwittingly, be damaging the prospects of educational advance, since countries that restrict the search for 'good practice' only to those educational settings within their own boundaries of necessity miss potentially valuable practices from outside those boundaries. Countries that refuse to adopt an international reach may fail to acquire innovations which certain countries have discovered and are profitably utilising, such as the highly effective Success for All programme from the United States (Slavin, 1996) or indeed the constructivist technologies being developed in the United States and the Netherlands (see Teddlie and Reynolds, 2000, Chapter 12).

Some recommendations

Since we remain certain that, on the basis of our results, there is everything to gain and nothing to lose from an international reach in the attempt to improve education systems, we clearly reject the critics' views. Indeed, it is difficult to understand them or the factors that have prompted them.

We would argue, additionally, that our experiences have made us aware not just of classroom and school factors that are in some cases conceptual and/or practical universals but have given us 'world views' about education that we believe can facilitate educational advance, world views that are couched at a level of generality above that of 'effectiveness factors' but which have clear practical utility, nonetheless. It is with these 'world views' that we conclude, couched as a series of recommendations.

Recommendation One: creating world-class schools requires systems not people

We noted in the first section of Chapter 13 that there were differences between the English-speaking societies and others in the school characteristics that were useful to the research teams in explaining effectiveness. In English-speaking countries, *personal* factors such as the quality of the principal, or relational factors such as the nature of the relations between teachers, were relatively more associated with whether schools 'added value' or not. By contrast, in Pacific Rim societies, the factors that were most useful in explaining 'effectiveness' and 'ineffectiveness' were *systemic*, not *personal*, ones, and were concerned with the degree of implementation of quality curricula, high quality organisational structures and the like.

It is clear to us that enormous advantages accrue to those societies which possess 'strong systems', rather than rely heavily on 'strong people' or 'unusual persons' to run their schools. Strong systems minimise the variance in the quality of education provided, increase the likelihood of continuance over time and assure continuance after any key personnel leave the employment of their institution. Systems, on the other hand, that rely on persons to generate their own methods, inevitably persons of different levels of competence, will generate variance in the quality of the methods used according to how much competence persons possess initially. Strong systems can probably generate a higher proportion of educational professionals with the requisite skills to run effective schools, whereas systems that rely on personal characteristics are restricted to the number of persons who possess the requisite personal characteristics. When what is required for being successful in the occupational role of teacher is constantly being increased in quantity and difficulty, the chance of individuals already having what is required is correspondingly lessened.

What are examples of strong systems? We do have examples of strong systems that go beyond personal characteristics, yet are not as embedded in the culture as the practices noted in our discussions of the Asian classrooms in the study. Examples from US society would be programmes such as Success for All (Slavin, 1996), which was externally created and is now delivered to schools through provision of curriculum, training and feedback. Over the years, continued expansion of this model not only incorporated curricular and institutional training, but developed sophisticated evaluation and assessment materials to more effectively meet the programme goals. Comprehensive systems of schooling can be found in other models such as those of the New American School Designs or High Reliability Schools. The specifics of the system employed in each programme may differ, but the provision of a coherent system is core.

Recommendation Two: creating world-class schools requires it to be taken for granted

In some countries that we have studied, there are core beliefs held in the society regarding children, teaching and schools, that form a basis for the development of a 'technology of practice' amongst educational professionals across the schools. The elements of this technology and the beliefs that support it are, however, very different from country to country. In Pacific Rim societies or Norway, for example, there are shared values that virtually all educational professionals share about 'what should happen' in a classroom or a school. In part, such cohesion reflects the very nature of the societies themselves, with their shared values of desired educational practice being derived from Confucian traditions in the case of the Pacific Rim and from a strong national community in the case of Norway.

But it is clear that educational factors can mould these cohesive values also, in addition to reflecting them. Most elementary school teachers in Taiwan, for example, receive training from nine institutions whose faculty come from the same institutions. Educational meetings to determine national policy include the major educational players, and changes can be rapidly conveyed to teachers who share the general national values about which educational values are important and which practices appropriate. There is, of course, variation among educational professionals in their practice, but it appears to be concerned with the degree of implementation of the particular practice rather than being based upon varying definitions about the purposes of teaching and the goals of the educational system in the first place.

Whereas some societies have this shared set of understandings about what schools should be doing, and particularly Norway, Taiwan, and Hong Kong spring to mind here, English-speaking countries evidenced huge variation in what was seen as appropriate, or at least acceptable, practice, reflecting unresolved values debates at national level about what the purpose of education should be, and what therefore 'good practice' is. These characteristics reflect national values of individualism and local control. In such situations, children in the early age phases of schooling may be the losers. They are exposed to variation in practice, in part because teachers have unclear or differing sets of goals, and are exposed to variation in the quality of the implementation of the practice by the different sets of teachers with the different sets of goals. This results in schools and classrooms being unpredictable and lacking in consistency, constancy, and cohesion.

The creation of world-class schools clearly requires agreement upon goals amongst educationalists as educationalists, if not as individuals. While there seems to be little useful purpose to be served by a continued professional debate about values present in a number of societies that we have studied until the educational system can effectively deliver any of the values, it cannot do this at present because it has ineffective and varied 'means' that have been produced by the absence of clarity of mission and consistent delivery.

Recommendation Three: creating world-class schools requires technologies of practice

We noted in Chapter 13 that there were interesting differences between countries in the extent to which children's achievements were associated with their parents' social backgrounds. In the United States and United Kingdom, children's mathematics achievement was strongly related to such factors as parental occupation and parental education. By contrast, in societies such as Taiwan and Hong Kong the relationship was less.

It is easy to explain this paradox, since the English-speaking societies have largely permitted teachers to self-determine much of their practice. In this setting, expectations of how children are influenced by their parents' lower expectations form part of the nationally based value systems about children from lower social classes that can easily be reflected in classroom practices that discriminate against such children. Put simply, if there is an absence of a shared technology of practice transmitted through programmes of professional education, then the 'hole' will be filled by practices that are determined by the personal views of teachers and principals.

The alternative, and some societies evidence this, is to ensure that professional education gives all teachers a technology that is to be applied uniformly and evenly to all children independent of any background factors that may exist. In such countries as the Netherlands and Taiwan, therefore, all teachers receive the 'technology' of their profession through instructional theory courses that bring to all trainees the world's great knowledge bases about effective instruction, intervention programmes, novel approaches such as metacognitive strategies, and the like. Undergirding this technology is the belief that effort is the basis for success rather than family or intelligence. The attempt is made to, in a structured fashion, fill the circle of professional practice that would largely be filled by a process of self invention or 'do-it-yourself' or 'finding what works best for me' in other societies. The specification of a teaching technology is also associated with a clearly specified professional ideology that minimises the chance of children from disadvantaged homes being educated by discriminating practices. In Taiwan, for example, the belief is inculcated that all children can learn, that the school should educate all children whether their background is advantaged or disadvantaged, and that education is the right of all. Correspondingly, there is limited discussion about children's family backgrounds, since they are not seen as relevant to the job of the school, since the role of the school is to educate all children independently of their backgrounds.

Specification of a teaching technology, and its possession by all members of a teaching profession, may in the circumstances of the societies that we studied, be of value to more than only the disadvantaged. Whilst societies such as the United Kingdom have had teacher education which has been orientated towards the needs of the teacher 'artists' to be allowed to invent their own practice and therefore create potentially better practice than that they would have been given as a technology, this may result in less than good practice for those teachers who have not possessed the 'art' but could have acquired the science. The range in the quality of education provided in such societies as the United States, England, and the Republic of Ireland, as shown by the relatively high variance locatable at school level, in part reflects this lack of an agreed technology of practice.

Recommendation Four: creating world-class schools requires societal support

At the level of the school, but even more in the level above the school, it became clear that higher level conditions can be created for classroom teaching and the effectiveness that has to be achieved in classrooms. In the ISERP study, countries with more and less centralised educational policies were all included. We could not find much influence of the degree of centralisation (or decentralisation) on the results of students or on the way schools and teachers operate. It is the variation *within* (centralised and decentralised) systems with respect to schools and classrooms that is greater than that *between* the centralised and decentralised systems.

The differences between countries we noted above were related to the coherence and the strength of the system itself. The place of the educational system and the value that is placed on it indicates how much strength the system has. It became apparent that an effective education system level can (but not necessarily will) create effective, strong schools and classrooms, but that depends partly on the value that is placed within the society on the educational system and the importance of the teaching profession. We found in our study that the emphasis on education is different in specific countries and relates to the value that is placed upon the educational profession in different societies. In some countries, education is not regarded highly and is seen as something that only schools have to deliver. In other societies education is seen as a task for society as a whole, in which teachers and schools are important and highly respected. In the first case, one can imagine that the well-being of teachers, their own idea about their profession, and the work they are doing is affected negatively by their own position and the position of education in general in the society. In this case, it is difficult for schools and teachers to ask for or to expect assistance from the family, and for the wider society to be involved and to assist in what schools are doing. For example, in the UK there is a lot of criticism of schools and education that has negatively affected the perceptions of their competence and the well being of teachers by comparison with the societal support in Ireland. These negative attitudes again affect the functioning of schools, teachers, and classrooms.

What is needed for educational effectiveness is a paradoxical, complicated set of societal features, namely the perception that education and teachers matter and are worthy of support, but a culture that in its day to day functioning does the job of educating its young itself because it feels that education is *not* just a school responsibility.

Recommendation Five: creating world-class schools requires thinking the unthinkable

Knowledge of such things as how to teach reading has advanced tremendously over the past 50 years. The content of any recent elementary text series integrates concepts from algebra, geometry, and statistics into the primary grades. Reflecting the geometrically expanding knowledge base of the fields, the content of a modern science lesson is fantastically more complex than that of even 40 years ago. Yet we English-speaking countries organise the provision of primary school instruction much as we did 100 years ago: one teacher, as few students as the government can afford, and the full range of subject areas.

Perhaps because universal free public education came later in Asia, those countries have clearly adapted primary education to the realities of an increasingly complex world. For whatever reason, both Hong Kong and Taiwan (and through other studies, we are aware of the same organisational arrangements in other Asian countries) assign teachers to the specialities of mathematics and science. Because these teachers are expected to deliver those courses not in a 'drill and kill', but in an intellectually stimulating fashion, the teachers have been provided more planning time than teaching time in a school day. Teachers need time to think about and plan lessons that require active engagement and 'higher order' thinking on the part of the students. The well-known TIMSS video series of Japanese, German and

US teachers clearly presents more Japanese lessons that are more likely to demand the fullest of each child's intellect. What the videos show much less well is the amount of planning time built into all Japanese teachers' days. Here are countries that have responded to changes in the modern world by themselves innovating their practices. In our Anglo-Saxon terms, they are thinking the unthinkable. We need to do the same, or similar.

Conclusions

In virtually every field of human endeavour and achievement, an increasingly internationalised world is now adopting a global reach. Drugs that have been developed as effective are utilised internationally in months. New schools of thought in the Humanities, such as post-modernism, spread with viral speed. In such areas as management, the practices utilised by successful companies are used by all countries within months if not years, since companies know they will simply go out of business if they do not rapidly change and improve. If in virtually every area of its existence, humanity is using a world of experience to draw on to improve itself, why should we in education not do the same? Rather than being frightened by a world of educational experiences, it is surely time for us to learn from them. It is time to look broadly across the planet, and then integrate what we see with what we do, so that we may do it better. The children of the world deserve it, now.

Acknowledgement

First published as Reynolds, D., Creemers, B. P. M., Stringfield, S., Teddlie, C. and Schaffer, E. 'Creating world-class schools: What have we learned?' in D. Reynolds, B. P. M. Creemers, S. Stringfield, C. Teddlie and E. Schaffer (2002) *World Class Schools: International Perspectives in School Effectiveness*. London: Routledge. Reprinted here with permission from Taylor & Francis.

6

Teacher effectiveness
Better teachers, better schools

Were a Martian educationalist to arrive in Britain today, I am confident that what would most surprise him or her is that we have no applied science of teaching, that we have no plans to generate one and that many people are happy with this situation. Teaching is the core technology of what teachers do. It is more and more prescribed as politicians and others start to, quite rightly, intervene in the teaching methods that are used. It is the distinct area of teaching that provides for me the most likely explanation for why educational reforms in Britain have hitherto always failed, namely that in pulling the 'lever' of the school we have missed pulling the 'lever' of the teacher.

Our ignorance in the area of teacher effectiveness is virtually total. I can find us more studies on the minute phenomenon of 'wait time' (the number of seconds of silence one should tolerate in a class after asking a question) from one country, the United States, than I can on the whole issue of 'what makes a good teacher' in the UK. I can find us literally thousands of studies from around the world into teacher effectiveness but only a handful from Britain. Why is this? What has kept us from seeing things as others see them?

Firstly, there is the quaint, old fashioned and ultimately highly damaging British view that teaching is an art, not an applied science, and that, therefore, teachers are born like an artist rather than made like an applied scientist. This view of course restricts us to possessing only the number of talented individuals who are born the artists, who are of course unlikely to be enough to staff our schools. Higher education carries much of the blame for this view, since its purpose in teacher education has been to protect the interests of the artists by letting them discover their methods and therefore become great teachers, greater than they would have been if they had been taught their methods. Unfortunately, the large proportion of trainee teachers who are not born 'teacher artists' have not therefore been given the technology that they need.

Higher education is responsible also for the second factor that prevents an applied science of teaching – the low status of applied and practical work in educational research. In British educational research, the most useless research has the highest status and those of us who are in fields like school effectiveness are regarded with the same disdain as the Victorians viewed engineers. High status goes either to those who research the outside school determinants of pupils' achievement about which we can do little, or to those who celebrate a values debate and discuss the 'ends' of education. It does not go to those who want to try to find better 'means'.

Thirdly, the absence of routinely collected assessment data has hindered research. Historically, the primary sector has been far from 'data rich' but it is precisely in the primary sector that there has been the best chance of establishing which teacher behaviours affect learning gain, because a child gets only one teacher within this sector.

Fourthly, and in my view most importantly, our inability to create a science of teaching reflects on our inability as an educational culture to handle the issues concerning the variation between teachers in their quality. When Rutter et al. (1979) showed that schools made a difference, he was greeted with a storm of abuse, a symptom of our inability then to handle the issue of differences between schools. When Woodhead talked about the trailing edge of teachers in my *Panorama* programme in 1996, he too was rubbished, a symptom of our contemporary inability to handle between-teacher variation and to learn from it. Because we fear that identifying and learning from the leading edge of the profession identifies the remainder as less than leading edge, we fear to recognise and learn from the variation.

These are not the only reasons of course for the absence of a teacher effectiveness literature – school effectiveness researchers wanted to disprove the 'schools make a difference' thesis, and so got obsessed with the level of the school rather than the classrooms. There are no British traditions in the areas of 'learning and instruction' that have had such an effect on Continental educational research. Vulgarised Piagetian notions concerning the large variation between children in what they bring to school have been used to support the frankly absurd notion that some children will learn from any kind of teacher behaviour. Because of this emphasis upon individual differences, we have celebrated the utility of a related diversity of teaching styles.

This ignorance in our educational culture is costing us heavily, however, both intellectually and practically. Firstly, school effectiveness research has shown that teachers and the learning level are three to four times more powerful than the l level. In order of descending importance, the teacher is the most important ﾐinant of outcomes, then the school, then the LEA.

ﾟndly, we are harming ourselves since, because of our ignorance, we are to adequately address at a practical and policy level the very large variation that exists between teachers in their behaviours. In our own International School Effectiveness Research Project (ISERP) (see Reynolds *et al.*, 2002), across nine countries including those educational heavyweights of Taiwan and Hong Kong, probably the only teacher in the world I saw who could generate 100% time on task from her children was British, but Britain also evidenced teachers who scored as low as 30% time on task in these primary classrooms. Taiwan, by contrast, had few teachers above 96% or 97%, but none that I ever saw below 85%. We have the validity – we have excellent teachers – but we do not have the reliability that would deliver to all children effective teaching.

Thirdly, the absence of a discourse about teacher effectiveness costs us the ability to conceptualise and understand those many programmes from other societies that are effectively combating underachievement. Virtually every effective programme of educational intervention internationally is classroom or instructionally based, a factor that should worry us in Britain as we continue to pull the school levers. Our inability to understand Taiwanese whole-class interactive instruction – which many persist in calling whole-class teaching – makes the same point.

Fourthly, our inability to understand and learn from the within school variation of teachers costs us valuable within school 'drivers'. A 'learning level' or 'teacher level' orientation – that we cannot possess at present because we haven't got the valid knowledge base – could bring us so much of use.

Whilst not every school is an effective school, every school has within itself some practice that is more effective than some other practice. Many schools will have within themselves practice that is absolutely effective, across all schools. With a learning level orientation, every school can work on its own internal conditions.

Focusing 'within' schools may be a way of permitting greater levels of competence to emerge at the school level, since it is possible that the absence of strategic thinking at school level in many parts of the educational system is related to the overload of pressures amongst Headteachers, who are having referred to them problems which should be dealt with by the day-to-day operation of the middle management system of Department Heads, Year Heads, Subject Co-ordinators and the like.

Within school units of policy intervention such as years or subjects are smaller and therefore potentially more malleable than those at 'whole school' level.

Teachers, in general, and those teachers in less effective settings in particular, may be more influenced by classroom-based policies and a classroom level discourse that are close to their focal concerns of teaching and curriculum, rather than by policies that are 'managerial' and orientated to the school level.

The possibility of obtaining 'school level to school level' transfer of good practice, plus any possible transfer from LEAs in connection with their role as monitors of school quality through their involvement in the approval of schools' development plans, may be more difficult to obtain than the possibility of obtaining 'within school' transfer of practice between people who at least work within the same building.

So, my argument is that we are impoverishing ourselves as an educational culture and harming the educational prospects of our children, by not developing an applied science of teaching. If we look at those countries that possess this – and I must be honest and say that virtually every industrialised society that I know, except Britain, possesses this – we see the existence of a codified, scientifically established body of knowledge than can guide these nations and their teachers towards better practice. What are the 'effective' teacher behaviours that other countries' knowledge bases have established as effective?

They include:

- lesson clarity (because of lack of clarity costs time in further elaboration/ exploration);
- instructional variety (using varying styles of questioning, instruction, etc.);
- teachers' effective time management (having routines so well established that no time is lost on administration/behavioural routines);
- high student levels of time on task;
- maintaining a high success rate for pupils (this should be 75/80%).

Other factors of importance are:

- using and incorporating pupil ideas;
- strong structuring;
- appropriate and varied questioning;
- probing for knowledge (an example here is the Japanese tradition of asking repeated questions, maybe six or seven, to the same child);
- frequent feedback, and linked with this corrective instruction and feedback;
- high expectations of what pupils can achieve;
- clear, and restricted, goals (or 'strong mission').

This body of knowledge is even available for such fine-grained issues as the types of teaching behaviours that are especially useful for teachers in disadvantaged areas (these include presenting materials in small bits, emphasising the application of knowledge, giving immediate help if pupils are getting material wrong, and providing a warm and supportive atmosphere in which pupils know help is available). For more advantaged children, appropriate methods are: giving difficult material, emphasising learners' independent roles, encouraging very rich verbalising and requiring extended reasoning.

The technology of effective teaching in other countries even extends to knowledge concerning the methods that are appropriate for different subjects, like mathematics for example. Effectiveness in mathematics is related to severely limiting individual work, to whole-class interactive instruction and to the maximisation of coverage in a heavily hierarchical subject by use of steeply graded and differentiated materials, all factors that were featured I am pleased to say in the Numeracy Task Force Report *Numeracy Matters.*

So what do I propose that we do in this situation?

Generally, I believe that we need to move beyond our national discourse about 'schools' and 'schooling' to one concerning 'teachers' and 'teaching'. School-level interventions and policies are necessary – but I believe they are sufficient to generate the educational outcomes that we need.

Specifically, I believe:

1   We need to develop the technology of teaching by more research, in order to give us the teacher behaviours that are appropriate for children of different ages, subjects, catchment areas and districts. In Britain we have celebrated a 'one size fits all' notion of teaching rather than celebrate and plan for a diversity of teaching methods within different age phases, subjects, etc. with of course a common core of effective practices throughout.

2   We need to ensure that all pre-service teachers receive the technology of their profession, as would any other group of professionals. To use an aeronautical analogy, it is not enough that we know how to land a plane. All planes have to land, or the consequences are a disaster. It is similarly not enough that we know how to teach. All teachers must practise these effective methods or the consequences are disastrous.

The TTA have in fairness done sterling service in putting educational foundations for all trainees in place. I should add that the evidence is overwhelming that all professional development needs the teaching of theory, in this case teaching theory, as well as professional methods in order for it to be successful. The training cycle should therefore go:

- teaching of instructional theory;
- teaching methods (that are only understandable if one can link them together theoretically);
- practice of the methods;
- re-teaching and coaching in the methods as appropriate.

In fairness to the TTA, I have no doubt that were they to insist, as they should, that all trainees receive instructional theory, the problem would lie in the ability and unwillingness of Higher Education to do it, given that schools could not be expected to do so.

3   We must remember that teachers need to be more than the passive recipients of existing knowledge bases. In a world so rapidly changing, the knowledge needed to teach will be changing too. We need – and again the TTA has done sterling service here – to insist that all teachers are able to research in their schools, to use the empirical rational model to create knowledge about effective practices that is better than that which they should have been given as their intellectual and practical foundations.

I have no doubt that my desire for teachers to be seen as technologists, rather than as philosopher kings, may not appeal to all. In defence, I would point to the success of another profession, the medical profession, lionised in this same slot by David Hargreaves two years ago, which in the decades of the early part of this century reminds one of what teachers may be close to being now – they were relatively poor, demoralised, and self-destructive, attempting to get their emotional professional satisfaction out of inventing their own, invariably ineffective, methods. Everyone tried to invent their own cure for TB, few did so. Now they use methods which research has established as valid and, based upon an audit of the patient, obtain their professional fulfilment and emotional satisfaction from seeing the sick become well and the lame become whole. The few that did find the cure for TB have had that discovery given to all.

I believe teachers need, similarly, to reject the demoralising nonsense that they should re-invent the teaching wheel, and that their professional satisfaction is linked to their exhausting yet doomed attempt at educational and instructional D-I-Y, the educational equivalent of the invention of a cure for TB.

Instead, they should be encouraged to use known to be valid methods, whilst at the same time always enquiring as to how they can make them better. They should be encouraged to gain their satisfaction not from the D-I-Y but from seeing children learn and from seeing the educationally lame then walk.

The result would be a more self-respecting and emotionally fulfilled teaching profession, more educated children and a more prosperous and cohesive society.

All this is achievable if we develop a science of teacher effectiveness.

Acknowledgement

First published in *Research Intelligence* No. 26 (1998). Reprinted here with permission from the British Educational Research Association (BERA).

7

School effectiveness and teacher effectiveness in mathematics

Some preliminary findings from the evaluation of the Mathematics Enhancement Programme (Primary)

Introduction

In the past 20 years, an ever-growing knowledge base on effective teaching has been built up. Starting with research in classrooms looking purely at 'quantity' of behaviours (e.g., Stallings and Kaskowitz, 1974), research has now moved on to consider 'quality' of behaviours as well. A number of scales have been developed to this end, and have further enhanced the teacher effectiveness knowledge base.

This, mainly American, research has produced a large number of factors that are associated with higher pupil achievement. Although these findings are usually presented in general terms, a lot of the research has been done in connection with mathematics teaching, making these findings probably especially relevant to this subject (Reynolds and Muijs, 1999b). One of the main factors related to mathematics achievement scores in this body of research is *opportunity to learn,* usually measured as either number of pages of the curriculum covered or percentage of test items taught. This variable is clearly related to factors such as length of the school day and year, but also to effective classroom management, which manages to maximise *time-on-task*, the amount of time pupils spend actively engaging with the curriculum (Brophy and Good, 1986; Creemers and Reezigt, 1996; Hafner, 1993).

Another consistent finding is that effective teachers emphasise academic instruction as their main classroom goal, and have an *academic orientation.* They therefore create a businesslike, task-oriented environment and spend classroom time on academic activities rather than on socialising, free time, etc. This factor would seem to operate at the school as well as at the classroom level, and in a wide range of contexts and countries (Borich, 1996; Brophy and Good, 1986; Cooney, 1994; Creemers, 1994; Griffin and Barnes, 1986; Reynolds, Sammons, Stoll, Barber, and Hillman, 1996; Scheerens and Creemers, 1996).

Time on task is, as mentioned above, strongly influenced by *classroom management*. Effective teachers are able to organise and manage classrooms as effective teaching environments in which academic activities run smoothly, transitions are brief, and little time is spent getting organised or dealing with resistance (Brophy and Good, 1986). The latter is obviously related to good *behaviour management*, which entails clearly instructing pupils on proper behaviour procedures at the start of the year, so that pupils know what is expected of them during lessons, closely monitoring the classroom, and reinforcing wanted behaviour, along with discouraging undesired behaviour (Borich, 1996; Brophy, 1986; Brophy and Good, 1986; Evertson, Anderson, *et al.*, 1980; Lampert, 1988; Secada, 1992).

Moving to the actual teaching, research has found that pupils learn more in classes where they spend most of their time being taught or supervised by their teachers, rather than working on their own. In these classes teachers spend most of their time presenting information through lecture or demonstration. Teacher-led discussion as opposed to individual seat-work dominates. The teacher carries the content personally to the student, as opposed to relying on textbooks or maths schemes to do this. Information is mainly conveyed in brief presentations, followed by recitation and application opportunities. In this type of instruction, the teacher takes an active role, rather than just 'facilitating' pupils' learning. Use of examples is important, and teachers should strive to make presentations lively and engaging to maximise gain. This type of instruction is usually referred to as *direct instruction* (Borich, 1996; Brophy and Good, 1986; Galton, 1987; Lampert, 1988).

Achievement is maximised when the teacher not only presents material actively, but does so in a structured way, by beginning with an overview and/or review of objectives. Teachers need to outline the content to be covered and signal transitions between lesson parts. Attention must be drawn to the key points of the lesson, subparts of the lesson should be summarised as it proceeds, and the main ideas should be reviewed at the end of the lesson. In this way the information is not only better remembered by the students, but also more easily understood as a whole rather than as a series of isolated skills. In this respect, it has been found to be especially important in mathematics to clearly link different parts of the lesson and of the curriculum. New knowledge needs to be linked to pupils' prior knowledge, and mathematical ideas must be linked and not taught in isolation (Borich, 1996; Brophy and Good, 1986; Lampert, 1988). Information must be presented with a high degree of clarity and enthusiasm, and, for basic skills instruction, the lesson needs to proceed at a brisk pace (Brophy and Good, 1986; Good, Grouws, *et al.*, 1983; Griffin and Barnes, 1986; Silver, 1987; Walberg, 1986).

Although we have noted above that teachers need to spend a significant amount of time instructing the class, this does not mean that all seatwork is negative. Individual seatwork or small group tasks are a vital component of an effective lesson, as they allow pupils to *review and practise* what they have learnt during instruction. To be effective, however, tasks must be explained clearly to pupils, and the teacher must actively monitor the class and go round the classroom to help pupils, rather than sitting at her/his desk waiting for pupils to come to her/him. The teacher needs to be approachable to pupils during seatwork (Borich, 1996; Brophy and Good, 1986).

This focus on the teacher actively presenting material should also not be equated to a traditional lecturing and drill approach, in which the students remain passive during the lesson. Effective teachers ask a lot of questions and involve pupils in class discussion. In this way, students are kept involved in the lesson, while the teacher has the chance to monitor pupils' progress and understanding. If pupils are found not to understand a concept properly, it should be re-taught by the teacher. Teachers must provide substantive feedback to students resulting either from pupil questions or from answers to teacher questions. Most questions should elicit correct or at least substantive answers. The cognitive level of questions needs to be varied depending on the skills to be mastered. The best strategy would appear to be to use a mix of low-level and higher level questions, increasing the latter as level of the subject matter taught gets higher. There should also be a mix of product questions (calling for a single response from students) and process questions (calling for explanations from the students), and effective teachers have been found to ask more process questions than ineffective teachers (Askew and William, 1995; Brophy and Good, 1986; Evertson, Anderson, et al., 1980).

When students answer a question correctly, this should always be acknowledged. However, this does not mean that teachers should use praise indiscriminately. Effective teachers are usually quite sparing in their use of praise, as, when overused, praise can become meaningless. More praise is needed in low ability and low SES classrooms, as pupils tend to be less self-confident. If students give an incorrect response, the teacher should indicate that the response is incorrect in the form of a simple negation, avoiding personal criticism of students, which may deter them from participating in classroom activities. Teachers should try to rephrase questions and provide prompts when pupils are unable to answer them. Students should be encouraged to ask questions, which should be redirected to the class before being answered by the teacher. Relevant student comments should be incorporated into the lesson (Borich, 1996; Brophy and Good, 1986). It is therefore clear that effective teaching is not just active, but *interactive* as well.

In addition, effective teachers have been found to use a *varied teaching* approach to keep pupils engaged, and to vary both content and presentation of lessons. Specifically with respect to mathematics, a lot of research has attested to the importance of using a variety of materials and manipulatives, in order to be able to assist mental strategies and to more easily transfer mathematical knowledge to other situations and contexts.

Classroom climate is the final factor that teacher effectiveness research has found to be significant. As well as businesslike, the classroom environment also needs to be suitably relaxed and supportive for pupils. Teacher expectations need to be high. The teacher should expect every pupil to be able to succeed. They need to emphasise the positive in each child; for example, if a pupil is not particularly good at algebra, s/he may still be good at another area of mathematics such as data handling. These positive expectations need to be transmitted to the children (Brophy and Good, 1986).

In recent years, a lot of attention in mathematics research has focused on issues connected to children's construction of knowledge. The main assumption of this *constructivist* school, which builds heavily on the work of Jean Piaget, is that children actively construct their own knowledge rather than passively receiving it. Children, according to this view, do not acquire learning from the teacher, but through seeking out meaning and making mental connections in an active manner (Anghileri, 1995; Askew, Rhodes, Brown, William, and Johnson, 1997; Nunes and Bryant, 1996). Use of correct mathematical language has also been considered an important aspect of effective mathematics teaching by some commentators.

Most of the research undertaken has, as mentioned above, been in the US. In Britain, only three major studies of teacher effectiveness have taken place so far. The first of these, Galton's ORACLE project, found that teachers labelled as 'Class Enquirers' generated the greatest gains in the areas of mathematics and language, but that this finding did not extend to reading. By contrast, the group of 'Individual Monitoring' teachers made amongst the least progress. It is important to note that the more successful 'Class Enquirers' group utilised four times as much time in whole-class interactive teaching as the 'Individual Monitors' (Croll, 1996; Galton and Croll, 1980).

The second important British teacher effectiveness study is the Junior School Project (JSP) of Mortimore, Sammons, Stoll, Lewis, and Ecob (1988), based upon a four-year cohort study of 50 primary schools, which involved collection of a considerable volume of data on children and their family backgrounds ('intakes'), school and classroom 'processes' and 'outcomes' in academic (reading, mathematics) and affective (e.g., self conception, attendance, behaviour) areas.

This study reported 12 factors that were associated with effectiveness both across outcome areas and within specific subjects such as mathematics. Significant positive relationships were found with such factors as structured sessions, use of higher-order questions and statements, frequent questioning, restricting sessions to a single area of work, involvement of pupils and the proportion of time utilised in communicating with the whole class. Negative relationships were found with teachers spending a high proportion of their time communicating with individual pupils (Mortimore *et al.*, 1988).

A recent, more qualitatively oriented study by a team from King's College London (Askew *et al.*, 1997) looked at teachers' beliefs, knowledge and attitudes rather than behaviours. The researchers identified three types of teachers described as discovery oriented (strongly constructivistically oriented with the teacher seen as facilitator), transmission oriented (teachers using purely direct instruction with little interaction) and connectionist (balancing a focus on the teacher, as in the transmission orientation, with a focus on the learner as in the discovery orientation) and found the last of those to be the most effective. Results also pointed to the importance of making connections between different parts of the curriculum.

A number of teacher effectiveness factors have also been studied in continental Europe, most notably in the Netherlands. However, a review of Dutch research found disappointing results, with teaching factors such as whole-class teaching, achievement orientation and time spent on homework being positively related to pupil outcomes at the primary level in respectively three, four and four studies out of 29 (and negatively related in none), while differentiation and cooperation were negatively related to outcomes in two and three studies respectively, and positively related to outcomes in none (Scheerens and Creemers, 1996). However, where significant results are obtained, they tend to support the conclusions of the American and British studies, Westerhof (1992) for example finding that a large proportion of variance could be explained by the factors 'interactive teaching', 'giving instructions', 'criticising' (a factor better described as correcting errors), 'soliciting responses' and 'conditioning'.

The limited number of British studies into what makes teachers differentially effective makes this study timely and important, as, in view of this dearth of research and the mixed results of the research in the Netherlands, it is clearly necessary to explore whether the American research base readily translates to a British context. Traditionally, teacher effectiveness has not been at the heart of British educational research, which has often been sociologically inspired and lacking in a strong pedagogy tradition such as that existing in continental Europe, while the powerful school effectiveness tradition has tended to concentrate on the school level to the exclusion of classroom level factors (Reynolds et al., 1996). Recently, however, British interest in this research base has grown, largely as a result of weak performance in the Third International Maths and Science study, and the publication of the *Worlds Apart* report (Reynolds and Farrell, 1996), which focused on the effectiveness of the whole-class interactive teaching methods employed in educationally successful East Asian countries such as Taiwan, which led to the government adopting a whole-class interactive strategy for maths teaching in primary schools, the 'National Numeracy Strategy' (Department for Education and Employment [DfEE], 1998). In view of the recent enthusiasm for this method, the question needs addressing of whether whole-class interactive teaching really is effective in raising mathematical achievement.

We agree with Brophy's (1986) contention that effective teaching is likely to be a conglomerate of behaviours. It is unlikely that one isolated behaviour will make the difference. Rather, it is the combination of effective teaching behaviours that will lead to better performance in pupils. As for the debate on whole-class interactive teaching, whenever it is found that spending more time teaching the whole class together is effective, the question arises of why this should be the case. We propose here that the so-called 'black box' between teaching the whole class and gain scores is in fact filled by the effective teaching behaviours, whole-class teaching thus allowing teachers to teach (effectively). It is this hypothesis that will be explored in this study. Furthermore, while researchers such as Brophy (1986) have hypothesised that it is the cumulative impact of effective teaching behaviours rather than any one or group of behaviours that makes the difference, neither the interrelationship between behaviours nor their cumulative impact have so far been studied using the sophisticated statistical techniques we now possess. In this study we will propose a model in which the separate teacher behaviours form a number of scales that are classroom management, behaviour management, direct teaching, interactive teaching, individual practice, classroom climate, varied teaching, constructivist methods and mathematical language. It is hypothesised that these scales will be influenced by the percentage of time spent in whole-class teaching, as this type of teaching is expected to create the conditions for effective teaching to occur (Reynolds and Muijs, 1999b, 1999c).

The Gatsby Mathematics Enhancement Programme (Primary)

Notwithstanding the evidence discussed above, there has long been a tendency in Britain to prefer methods of teaching based on an individual learning approach, in which the student is expected to learn at his/her own pace during most of the lesson, usually going through maths schemes/workbooks, while the teacher sits behind his/her desk marking pupils' work. Recently, partly as a result of the poor performance of British pupils in international comparative tests (e.g. TIMSS), and partly because of the poor numeracy of British adults as evidenced by a number of national and international studies (e.g. Department for Education and Employment, 1998), the effectiveness of these methods has come under ever closer scrutiny, which has led to a number of reform programmes in mathematics education, emanating from both the national government and local education authorities and charitable trusts.

One such reform programme is the Gatsby Mathematics Enhancement Programme (Primary), funded by the Gatsby Charitable Foundation (a Sainsbury family charitable trust), which aims to improve mathematics teaching at the primary level, in part through helping teachers to attain more effective whole-class teaching strategies. An evaluation of this programme was funded by the Gatsby Charitable Foundation, and carried out by the Newcastle Educational Effectiveness and Improvement Centre at the University of Newcastle. The evaluation of the success or otherwise of the project will be discussed in other publications. In this article, we will look at what the data have shown us about effective whole-class interactive teaching in primary schools. Looking at the effectiveness of whole-class interactive teaching in this way is particularly timely, in view of the fact that the British government is advocating this teaching method through its National Numeracy Strategy (DfEE, 1998), which all schools are advised to follow, although it has to be pointed out that the fact that all teachers in the project have been trained to use whole-class interactive teaching methods will limit the variance in teacher behaviours we can observe in this study.

Sample and methods

Data on 16 primary schools in two local education authorities involved in the Gatsby project, along with three control schools in another local education authority, are included in this analysis. All teachers in years 1, 3 and 5 were observed during maths lessons by trained observers, making a total of 24 teachers in year 1, 26 in year 3 and 28 in year 5. Inter-observer reliability had earlier been established by all observers observing the same four lessons as .81 (sig. < .001) using Cohen's Kappa. A total of 2,128 pupils were involved. An observation schedule developed for the project, the Mathematics Enhancement Classroom Observation Record (Schaffer, Muijs, Kitson, and Reynolds, 1998), which was based on a number of existing reliable instruments such as the SSOS, was used in the classroom.

During lessons observers counted the number of pupils on/off task every five minutes, and wrote down what was going on during the lesson in a detailed fashion. This included classroom organisation, which was coded as either whole-class interactive teaching (the teacher is teaching the whole class in an interactive way), individual seatwork (pupils are working on their own, for example doing an exercise on a worksheet or in a workbook), small group work (pupils are working collaboratively on a task, in either pairs or larger groups), and lecturing the whole class (the teacher is teaching the whole class in a non-interactive way, lecturing pupils and not engaging them through asking questions or discussion).

The amount of time in minutes spent in each of these types of classroom organisation could then be calculated for each lesson. After each lesson the occurrence and quality of 65 teacher behaviours was rated on a scale of 1–5, coded as follows: 1 = behaviour rarely observed, 2 = behaviour occasionally observed, 3 = behaviour often observed, 4 = behaviour frequently observed, 5 = behaviour consistently observed, and na = not applicable. It is the rating of behaviours, classroom organisation and time on task measures which will form the basis of this article. The detailed lesson scripts are more qualitative in nature, and will be qualitatively analysed at a later date.

As mentioned earlier, these behaviours were hypothesised to form nine subscales: classroom management, behaviour management, direct teaching, individual practice, interactive teaching, varied teaching, mathematical language, classroom climate and constructivist methods (a number of items which were culled from constructively oriented theory and research mentioned above were included to reflect this position. These include encouraging pupils to use their own problem solving strategies and connecting different areas of maths to each other and other curriculum areas). Internal consistency of the scale scores (measured using Cronbach's Alpha) was over .8 for all scales.

All pupils were tested using the National Foundation for Educational Research's Numeracy tests, which were administered twice, in March and in July of 1998. These tests consist of two sections for each year, one written and one mental, and are designed to accord with the English National Curriculum in mathematics. The scores of the tests had a reliability based on Cronbach's Alpha of over .8 in all years in this study (see Table 7.1). Data on free school meal eligibility, English comprehension, special needs status and gender were also collected from the school.

Results

Means and correlations

Means and standard deviations of the test scores and teaching scales used in these analyses are given in Table 7.2. Pupil gain scores were calculated by subtracting

Table 7.1 Internal consistency of test scores (using Cronbach's Alpha)

	Year 1 written A	Year 1 written B	Year 1 mental	Year 3 written	Year 3 mental	Year 5 written	Year 5 mental
March	0.93	0.89	0.90	0.97	0.96	0.98	0.96
July	0.96	0.93	0.94	0.98	0.96	0.98	0.98

Table 7.2 Means and standard deviations of test scores and scales

	M	(SD)
Year 1 written test A – March	7.55	(3.03)
Year 1 written test B – March	3.51	(2.94)
Year 1 mental test – March	4.37	(3.52)
Year 3 written test – March	16.06	(8.15)
Year 3 mental test – March	9.18	(5.28)
Year 5 written test – March	21.77	(9.47)
Year 5 mental test – March	12.96	(5.90)
Year 1 written test A – July	9.88	(3.70)
Year 1 written test B – July	5.34	(3.53)
Year 1 mental test – July	7.32	(4.26)
Year 3 written test – July	20.26	(9.46)
Year 3 mental test – July	11.57	(5.36)
Year 5 written test – July	24.53	(10.64)
Year 5 mental test – July	15.04	(6.66)
Classroom management	15.39	(3.09)
Behaviour management	13.79	(2.85)
Direct teaching	28.85	(5.81)
Individual practice	13.85	(2.48)
Interactive teaching	47.92	(8.48)
Constructivist methods	10.58	(3.34)
Mathematical language	6.87	(1.50)
Varied teaching	9.45	(2.69)
Classroom climate	27.03	(4.41)
Time on task	90.55	(6.32)
Percent whole-class interactive	51.63	(14.30)
Percentage seatwork	31.45	(13.30)
Percentage small group work	5.55	(11.22)
Percentage whole-class lecture	3.85	(5.16)
Percentage transitions	12.04	(6.75)

scores on the March test from scores on the July test. In Table 7.3 the correlations of the teaching scales, classroom organisation, and time on task measures with each other and with pupil gain scores from the March to July tests are given. As can be seen in Table 7.3, seven teaching factors – classroom management, behaviour management, direct instruction, review and practice, interactive teaching, varied teaching and classroom climate – are consistently significantly positively correlated with pupil gain scores in all three years. Correlations were strongest in years 3 and 5 on the written test. All these factors were significantly correlated with gain scores in all years. The use of correct mathematical language was significant only in year 1 and on the written test in year 5, and the use of constructivist methods was not significant in any of the tests except the year 3 mental test, where the relationship was negative. Possibly, positive effects of these methods may take longer to translate into achievement gains than the three-month period discussed here.

Time on task percentage and percentage of time spent on seatwork, teaching the whole class interactively, lecturing the whole class, small group work and percentage of time spent on transitions were not strongly related to pupil gain scores, although some weak positive correlations with gain scores and some weak negative relations with seatwork were found in years 1 and 3, but not in year 5. Time on task was likewise only weakly related to gain scores, although the direction of the relationship was positive in all cases.

The teaching factors are strongly correlated with one another (all correlations over .55), with the exception of the constructivist methods and mathematical language scales, which are weakly to moderately (but still positively) related to the other scales (see Table 7.4).

The classroom organisation factors, percentage time spent on whole-class interactive teaching, percentage time spent on seatwork, percentage time spent on group work, percentage time spent on whole-class lecturing and percentage time spent on transitions, were also related to the teacher behaviour factors. The main positive relationship was with whole-class interactive teaching, which was significantly correlated with the seven 'behaviourist' effective teaching factors (termed effective teaching scale). Time spent on seatwork was (more weakly) negatively correlated with the teaching factors, as was time spent on small group work and time spent on transitions. Lecturing the whole class was only weakly related to the effective teaching factors, but was more strongly positively related to the use of mathematical language and constructivist methods. Time on task was significantly positively related to all nine teaching factors, with correlations ranging from .32 to .59.

Multilevel analyses

In order to see whether the teaching factors are still related to pupil test score gains once pupil background is controlled for, multilevel models were computed. This technique partitions the variance between the different levels at which it is measured (e.g., pupils and classrooms), thus both attenuating the problem of underestimating standard errors in single-level analyses of clustered sample data, and allowing us to look at whether there are actually significant differences in pupil

Table 7.3 Pearson correlation coefficients of teacher behaviour scales with pupil gain scores

Scales	Year 1 written test form A	Year 1 written test form B	Year 1 mental test	Year 3 written test	Year 3 mental test	Year 5 written test	Year 5 mental test
Classroom management	0.12★★	0.21★★	0.26★★	0.34★★	0.15★★	0.34★★	0.17★★
Behaviour management	0.13★	0.19★★	0.25★★	0.40★★	0.16★★	0.32★★	0.15★★
Direct teaching	0.24★★	0.22★★	0.32★★	0.32★★	0.14★★	0.36★★	0.22★★
Individual practice	0.18★★	0.17★★	0.26★★	0.35★★	0.15★★	0.34★★	0.21★★
Interactive teaching	0.20★★	0.24★★	0.24★★	0.38★★	0.18★★	0.39★★	0.18★★
Constructivist methods	0.09	0.03	0.07	0.04	−0.18★★	0.03	−0.09
Mathematical language	0.22★★	0.19★★	0.12★	−0.01	0.09	0.13★★	0.01
Varied teaching	0.20★★	0.24★★	0.28★★	0.37★★	0.25★★	0.34★★	0.14★★
Classroom climate	0.17★★	0.23★★	0.21★★	0.28★★	0.13★★	0.36★★	0.16★★
Time on task	0.05	0.10★	0.15★★	0.21★★	0.05	0.02	0.10★
% whole–class interactive	0.16★★	0.11★★	0.16★★	0.26★★	0.10★	0.03	0.01
Percentage seatwork	−0.12★	−0.13★★	−0.13★★	−0.20★★	−0.07	−0.06	−0.03
% small group work	0.02	0.00	0.00	−0.14★★	−0.10★	−0.14★★	−0.12★★
% whole–class lecture	−0.02	−0.05	−0.06	−0.07	−0.22★★	0.30★★	0.07
Percentage transitions	−0.10★	0.04	−0.06	−0.04	−0.08	−0.13★★	−0.02

Notes

★ = Significant at the 0.05 level

★★ = Significant at the 0.01 level

Table 7.4 Pearson correlation coefficients between teacher behaviours, classroom organisation and time on task

	1	2	3	4	5	6	7	8	9	10	11	12	13	14	15
1. manage		0.75**	0.67**	0.79**	0.75**	0.08**	0.19**	0.57**	0.72**	0.17**	-0.08**	-0.14**	-0.22**	0.04	0.58**
2. behave			0.77**	0.75**	0.79**	0.12**	0.24**	0.67**	0.81**	0.37**	0.07**	-0.31**	-0.25**	-0.07**	0.55**
3. direct				0.76**	0.78**	0.11**	0.36**	0.70**	0.80**	0.23**	0.01	-0.13**	-0.25**	-0.18**	0.36**
4. indprac					0.89**	0.22**	0.24**	0.74**	0.82**	0.19**	-0.07**	-0.04	-0.31**	-0.17**	0.44**
5. interact						0.25**	0.38**	0.75**	0.85**	0.22**	0.03	-0.13**	-0.20**	-0.17**	0.42**
6. cons							0.20**	0.07**	0.13**	-0.09**	0.24**	0.13**	0.08**	-0.23**	0.32**
7. matlang								0.45**	0.35**	-0.02	0.14**	0.08**	-0.04	-0.20**	0.05*
8. varteach									0.80**	0.41**	-0.02	-0.32**	-0.16**	-0.13**	0.13**
9. climate										0.30**	0.04	-0.19**	-0.22**	-0.20**	0.42**
10. pctlec											-0.09**	-0.86**	-0.12**	-0.21**	0.03
11. pctseat												-0.12**	0.10**	-0.31**	0.14**
12. pctgrp													0.05*	-0.13**	-0.05
13. pcttrans														0.05*	-0.09**
14. time ot	0.59**	0.55**	0.36**	0.44**	0.42**	0.32**	0.05*	0.13**	0.42**	0.03	0.14**	0.13**	0.09**		-0.04

Notes

* = Significant at the 0.05 level

** = Significant at the 0.01 level

gain scores at the classroom level before enabling us to look at the explanatory power of the variables at the different levels.

In these multilevel analyses, we will look at pupil scores on the July 1998 tests, controlling for performance on the March tests, which are entered as a predictor of July test scores in order to gauge the effect of the predictor variables on pupil gains in mathematics. We will also introduce the main pupil background variables, free school meal eligibility (a dummy variable: eligible or not), gender, English comprehension (English first language or not), and the pupil's age in months at the time s/he took the test. In a second phase, rather than entering the effective teaching scales separately, a composite effective teaching variable will be entered (calculated by summing the scores on the scales for classroom management, behaviour management, direct teaching, individual practice, interactive teaching, varied teaching and classroom climate), this to help avoid multi-collinearity which could otherwise result from using the highly intercorrelated teaching scales as predictors in the analyses. Time on task, and percentage whole-class interactive teaching will also be introduced, as will constructivist teaching and use of mathematical language. A dummy variable indicating whether or not the school was involved in the Gatsby project (interven) will also be added. Results can be found in Tables 7.5–7.7.

As can be seen in Table 7.5, the percentage of unexplained variance in pupil attainment in maths between March and July at the classroom level ranged between 7.2% (year 5 mental test) and 23.4% (year 1 mental test), and was significant in all analyses. This does not, of course, necessarily mean that this variance is all down to teacher factors, as classrooms differ from each other on other dimensions as well.

In the second model pupil background variables, free school meal eligibility, pupil age at test, English comprehension and gender were added. These variables

Table 7.5 Multilevel model 1: intercept only

	Year 1 written A	Year 1 written B	Year 1 mental	Year 3 written	Year 3 mental	Year 5 written	Year 5 mental
FIXED							
Intercept	4.03	3.09	4.68	5.43	4.88	6.25	4.86
(Constant)	(0.42)	(0.27)	(0.42)	(0.58)	(0.36)	(0.93)	(0.56)
March	0.78	0.69	0.66	0.90	0.72	0.83	0.78
test score	(0.04)	(0.04)	(0.04)	(0.02)	(0.03)	(0.03)	(0.04)
RANDOM							
Variance	0.74	0.67	2.58	3.19	1.17	5.96	1.47
level 2	(0.31)	(0.29)	(0.90)	(1.14)	(0.45)	(2.23)	(0.68)
Variance	6.37	6.44	8.45	20.63	10.21	37.93	18.88
level 1	(0.41)	(0.41)	(0.54)	(1.20)	(0.59)	(2.32)	(1.16)
% Var. level 2	10.4%	9.5%	23.4%	13.4%	10.2%	13.5%	7.2%

(see Table 7.6) explain less than 5% of the variance in gains on the tests from March to July. Free school meal eligibility was the most consistently significant variable, being significant in year 1 and on the written test in year 5, and almost reaching significance on both tests in year 3. Age in months was significant for the written test form b in year 1 and the written test in year 3, with older pupils making more progress, and English comprehension was significant for progress on the written test form a in year 1 and the written test in year 5, in both cases pupils with English as their first language making more progress.

Table 7.6 Multilevel model 2: intercept and pupil background

	Year 1 written A	Year 1 written B	Year 1 mental	Year 3 written	Year 3 mental	Year 5 written	Year 5 mental
FIXED							
Intercept	−0.35 (2.67)	−1.85 (2.71)	0.25 (3.17)	−11.79 (5.56)	−0.31 (3.93)	−0.98 (9.32)	−2.80 (6.56)
March test scores	0.73 (0.05)	0.66 (0.05)	0.63 (0.04)	0.88 (0.03)	0.70 (0.03)	0.81 (0.03)	0.76 (0.04)
Age in months	0.04 (0.03)	0.06 (0.03)	0.04 (0.04)	0.17 (0.06)	0.05 (0.04)	0.05 (0.07)	0.06 (0.05)
Gender	−0.42 (0.22)	−0.40 (0.22)	−0.03 (0.26)	−0.34 (0.37)	0.29 (0.26)	−0.17 (0.53)	0.14 (0.37)
English comprehension	1.27 (0.51)	0.39 (0.51)	0.58 (0.62)	1.32 (0.78)	0.70 (0.54)	2.26 (0.98)	1.09 (0.66)
FSM eligibility	0.75 (0.25)	0.46 (0.26)	0.80 (0.29)	0.72 (0.42)	0.57 (0.30)	1.34 (0.59)	0.45 (0.41)
RANDOM							
Level 2 intercept	0.64 (0.27)	0.61 (0.27)	2.39 (0.85)	3.16 (1.13)	1.11 (0.43)	4.33 (1.57)	1.14 (0.50)
Level 1 intercept	6.16 (0.39)	6.34 (0.40)	8.32 (0.53)	20.16 (1.71)	10.10 (0.59)	37.55 (2.30)	18.84 (1.15)
% Variance level 2	9.4%	8.8%	22.3%	13.6%	9.9%	10.3%	5.7%
EXPLAINED VAR. Compared to previous model							
Total	4.4%	2.2%	2.9%	2.1%	1.5%	4.6%	1.8%
Level 2	13.5%	11.6%	7.4%	0.1%	5.1%	27.3%	22.4%
Level 1	3.3%	1.6%	1.5%	2.3%	1.1%	1.0%	0.2%

Table 7.7 Multilevel model 6: intercept, pupil background and classroom variables

	Year 1 written A	Year 1 written B	Year 1 mental	Year 3 written	Year 3 mental	Year 5 written	Year 5 mental
FIXED							
Intercept	−0.36 (3.27)	−5.11 (3.36)	−3.06 (5.30)	−21.16 (6.58)	−1.26 (5.14)	0.49 (10.42)	−7.45 (7.91)
March test score	0.71 (0.02)	0.64 (0.04)	0.62 (0.04)	0.89 (0.02)	0.71 (0.03)	0.82 (0.03)	0.76 (0.04)
Gender	−0.38 (0.22)	−0.36 (0.22)	0.00 (0.26)	−0.41 (0.36)	0.28 (0.26)	−0.34 (0.52)	0.09 (0.37)
English comprehension	1.00 (0.50)	−0.01 (0.51)	0.39 (0.62)	1.36 (0.72)	0.73 (0.53)	1.97 (0.91)	0.88 (0.68)
FSM eligibility	0.71 (0.25)	0.42 (0.26)	0.81 (0.29)	1.00 (0.40)	0.69 (0.29)	−1.19 (0.57)	0.39 (0.41)
Age in months	0.06 (0.03)	0.05 (0.03)	0.04 (0.04)	0.15 (0.01)	0.05 (0.04)	0.05 (0.07)	0.06 (0.05)
Intervention	−0.05 (0.70)	−0.76 (0.73)	−2.10 (1.37)	0.08 (0.60)	0.16 (0.53)	−0.24 (1.03)	0.08 (0.08)
Whole–class interactive	0.01 (0.01)	0.015 (0.010)	0.04 (0.02)	0.01 (0.02)	−0.01 (0.02)	0.00 (0.02)	0.02 (0.02)
Time on task	0.08 (0.02)	0.00 (0.23)	−0.02 (0.04)	0.00 (0.04)	−0.04 (0.04)	0.16 (0.06)	0.01 (0.05)
Constructivist methods	0.16 (0.06)	−0.03 (0.06)	0.09 (0.11)	0.04 (0.06)	−0.12 (0.06)	0.10 (0.09)	−0.08 (0.08)
Mathematical language	0.09 (0.14)	0.28 (0.14)	−0.12 (0.26)	0.01 (0.20)	0.10 (0.18)	−0.20 (0.17)	−0.08 (0.15)
Effective teaching	0.02 (0.01)	0.03 (0.01)	0.05 (0.02)	0.06 (0.01)	0.03 (0.01)	0.08 (0.01)	0.04 (0.01)
RANDOM							
Level 2 intercept	0.06 (0.10)	0.08 (0.10)	0.92 (0.39)	0.18 (0.28)	0.41 (0.24)	0.00 (0.00)	0.38 (0.34)
Level 1 intercept	6.15 (0.39)	6.34 (0.40)	8.32 (0.53)	20.22 (1.17)	10.12 (0.59)	37.34 (2.24)	18.82 (1.15)
% variance level 2	1.0%	1.2%	9.9%	0.9%	3.9%	0.0%	2.0%
EXPLAINED VAR. Compared to prev. model (total)							
Total	8.6%	7.6%	13.7%	12.5%	6.1%	10.9%	3.9%
Level 2	90.6%	86.9%	61.5%	94.3%	63.1%	100%	66.7%
Level 1	0.2%	0.0%	0.0%	0.0%	0.0%	0.5%	0.0%

An interesting finding is the fact that these background variables explained a larger proportion of level 2 variance than of level 1 variance. This points to the homogeneity of primary classrooms, which tend to recruit pupils from relatively homogeneous catchment areas with respect to socio-economic status. On the whole, though, it has to be pointed out that these variables did not explain pupils' progress on the Numeracy tests well. This is not to say that these background variables are unimportant to pupils' achievement in mathematics. Rather, it seems likely that the effects of pupil background are already incorporated into their performance on the March test, and therefore do not strongly affect their progress in the short time-span studied here.

In the third model the effective teaching scale and the other classroom teaching factors were introduced in order to ascertain whether they were able to explain part of the remaining between-classroom variance once pupil background had been taken into account.

It is clear from the results presented in Table 7.7 that the effective teaching scale explains a significant percentage of between-classroom variance, once pupil characteristics have been controlled for. This variable was highly significant in all years and on all tests, and the teaching variables together explained between 61.5% and 100% of the remaining between-classroom variance, causing between-classroom variation to become insignificant in most cases. Explained variance was highest in year 5. Of the other two variables, only the percentage of time spent teaching the whole class interactively, as opposed to time spent on seatwork or group work, was (weakly) significant in the year 1 mental test analyses but not in the higher years. Time on task was only significantly positively related to progress in mathematics on the written test in year 5 and the written test form a in year 1. Constructivist teaching methods were significantly positively related to gains in year 1 on the written test form a and negatively to gains on the mental test in year 3. Use of mathematical language was significantly related to gains on the form b test in year 1.

These percentages make clear that the aggregate effect of effective teaching behaviours is highly practically significant, explaining as it does in this sample the majority of the variance in between-classroom test gains not explained by pupil background factors. The significance of the difference between effective teaching behaviours is illustrated in Table 7.8, from which it becomes clear that, holding all other variables constant, being taught by the teacher scoring highest as opposed to the teacher scoring lowest on the effective teaching scale can increase a pupil's scores on the test by between 10% and 25%. It would seem that the effective teaching scale, which accounted for by far the majority of the predictive power in these analyses, is quite well able to distinguish effective from less effective teachers at the primary level and for the elements studied here, although it must be remarked that, due to the short time elapsed between the two testing instances, the total variance in gain scores to be explained was quite limited.

Table 7.8 Predicted differences in scores on the July numeracy tests for pupils taught by the weakest and strongest teachers, holding all other variables constant

	Year 1 written A	Year 1 written B	Year 1 mental	Year 3 written	Year 3 mental	Year 5 written	Year 5 mental
Difference in point score	2.05	2.05	4.46	5.70	2.85	8.57	3.88
% difference	10.7%	14.6%	24.7%	12.9%	12.4%	17.8%	12.9%
Test range	0–19	0–14	0–18	0–44	0–23	0–48	0–30

Structural equation models

While these analyses did not find much evidence for a direct effect of classroom organisation (whole-class interactive) or time on task on pupil gains, this does not necessarily invalidate the aforementioned hypothesis, as long as there is evidence of an indirect relationship as hypothesised above. Some tentative evidence for such a relationship may be garnered from the correlations between these variables and pupil gain scores, as evident in Table 7.3 above.

To test whether the theoretical model we proposed above, in which whole-class teaching affects effective teaching behaviours and time on task, which in turn affect pupil gain scores, it was decided to use structural equation modelling. This technique, which measures the fit of pre-specified directional relationships between the variables to the covariance matrix used, allows us to model directional relationships between variables, while also taking into account measurement error in the data. The LISREL programme was used to calculate the models.

Structural equation models were tested for each of three years. In order to allow the sample sizes to be such that the Chi-Square test would give us an accurate estimate of goodness of fit, the sample was split in two for each of the three years. In this way it was also possible to obtain an impression of the reliability of the model.

In this model, in which only the classroom factors were included, March test scores were posited to strongly affect July test scores, while the teaching factors in turn were hypothesised to also have a significant effect on the July test scores, albeit clearly weaker than that of March test scores. Classroom organisation (whole-class interactive teaching) was hypothesised to affect effective teaching behaviours, and thus exert an indirect influence on pupil gain scores (July test scores controlled for March test scores), because it was hypothesised that spending more time teaching the whole class would allow teachers to display more effective teaching behaviours than allowing pupils to work on their own for a larger part of the lesson.

In view of the correlation between the constructivist scale and the mathematical language scale, it was decided to let both load on a latent non-behavioural teaching variable. This was hypothesised to affect July test scores. Whole-class teaching was expected to lead to higher time on task rates, as it was hypothesised that spending more time teaching the whole class as opposed to allowing pupils to work on their own for most of the lesson would allow the teacher to monitor pupils' behaviour more easily, and would be less likely to lead to pupils getting distracted from the lesson. Time on task was in turn hypothesised to help create the conditions for effective teaching to occur. While we would assume that the relationship between effective teaching and time on task would in fact be reciprocal, the modelling of reciprocal effects in LISREL is highly problematic at present. Models were tested separately for the three years studied. The errors of the teaching factors were allowed to correlate with each other, as, due to the way they were measured (by one classroom observer during the same observation), they were expected to covary to some extent. These models are depicted in Figures 7.1–7.6. A problem with this model is the fact that they do not take into account the multilevel structure of the data, as classroom level data is in this case disaggregated to the individual level. This clearly is cause for some caution when interpreting the results, as standard error, for example, is liable to be underestimated.

As can be seen in Table 7.9, the model fits in years 3 and 5, and the similar fit indices for the two subsamples suggest this model is quite stable in these years. Chi-square remained significant for the year 1 models, however, suggesting that the hypothesis is less well supported in this year. This confirms the weaker relationship between teacher factor and progress in mathematics in year 1 found in the analyses mentioned above. Most paths suggested in the theoretical model also reached significance, the only one failing to do so in a number of models being that from time on task to non-behavioural teaching, which was not significant in year 5, and the path from non-behavioural teaching to test scores, which was not significant in any of the models. It also has to be remarked that the loadings of the non-behavioural scales on that factor were weak in a number of models.

Some other differences were found between the years in the strength of the significant paths in the models: the effect of whole-class teaching on teaching behaviours and time on task was strongest in year 1, and the effect of effective teaching on test scores was strongest in year 3 and weakest in year 1. The path from whole-class interactive teaching to time on task was not significant in year 1. Overall these differences suggest that year 1 differs somewhat from the older years.

However, despite these differences the overall similarity of the models is striking. As would be expected, especially in light of the short period that has elapsed between testing, test scores are quite stable over time. However, over and above the effect of test stability, differences in pupils' progress clearly do occur, and they would seem to be affected by teacher effectiveness, the path from which to July test results is significant in all cases. Effective teaching behaviours are in turn influenced by both time on task and classroom organisation, and classroom organisation (the percentage of time spent on whole-class interactive teaching) in turn strongly influences time on task. The only paths that failed to reach significance in a number of cases were the ones involving non-behaviourist methods. Both the influence of non-behaviourist methods on achievement and the influence of time on task on non-behaviourist methods were not strongly supported by these models.

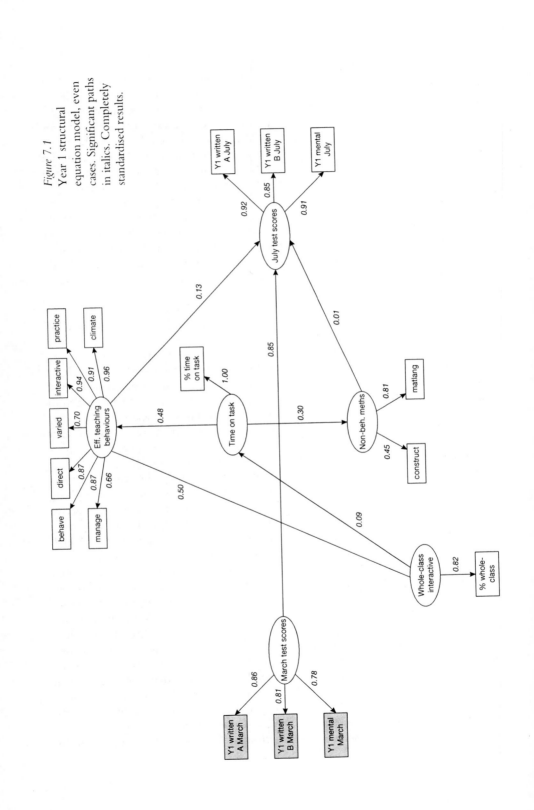

Figure 7.1
Year 1 structural equation model, even cases. Significant paths in italics. Completely standardised results.

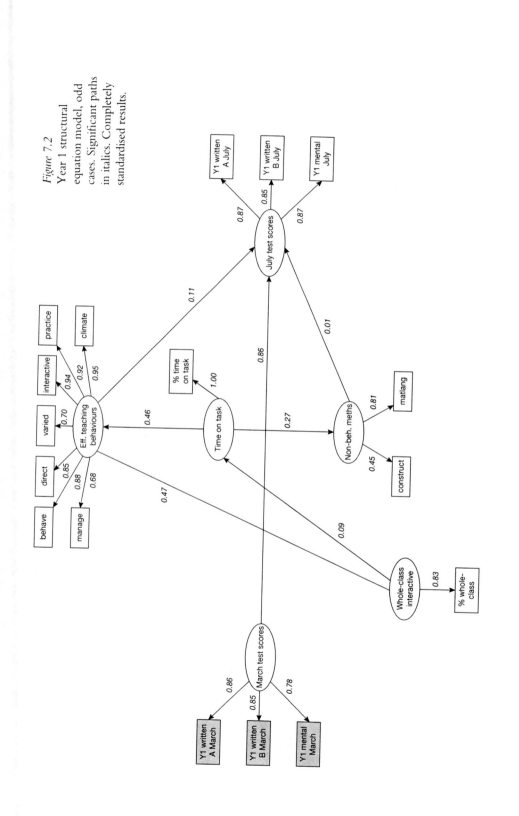

Figure 7.2
Year 1 structural equation model, odd cases. Significant paths in italics. Completely standardised results.

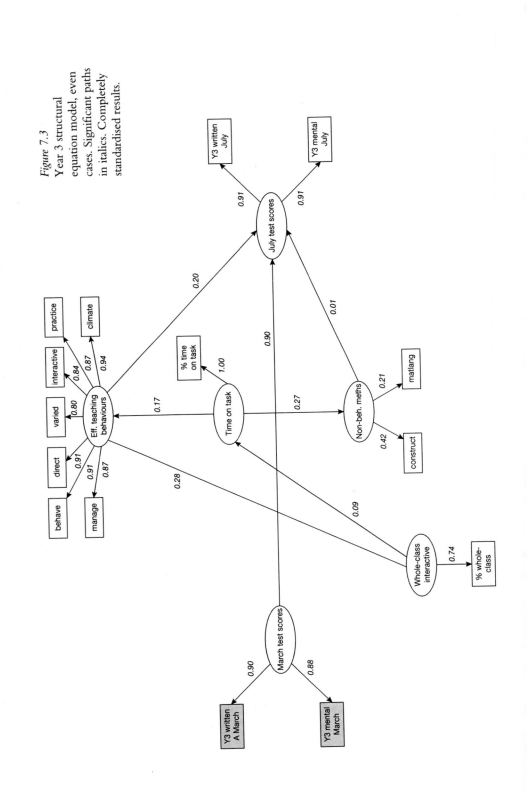

Figure 7.3
Year 3 structural equation model, even cases. Significant paths in italics. Completely standardised results.

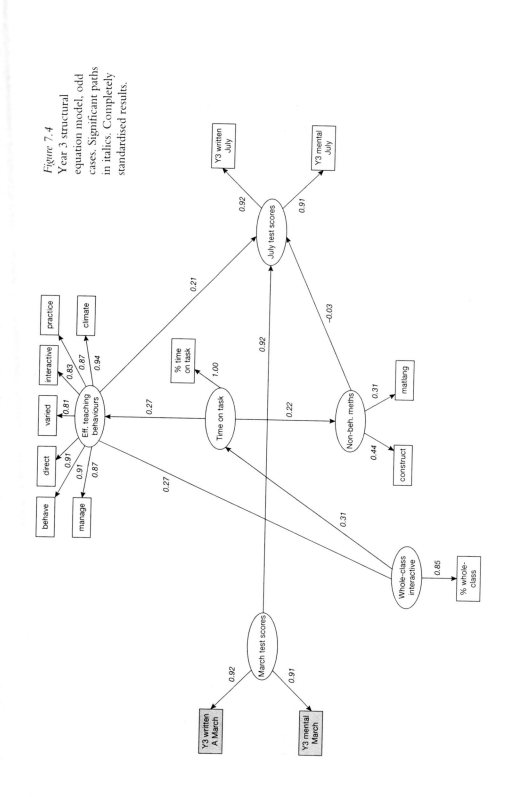

Figure 7.4
Year 3 structural
equation model, odd
cases. Significant paths
in italics. Completely
standardised results.

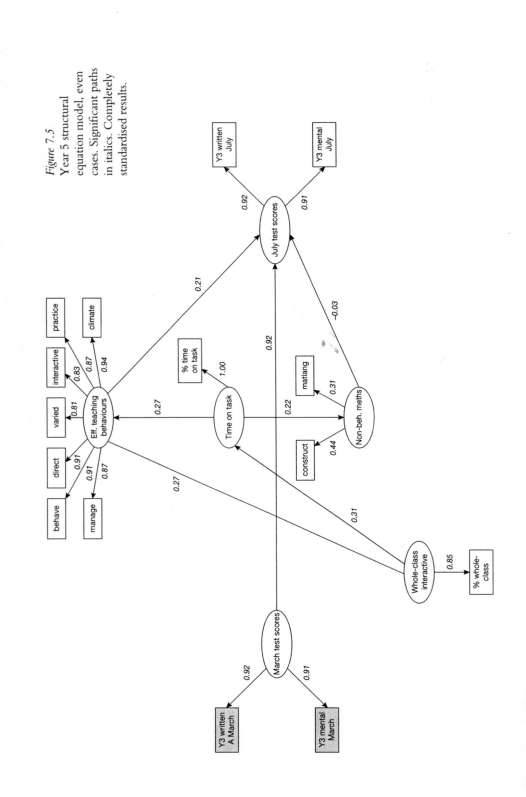

Figure 7.5
Year 5 structural equation model, even cases. Significant paths in italics. Completely standardised results.

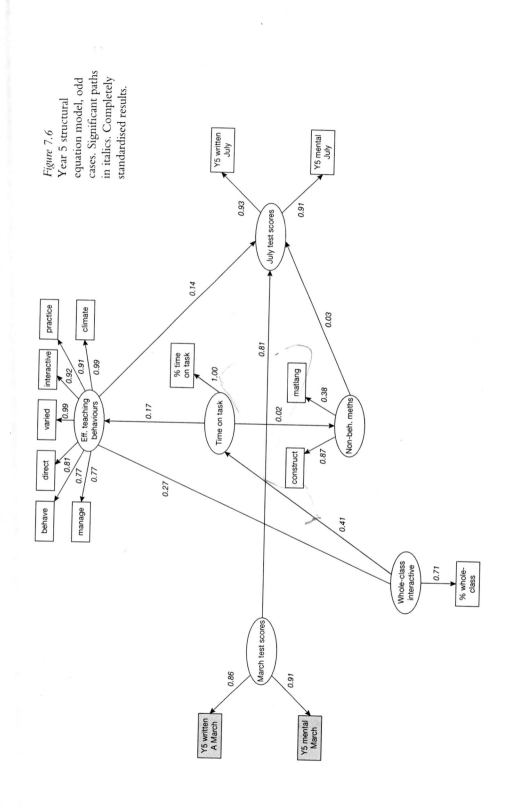

Figure 7.6
Year 5 structural equation model, odd cases. Significant paths in italics. Completely standardised results.

Table 7.9 Structural equation model fit indices

	Chi square (df)	RMSEA	GFI	NFI	CFI
Year 1, odd cases	174.49 (77)	0.06	0.94	0.96	0.98
Year 1, even cases	193.35 (77)	0.07	0.93	0.96	0.97
Year 3, odd cases	69.49 (56)	0.03	0.97	0.99	1.00
Year 3, even cases	72.61 (56)	0.04	0.97	0.98	0.99
Year 5, odd cases	79.64 (56)	0.04	0.97	0.98	0.99
Year 5, even cases	77.66 (56)	0.04	0.97	0.98	0.99

Discussion and conclusion

This study clearly points to the importance of the effective teaching behaviours as outlined in the teacher effectiveness research to successful mathematics teaching in the UK. It has become clear that, while individual behaviours may only explain a very small percentage of variance in pupil gains over time, taken together they are significant. This study also lends support to the view that these behaviours do indeed occur together in effective teachers, thus forming a cluster of effective teaching behaviours. The relationship of pupil gains to classroom organisation would seem to be an indirect one. It would seem that, rather than directly affecting pupil progress, whole-class teaching creates the conditions for effective teaching to occur, a result that could explain the fact that the amount of time spent teaching the whole class, while found to be effective in a number of American studies, was only found to be significant in three out of 29 primary level studies in the Netherlands reviewed by Scheerens and Creemers (1996).

More whole-class teaching allows teachers to be effective, in a way that individualised approaches do not. That this finding emerged even from a study in which, through its nature, the vast majority of teachers used a whole-class interactive approach is significant. However, it would be dangerous to generalise this finding ad infinitum. It is clear that while spending a large proportion of the lesson teaching the whole class is beneficial, individual or group practice (as evidenced by the significance of this teacher scale) is clearly necessary to enhance pupil learning. To spend 100% of all lessons teaching the whole class together would probably be harmful. In this sense, the relationship between classroom organisation and gains is probably a curvilinear one. The mistake some American educators have made, in extrapolating findings on the importance of academic learning time to such an extent that play times have been virtually abolished, should not be repeated here.

The centrality of the teacher in pupils' learning processes is clear, however. Any approach designed to let pupils learn on their own, with the teacher acting merely as a 'facilitator', is likely to fall short of the cognitive demands of primary age children.

As is clear from the items included in the scales, it would be wrong to describe this whole-class interactive teaching style as a 'chalk and talk' drill-and-practice approach. The importance of engaging with students at a cognitively higher as well as lower level is clear from the inclusion of items such as asking open questions, allowing multiple answers etc. As such, this teaching style by no means precludes attention to higher-level learning goals. An explanation for the value of these behaviours and related classroom observation factors can be found in the need for pupils at this age for a good deal of explicit cognitive structuring (Stallings, Weisler, Chase, Feinstein, Garfield, and Risland, 1995).

While this study thus clearly supports whole-class interactive teaching, a number of limitations of this study need to be pointed out.

The tests used in this study, while reflecting the English National Curriculum, and the short-term nature of this study, mean that we have studied typical basic skills achievement gains only. It is not clear from this study whether these effective teaching behaviours are also, or as strongly, related to longer-term and more cognitive outcomes, such as independent learning goals or metacognitive development. It is possible, and indeed likely, that other teaching methods are needed alongside of the whole-class interactive approach found to be effective in this study to attain these goals. Joyce and Weil (1996), for example, point to the possible utility of methods such as synectics or thinking skills approaches for achieving this type of goal, while Slavin's (1996) research points to the importance of cooperative small group work, an approach not often used in English education, as evidenced by the fact that less than 5% of lesson time was spent on average on group work (which was usually not organised to the standards suggested by Slavin) in the lessons observed in this study.

These comments do not, however, invalidate the results of this study, unless one believes that basic numeracy skills are entirely unimportant in children's mathematics learning. It should be clear that both basic skills and long-term cognitive goals have their place in any learning situation, and an either/or approach to this problem is unwise in the extreme.

A further limitation is that while proper hierarchical modelling techniques were used for the multilevel regression model, this was not the case for the structural equation model, for which the teacher level variables were disaggregated to the individual level. This was due to the fact that when using a two-level structural equation modelling approach, one is basically using a multiple group approach, which means that for both groups/levels the assumptions of the approach have to be met. This includes sample size, which in situations of perfect multivariate normality of the data set may be as low as 50, but under more prevalent conditions is usually closer to 200. Our sample clearly does not meet this requirement at the classroom level.

The short time-span between the two testing occasions is a further reason for caution with respect to these findings, and also explains why the total amount of variance in pupil gains is relatively small. This variance is further limited by the fact that schools in the Gatsby Mathematics Enhancement Programme (Primary) were encouraged to engage in whole-class interactive teaching styles, thus limiting the variance in classroom organisation as well as in teaching styles employed. The fact that all the teachers in the project were trained in whole-class teaching methods in the Gatsby project is presumably also responsible for the high overall time on task levels in this study.

Also, no data on teacher beliefs and attitudes were collected in this initial stage of the research. In view of the findings of amongst others Askew *et al.* (1997), this is a clear limitation, which will be addressed in the next phase of the project in which we will be looking at teacher beliefs about and attitudes towards mathematics, teachers and mathematics teaching and at their subject knowledge as well as continuing to look at behaviours.

A possible worry about this method of teaching is the finding in this study that boys made significantly more gains than girls did on many occasions. While it is not clear from this study whether this is a result of the teaching style, there is a danger that boys might dominate interaction with the teacher in an interactive classroom. This is clearly an issue that needs addressing, and teachers should be pointed to the need to involve girls in any interaction in the classroom.

This research has clear practical implications for teacher training in mathematics. If it is possible to identify clusters of behaviour that appear to be significantly related to pupil gains, then it would clearly be beneficial to devote a significant amount of energy to training teachers in the use of these methods, especially in the early phases of teacher training. This would also tie in well with the British government's literacy and numeracy strategies, which support whole-class teaching methods. As Brophy (1986) has pointed out, not all the results from this and similar studies are immediately easily transferable to the classroom, but, as the research is based in naturalistic classroom settings, it is certainly more so than a lot of the popular psychological research that is often used to justify impractical individualised and child-centred techniques. Knowing how children construct knowledge may be useful for teachers, but the practical utility of basing teaching strategies on such individual psychological theories must be questioned.

In future, longer-term research is needed to see how the relationships develop, and whether there is stability over the longer term, with respect both to measures of teacher effectiveness and to relationships between factors and achievement.

It is also imperative in future to do more fine-grained research, and to attempt to find 'thresholds' for the behaviours identified here as effective. Thus, while the results of this study would suggest that high levels of whole-class interactive teaching are beneficial, it would, as mentioned above, be useful to find out more about where overuse of a particular effective technique becomes harmful.

Future research also needs to take into account relationships between teacher behaviours and teacher beliefs and attitudes, which research (e.g., Askew *et al.*, 1997) has found to be related to teacher efficacy. As one could also expect that teacher behaviour is related to teacher beliefs, it is essential to study these relationships further.

Also, while this (and a lot of the American teacher effectiveness research, for example Good, Grouws, *et al.*, 1983) has concentrated on mathematics, it is obviously of equally strong interest to study what works in other subjects, such as

English, science, history, etc. Extension of research to other age groups would likewise seem appropriate. Finally, looking at the effectiveness of teachers in fostering different outcomes (e.g. higher cognitive level processes) might also be fruitful.

Overall, then, it would seem that there is plenty of work to do for researchers who want to extend the British and international teacher effectiveness research base, and thus contribute to a truly research-based profession of teaching in the UK and beyond.

Acknowledgement

First published as D. Muijs and D. Reynolds (2000) 'School effectiveness and teacher effectiveness: Some preliminary findings from the evaluation of the Mathematics Enhancement Programme', in *School Effectiveness and School Improvement*, Vol. 11 No. 2. Reprinted here with permission from Taylor & Francis.

8

The High Reliability Schools Project
Some preliminary results and analyses

Introduction

The last thirty years may well be the time of greatest ferment in public education in the history of developed nations. Whether an observer begins in England, the Netherlands, Canada, or any nation from Argentina around the Pacific Rim, including New Zealand and Australia, the calls for reform have been loud and growing louder. In a post-Cold War Global Information Economy, national government after national government has found that individual incomes and Gross Domestic Products are ever more closely tied to the education levels of their citizens. Specifically:

- social change means that there is a premium on reliability because of the interconnectedness of modern industrial societies;
- a trailing edge of uneducated labour has costs for the wider society in terms of lost production, potential costs of crime and social problems;
- the international mobility of capital means that production processes follow labour which is productive, whether this is in Pinner or the Pacific Rim;
- original and valid ideas that used to stay within geographical boundaries, where they may have been developed unreliably, now spread around the world in a millisecond.

In the current environment, school improvement discussions and, indeed, educational improvement 'programmes' and 'whole school reform designs' are all emerging within individual countries and travelling internationally at unprecedented levels and speeds. Examples abound. Reading Recovery (Pinnell, 1989) was developed in New Zealand, yet certified Reading Recovery teachers are practising from Hong Kong to Scotland. The Coalition of Essential Schools began as a volume about a fictional English teacher (Sizer, 1984), and has spread to over 1,000 schools including New Mexico Pueblos and the 'leafy suburbs' of London. Success for All (Slavin, et al., 1990, 1996) began in Baltimore, Maryland, and has spread to over 1,500 schools from Mexico to Israel.

Research has almost always been slow to follow reform efforts. Slavin et al. (1996) noted that high quality evaluations of educational reform efforts have typically not been conducted until after a reform has passed its zenith, and the great majority of educators have moved to the next fad. However, several strands of research now have long enough histories and have had enough staying power to allow studies. These in turn are able to provide useful information regarding the plausible impacts of ongoing educational improvement efforts.

The use of promising programmes

This concerns efforts to chart the effects of diverse school reform efforts. Over a 60-year period, a reasonably stable body of research has evolved, from the Eight Year Study (Aiken, 1942), the Follow-Through Planned Variation Study (Stallings and Kaskowitz, 1974), the RAND Change Agent Study (Berman and McLaughlin, 1977; McLaughlin, 1991), the DESSI studies (Crandall, et al., 1982), and the Special Strategies Studies (Stringfield, et al., 1997), to the New American Schools initiatives (Bodilly, 1996), and studies of specific reforms such as Success for All/Roots and Wings (Slavin, 1996).

Four of the major conclusions that can be drawn from this half-century-plus of large-scale studies follow. A first is that most, but not all, of the reforms can point to one or more schools that have greatly improved some combination of faculty attitudes, student deportment, and student attendance. A second is that all of the reforms that have 'scaled up' to significant numbers of schools have examples of schools in which the reform has had no measurable effect, and been discontinued. A third is that in virtually every case involving on-site observations of the reform implementation efforts, success has been greatest in schools where the design team and the local educators worked together to create the most efficacious interaction of the local realities with the reform design. Berman and McLaughlin (1977) referred to this as 'mutual adaptation'. More recently, others have described the process in a more active, engaging voice as 'co-construction' (Datnow, Hubbard and Mehan, 1998; Datnow & Stringfield, 2000). The important point is that there are virtually no sites described in any of the available studies in which a local school literally and uncritically adopts a reform 'whole hog'. Rather, in study after study, the sites obtaining the greatest multi-year effects actively engage ideas and practices, and eventually are full partners in the creation of an improved school.

A fourth general finding has been that, over diverse reform efforts and contexts, reforms have been substantially more likely to produce measured results if they focused on primary schools (see Teddlie and Reynolds, 2000). This is not to suggest that all primary-based reforms have proven equally effective. However, secondary school reforms have consistently found the achievement of measurable, long-term results challenging.

School effects

The ability of a school to engage with a design team in co-constructing school reform and thereby achieving reasonably strong implementation of most design components within a specific context implies a school that either possessed a substantially healthy or 'effective' school culture prior to engaging in a specific reform, or developed such a local environment as a result of the reform. Either possibility suggests the relevance of the school effects research base. Following initially promising work by Edmonds (1979), and Rutter *et al.* (1979), much of the academic field of school effectiveness fell relatively silent. A great deal of subsequent hucksterism in the name of 'effective schools' caused the field to fall into substantial disrepute. Cuban (1993) described the evolution of scholarly criticisms of the field as being such that 'By the late 1980s [the field of school effectiveness] had largely been banished to the netherworld of pop-research . . . '. However, a steady stream of school effects research subsequently evolved, such that a recent review of the fields of school effects and school restructuring described the primary difference between the two fields as simply being that school effects has a credible research base. The *International Handbook of School Effectiveness Research* (Teddlie and Reynolds, 2000) reviewed over 1,700 articles and books in the field. Paradoxically, the majority of school reform projects now assume the importance of basic school effects dimensions, typically without referencing such areas as 'instructional leadership', 'school culture/climate' and 'efficient use of school and classroom time' to the field.

A key finding from one longitudinal school effects study is particularly relevant to the issue of improving the reliability of reform. The Louisiana School Effectiveness Study (Stringfield and Teddlie, 1991; Teddlie and Stringfield, 1993) followed eight demographically matched pairs of schools for over a decade. One school in each pair had a stable history of relatively high academic achievement, and the other had a stable history of relatively low achievement. Multi-level analyses of qualitative data over the first six-year period led the team to the conclusion that the greatest difference between pairs of schools was neither consistent brilliance of administration or teaching in the positive outlier schools, nor universal incompetence in the negative outlier schools.

The authors in fact noted specific examples of exemplary teaching in some very dysfunctional schools. Rather, along several dimensions at the student, classroom and school levels, positive outlier schools were most clearly identifiable by an intolerance for large negatives. The less effective schools, regardless of the socioeconomic status of the communities they served, were substantially less consistent or stable, classroom to classroom and year to year, in the quality of services they provided to their students. Stated positively, the more effective schools were substantially more reliable.

If existing educational reforms, however promising, are most often successful when they are either introduced into, or help create, healthier, more effective schools, and if more effective schools are more reliable at multiple levels, it would follow that consciously building reliability into school reforms would be an avenue worth exploring.

High Reliability Organisations

For over a decade, scholars in fields as diverse as political science, organisational behaviour and engineering have studied non-educational organisations that are required to work under the very unusual demand of functioning correctly 'the first time, every time' (LaPorte and Consolini, 1991; Roberts, 1993). Such complex social organisations as air traffic control towers and operators of multi-state electric power grids continuously run the risk of disastrous and obviously unacceptable failure. Several thousand consecutive days of efficiently monitoring and controlling the very crowded skies over Chicago, or London, would be heavily discounted by the public if two jumbo jets were to collide over either city. Through fog, snow, computer system failures and nearby tornadoes, in spite of thousands of flights per day in busy skies, such a collision has never happened above either city, a remarkable level of performance reliability.

By contrast, in the USA, one of the most highly educated nations on earth, within any group of 100 students beginning first grade in a particular year, approximately 15 will not have obtained their high school diplomas 15 years later. In Britain, slightly less than half of all pupils will not have the 'benchmark' of 5 or more high level public examination passes. Obviously, many nations have even lower levels of educational performance.

Combining evidence from bodies of knowledge on school effects, school reform and educational organisational performance, and contrasting those data with studies of HROs, it seems appropriate to hypothesise that part of the explanation for the relative flatness of long term measures of such educational effectiveness measures as the US National Assessment of Educational Progress is not merely a lack of reform efforts. It seems likely that the efforts themselves, whether locally developed or co-constructed, have often lacked reliability. However valid, the lack of reliability has put a ceiling on validity.

Regardless of the sector of a society in which they work, High Reliability Organisations (HROs) share several characteristics. Twelve of them are described below (adapted from Stringfield, 1998):

1. High organisational reliability evolves under a particular circumstance. HROs evolve when both the larger society and the professionals involved in the working of the organisation come to believe that failure of the organisation to

achieve its key goals would be disastrous. Thus, individual airlines are allowed to add and subtract specific routes, but both commercial aircraft maintenance and air traffic control are very closely monitored. Changing routes has little consequence for the larger society; however, one flight's total failure is unacceptable. Similarly, one badly cascading error in the 40-year life of an otherwise superbly performing nuclear power station is simply not acceptable, either for the surrounding community or the professionals working within.

2. Organisational reliability requires a clear and finite set of goals, shared at all organisational levels. Reliability requires priority setting and focus.
3. An ongoing alertness to surprises or lapses. Small failures in key systems are monitored closely, because they can cascade into major problems. In order to sustain multi-level awareness, HROs build powerful databases.

   These databases can be described as possessing 'Four R's':

   (a) relevance to core goals;
   (b) rich triangulation on key dimensions;
   (c) real-time availability to all organisational levels;
   (d) regularly cross-checked by multiple, concerned groups, both inside and outside the organisation.

4. The extension of formal, logical decision-making analysis as far as extant knowledge allows. Regularly repeated tasks which are effective become standard operating procedures. This is in part to make 'best practice' universal, but also to allow a rich web of peer observation and communication.
5. Highly reliable organisations actively sustain initiatives that encourage all concerned to identify flaws in standard operating procedures, and honour the flaw finders.

Because high reliability is a social construction and requires high levels of individual professional decision making, HROs perpetually engage in the following three activities:

6. Active, extensive recruiting of new staff at all levels.
7. Constant, targeted training and retraining.
8. Rigorous performance evaluation. In HROs, monitoring is necessarily mutual, without counter-productive loss of overall professional autonomy and confidence. This achievement is possible because organisational goals are clearly and widely shared, and because experience has taught all concerned that reliable success evolves through frank, protected, multi-way performance feedback.

HROs have four more characteristics:

9. Because time is the perpetual enemy of reliability, HROs are hierarchically structured. However, during times of peak activity, whether anticipated or not, HROs display a second layer of behaviour that emphasises collegial decision-making, regardless of the formal position of the decision-maker.

10. Clear, regularly demonstrated valuing of the organisation by its supervising and surrounding organisations. All levels work to maintain active, respectful communication geared to the key goals of the HRO.
11. Short-term efficiency takes a back seat to very high reliability.
12. Equipment is kept in the highest working order.

Two additional points relate to the above HRO characteristics. The first is that while these characteristics must necessarily be described separately, their effect is multiplicative, not additive. The total absence of any one can nullify great efforts to obtain others. For example, Standard Operating Procedures can become mindless rigidity in the absence of ongoing honouring of flaw-finders. Active recruiting in the absence of supportive, long-term professional development is futile. The first ten characteristics, however laboriously put in place, cannot be sustained if an organisation continues a history of such poor accounting and economic prediction that it must periodically make drastic cuts in personnel, machinery, etc.

A second note concerns the description of the characteristics. It would be easy to read each of the above as a stable state. In fact, all are dynamic and regularly evolving. As technologies advance, systems have the opportunity to create much richer databases. Last year's teacher recruiting effort, however successful, merely becomes the baseline for measuring this year's effort, and so on.

Reliability analyses can be very useful for preventing failures in such diverse contexts as avoiding the future running aground of multi-billion dollar aircraft carriers or industrial catastrophes (Shrivastava, 1986). Far more often than not, catastrophic failures are the result of a cascading series of human errors or lapses in judgement. This relates to the 'social construction' of reliability.

Stringfield (1995, 1998) discussed each of these general principles in terms of educational reform efforts. Obviously many schools currently exhibit several of the HRO characteristics. Diverse reform efforts are also particularly well-/ill-designed to achieve one or more of the characteristics.

The current paper reports on the first five years of an ongoing effort to work on improving reliability with four clusters of secondary schools in Great Britain. The objective of the effort has not been the installation of any specific curricular package or set of reform characteristics, but rather to work with the clusters in co-constructing higher reliability in all schools' core activities.

The High Reliability Schools (HRS) Programme over time

The programme began in 1995 with a group of eight secondary schools in Area A, an English area more advantaged than the English mean of all local education authorities and an area producing slightly better than average achievement results, although in 'value added' terms these results perhaps should have been better, given the school intakes.

Initially, we were unsure exactly what the organisational processes were that could have been necessary to deliver the promise of the interesting ideas about high reliability that we were aware of and which were reviewed above. There were no alternatives to developing these processes with the schools themselves, on the principle that if we 'let the ideas go' through a programme of in-service education about high reliability, adding relevant bodies of academic knowledge, then we would be able to see over time which schools developed practical procedures and real life definitions of HRS which might deliver the reality of enhanced student gain.

In this first geographical area we did the following:

• generated an administrative structure of twice-a-term meetings of the HRS co-coordinators from each school (these were senior management persons responsible for activities in their schools, project liaison, etc.);
• brought to schools in training days the relevant material on high reliability concepts, plus also bringing knowledge on school effectiveness, some limited treatment of teacher effectiveness and some limited treatment of issues related to the induction of new teachers (because of the importance of minimising within-school range and unreliability);
• encouraged schools to significantly increase the volume of their assessment data through blanket testing of their intakes, use of performance indicator systems that picked up within-school variation and the like;
• asked schools to focus upon ambitious targets for their pupils in only four core areas, including the compulsory project-wide goals of academic achievement in public examinations and the attendance rates of pupils at school. The two additional targets were, for each school, to be school chosen, reflecting each school's historical developmental priorities and their context/culture;
• asked schools to constantly review their organisation and processes to eliminate cascading errors and to intervene with their pupils at risk of failure, in the attempt to raise performance.

The programme was also piloted in five English secondary schools in Area B, beginning in January 1997 two years after Area A but with a very similar programme structure. Certain additional bodies of knowledge were added – that on Departmental Effectiveness being a notable example – and there was an enhanced concentration on knowledge related to 'feeder' primary schools, since the intellectual quality of the intakes into the secondary schools was a particular problem in this area possessing very high levels of social disadvantage.

Both these two areas were used to 'pilot' and develop the programme, which in its most fully developed version, finally, was implemented in two groups of schools in a moderately disadvantaged area in Wales – Area C. It went first into four schools as 'pilots' from Autumn 1996 and then went into all the area's schools from Spring 1997, since all schools around the initial group of schools wished to be involved, adding eight further schools.

The final programme represented a very significant development of, and growth from, the very hesitant first steps of piloting in Areas A and B, in the following ways:

• The headteachers of all schools, as well as the HRS representatives, were involved in all project meetings, leading to an enhancement of programme understanding within schools and leading to the headteachers reinforcing the programme in their day-to-day management.

- There was enhanced cohesion and power in the project through the employment of a part-time project 'driver', who was one of the headteachers working a day per week.

- These schools had available to them a great deal of detail about the 'technology' of HRS that had been generated by the experimentation with HRS ideas within the Areas A and B samples. This covered, in depth, a technology to deliver the HRS 'principles' noted above. This material obviated the need for schools to 'discover' best practice and gave schools considerable foundations on which to build (we should note that the project eventually utilised ten HRS components, rather than the original twelve outlined above).

- The focus in the project on the 'broad brush' principles of HRS and the detailed organisational features of the HRS model as outlined in the components material was supplemented in Area C by a regular focus upon what we called 'the little things that matter'. All HRS meetings increasingly centred upon a key session in which each school explained to the whole group of Welsh schools the practical things that they had done at the 'micro' level to embed the concepts and the components in the form of practical organisational features at the point of delivery of education to pupils in classrooms and schools.

- The project added regionally based residential sessions for all headteachers and HRS representatives, and also added national residential sessions, all aimed at enhancing knowledge transfers across schools.

- The HRS representatives and headteachers were given additional bodies of knowledge to those given to all staff, to help them in their role. Additionally, bodies of knowledge were 'previewed' with them, before the exposure of the material to whole school staffs, so that they could answer staff questions and 'ease' the material into schools.

- The training days were changed to be more involving of staff, in the departmental effectiveness session for example involving meetings of staff arranged by department filling-in questionnaires that self reported on the extent to which individual departments were following the HRS technology.

As well as these changes to both the detail and general ethos of the project, the final version implemented in Area C exhibited substantial changes in both the knowledge base and the applications of it that were utilised, which reflected our increased knowledge over time of which knowledge bases were 'potent', and which of possible 'potency' had been missed:

- It was clear that the initial concentration upon the school level that had been reflected in the school effectiveness knowledge base was not powerful enough to affect key processes and outcomes. The classroom behaviours of teachers, the key determinants of pupil outcomes, appeared, unsurprisingly, to alter very little because of these knowledge inputs, so the knowledge bases on teacher effectiveness were greatly expanded and supplemented with those on advanced teaching methods (e.g. group work, constructivism). The knowledge base on departmental effectiveness was also added, reasoning that the department was closer to the learning level and that changes at that level might ripple through to affect outcomes.

This latter proved to be particularly powerful, since the department comprised people teaching the same subject and therefore had teachers with something in common, and since the department's performance was directly shown in the public examination performance indicator material that all schools possessed on performance on different subjects. The department was also a managerial entity that was, in practice, an alterable as well as a 'proximal' variable.

- It was also clear that the simple provision of information to schools about 'what works' in various areas was not sufficient to ensure change. Such foundational school effectiveness material is of course not 'owned' by schools or teachers since it comes predominantly from the research community. This material was also not sufficient for more than perhaps one year or 18 months of professional development activities, since teachers seemed to 'move past it' very quickly as their own professional development expanded.

Our focus shifted in Area C towards attempting to turn our schools into 'knowledge generators' rather than passive knowledge recipients. Particularly, we focused upon the introduction of peer observation systems to permit the charting, generation and transmission of good practice in classrooms, training some school personnel to use observation systems which were then cascaded around the entire school. Also, our focus upon improving schools' capacity to be 'intelligent' about their organisational functioning and outputs was enhanced, utilising additional training, the provision of sessions on the statistical analysis of data and the provision of the most advanced relational database that we could find which stored grades, background information and test scores of pupils.

- It was also clear that our earlier emphasis upon schools adopting standard operating procedures and the other detailed aspects of the HRS technology that we had outlined for their use was a 'one size fits all' approach to a situation in which schools were situated in highly variable local situations. Schools clearly differed in their:

  - levels of effectiveness;
  - levels of 'raw' outcomes;
  - improvement trajectory over time;
  - socio-economic status;
  - development history.

Over time we moved to an emphasis upon greater context specificity in terms of the precise organisational *practices* that we encouraged schools to adopt, whilst retaining the universality of the core HRS *concepts*. We encouraged schools to think of which might be 'universal' features of the HRS technology, that they should all apply in the same detail to the same degree (e.g. testing programmes), and which might be aspects of the technology that should be different in detail and degree in different situations.

- It was also clear in Area C that the very ambitious aims of the project to generate 'failure-free schools', as highly reliable industrial settings generated 'failure-free' outcomes (as with the example we historically used of landing planes), may have lost us valuable teacher commitment because of the project being perceived as wildly unrealistic in scope, typified by the comment of one teacher that 'air traffic controllers don't have to deal with planes that don't want to be landed' and that 'teachers have to deal with children who want to fly to Paris when they've been told to fly to London'. Over time, it was the practical problem solving usefulness of the HRS model that was stressed, rather than adherence to a set of ideas taken from outside school settings.
- The programme in its most fully developed version also began to take a close interest in the effectiveness of the primary feeder schools that were generating intakes of pupils which, in the case of most schools, were regarded as imposing 'low ceilings' on what it was possible to achieve. Primary senior management teams were in some cases invited to the secondary school's HRS training days. Some schools organised special help to their primary clusters on issues such as literacy and numeracy.

Results

We have collected a considerable volume of data on the effects of the project on schools and their outcomes, including 'audit' visits to all schools, questionnaires to participating school personnel, collation of all material used in the training of schools, and analysis of assessment data collected, and of course also have our own 'participant observer' recollections of programme content, impact and effects. Analysis of all this is now under way. We content ourselves here with looking at data relevant to two questions:

- Did the schools which utilised more of the HRS 'technology' show more gain in outcomes over time?
- Did the HRS schools do better than the national totality of schools in their gain in outcomes over time?

Looking at the first question, analysis of the increase in the proportion of pupils getting 5+ A*–C GCSE passes from 1994/5 school year to 2000/1, against a mean of all HRS school-based components, indicated that there were significant correlations at $P < 0.01$ level (Table 8.1).

Because of these results, HRS mean component scores and the increase in 5+ A*–C GCSE passes were analysed further. Table 8.2 shows that 71.1% of the HRS 'technology' correlated significantly with increases in the percentages of 5+ A*–C GCSE's obtained by HRS schools during this period. Furthermore, 44.9% correlated significantly at $P < 0.01$ level. Clearly, schools using more of the HRS constructs and associated practices showed more achievement gain than those using less. The detail of which precise HRS organisational features are most 'potent' in affecting achievement can be seen below.

Table 8.1 Spearman's rho correlation, mean of HRS components against increase in percentage of pupils with GCSE results 5+ A★–C

Schools	Correlation increase 5+ A★–C GCSE results 1994/5–2000/1 with mean of HRS components (rs)
All	0.366 ★★

Note
Correlation significant at P < 0.01 (1 tailed)

Table 8.2 Spearman's rho correlation between HRS school-based components mean scores and increase in GCSE results 1994/5–1999/2000

Individual HRS school-based components	r_s
1. A perception, held by the public and the employees, that failure within the organisation would be disastrous.	
The school involves parents in a commitment to improve the school and their child's learning	0.097
There is a shared belief in the school that pupil educational failure is completely unacceptable	**0.379★★**
The belief in school is that pupil exclusion is a major system failure	0.267★
2. Small number of clear goals, that are understood by staff and students. Strong sense of primary mission	
The school vision and mission encompass HRS philosophy	**0.384★★**
All stakeholders understand the school vision and mission	**0.333★★**
The school vision and mission are reflected in all aspects of the school	0.309★
The school is working to be reliable on no more than four goals	0.193
Two of the school's goals are improving attendance and performance in public exams	**0.342★★**
The School Development Plan reflects HRS principles	**0.347★★**
The School Development Plan aims to create an environment to promote learning and reduce failure	0.288★
The school evaluates the appropriateness of its goals and the progress towards them	0.287★
3. Consistent best practice, based on Standard Operating Procedures	
Within the school benchmarking against its own best practice takes place	**0.340★★**
Between-school benchmarking takes place	0.171
Best practice is shared between schools	0.122
School Standard Operating Procedures have been developed and are written down	0.166
School Standard Operating Procedures are consistently applied across the school	0.289★
Appropriate teaching strategies are being used which allow all pupils to experience success	0.156

Table 8.2 continued

Appropriate classroom management strategies are being used which allow all pupils to experience success	0.042
Pupils have high expectations of their own success	0.301*
Teachers have high expectations of pupil achievement	**0.329**★★
Opportunities to learn are maximised at every opportunity	0.177

4. **Have systems for identifying flaws in SOPs and validating appropriate changes**

There is ongoing monitoring of stakeholders (pupils, parents)	0.120
There is ongoing monitoring of external views of the school	0.107
The ongoing monitoring of Standard Operating Procedure Implementation does take place	**0.336**★★
There is ongoing monitoring of the effectiveness of Standard Operating Procedures	0.305*

5. **Extensive recruitment, training and retraining**

The school has sufficient, well-qualified staff to deliver its curriculum	**0.357**★★
The school has sufficient, well-qualified staff to deal with its pastoral responsibilities effectively	0.153
The school does recruit a high calibre of staff	0.250*
The school introduces all new staff to its values and ways of working	0.292*
There is additional support for the induction of NQTs into professional practice	0.234*
Staff in the school have good subject knowledge and expertise	0.123
Staff have good school effectiveness knowledge and expertise	**0.426**★★
Staff have good departmental effectiveness knowledge and expertise	0.164
Staff have good teacher effectiveness knowledge and expertise	0.265*
Staff with managerial responsibilities have good management knowledge and expertise	**0.411**★★
All teaching staff have been given training in best practice research	**0.384**★★
All staff have been given training in how to use best practice research findings	**0.338**★★
All staff have been trained in proven best practice, which underpins the SOPs of the school	**0.481**★★
Teachers reflect on and discuss their practice	0.133
Teachers continually strive for the improvement of classroom performance	−0.062
The school has a provision of wide ranging teacher development opportunities through a coherent programme	**0.438**★★
Development opportunities are designed to meet the needs identified in the School Development Plan	0.254*
Professional development focuses on the improvement of teaching and learning	0.313*
Professional development focuses on the improvement of pupil performance	0.287*
There are high expectations of staff performance	**0.577**★★

Table 8.2 continued

6. **Mutual monitoring of staff, without counterproductive**
   loss of overall autonomy and confidence
   The school has a culture of Peer Classroom Observation   0.423**
   There is ongoing monitoring of teacher performance   0.449**
   Ongoing monitoring of manager performance does take place   0.419**

7. **Data richness – take performance analysis very seriously to**
   improve the processes of the organisation
   Pupil input data is used to identify pupils in need of support   0.454**
      and intervention
   Pupil output data is used to assess value–added   0.579**
   Pupil attendance data is used to identify pupils at risk of underachieving   0.238*
   Pupil attendance data is used to assess individual pupil   0.327**
      performance
   Pupil attendance data is used to assess school performance   0.312**
   Pupil attitudinal data is used to assess school performance   0.081
   Tutors are used as academic monitors in tutor groups   0.279*
   The Heads of Department are academic monitors of pupil   0.371**
      performance in their respective departments
   Pupil data is shared with respective pupils   0.076
   Pupil data is shared with respective parents   0.154
   Data is used for coaching and tutoring pupils   0.269*
   Pupil data is shared with feeder schools   0.291*
   Pupil data is shared with feeder schools as part of collaboration   0.406**
      for improvement
   The implementation of all policies and development strategies   0.342**
      are monitored

8. **Are alert to surprises or lapses; prevent small failures from**
   cascading into major systems failures
   There is ongoing monitoring of pupil performance across the curriculum   0.290*
   There is early identification of pupils at risk of underperforming   0.406**
   Early intervention with pupils who are underperforming does   0.377**
      take place
   There is early intervention with pupils at risk of becoming   0.325**
      disaffected
   There is early intervention with pupils at risk of being excluded   0.170

9. **Hierarchically structured, but with an emphasis on collegial**
   decision-making and interdependence
   There is high quality leadership from the Headteacher   0.570**
   There is high quality leadership from the Senior Management   0.428**
      Team
   There are effective management structures   0.353**
   In the school significant responsibility is taken by middle managers   0.269*
   In the school there are positive collegial relationships between staff   0.172
   The staff work in interdependent, synergistic teams   0.304*

Table 8.2 continued

10. Equipment and the environment are maintained in the highest order; responsibility is shared equally by all who come in contact with it	
The school site is well maintained	**0.343★★**
The school site provides a pleasant working environment	**0.323★★**
Equipment is cared for by all who use it	0.144
Staff are smart in appearance	**0.366★★**
Wall displays are well designed and tidy	**0.331★★**

Note

Correlations at P <0.01 are in bold
★ Correlation significant at P < 0.05 level
★★ Correlation significant at P < 0.01 level

Moving on to look at the second issue, whether our HRS schools outperformed the national totality of schools, Table 8.3 shows the performance of schools in the three areas where we piloted and implemented the final programme. Area A schools where we first piloted performed much in line with other schools in the local authority, and both the local authority and our schools performed less well than the national totality of schools. Area B showed again a moderate pilot performance, probably because the local authority had allocated us a group of schools with the lowest results and which were most in need of improvement, which may explain our inability to impact much on outcomes. In Area C, however, where the fully developed version of the programme was implemented, levels of gain were running at close to double that for all Welsh schools, and at close to triple the improvement in all English schools. In Areas A and B also, as the programme developed coherence by 1998–1999, and 1999–2000, the schools' levels of achievement gain were significant.

The global area differences hid significant differences between schools in their levels of improvement over time which are a focus of our continuing research effort.

Variation between schools over time

The above description of the three LEA sites shows that there were distinctive contexts for the implementation of High Reliability Schools. For the purpose of this section, we have drawn on our case studies and audits of the 25 schools to describe the impact of context and school-level decisions on the implementation and the success of the project, since there was variability between schools and sites as to the quantity and quality of the HRS intervention.

The experience of some HRS schools in inner-city sites was quite promising. As in most settings, the comprehensive schools drew from a number of local primary schools in their area. At the time the study began, little data was collected

Table 8.3 School-level mean percentages of students with 5+ A★–C over time: HRS cohorts contrasted with English and Welsh means

5 or More A★–C GCSEs (%)

Region		School year							Overall gain
		1993/4	1994/5	1995/6	1996/7	1997/8	1998/9	1999/00	(00–start)
England	Mean	43.3	43.5	44.5	45.1	46	47.9	49	5.6
Area A Started Fall 95	Mean 46.9	48.5	45.3	46.6	47.0	45.6	46.5	50.6	3.7
Area B Began Jan 97	Mean 23.1	24.2	21.4	23.6	24.2	21.4	24.4	26.0	2.9
Wales	Mean	39	41	42	44	46	48	49	8.3
Area C – Old Welsh 4 Began Fall 96	Mean	20.8	26.5	26	28	34.5	37.3	40.0	15.6
Area C – New Welsh 8 Began Spring 97	Mean	36.1	34.8	36.6	42.3	44.9	47.6	51.0	15.2

Note
Light shading is years used to produce start levels of performance.

in the primary schools on student performance, including on reading. Following HRS principles, the comprehensive schools began to collect data on entry and found, in some schools, two-thirds of the entering students were two or more years behind in reading. The strategy of one of the most successful schools, Water Edge School, when it found itself in this circumstance was to employ reading teachers to work with the 11-year-old pupil population to assure basic-level reading and writing competence. They were so successful that many other schools requested their assistance in setting in place reading recovery and homework schemes. The success represents the results of a combination of use of data, focused goals and consistent application of a technology to create success.

Whilst this strategy was an excellent demonstration of the power of the school in stopping the problem before failing pupils cascaded throughout the school and impacted upon the school's performance in all subjects, one of us naively pointed out to the administrators of the Water Edge Comprehensive School that the reading problem was caused by the primary schools' inadequacy in teaching reading and that the primary schools, one in particular, had come up short. The head insisted that the school management had held a discussion with the primary school heads in the area, but could say little to them about what they might change or the schools would send their pupils to other comprehensive schools that did not make such demands!

The reading strategy that worked in one of the successful HRS schools did not work in all settings. One of the comprehensive schools, Limefield School, also experiencing similar reading problems among students from its intake schools, was taking from middle schools which taught students until they were 13 years old. Two-thirds of the middle school students were two or more years behind in reading when they arrived, but the middle/high school model gave the comprehensive school only two years to remediate in reading as well as to cover all the necessary subject matter to pass the GCSE examinations. They were unable to meet this difficult task and were closed and merged with another school, which had been unable to overcome its previous negative image and was on special measures. It is unfortunate that neither of these schools paired with successful HRS schools in order to emulate their success. As seen above, some of the HRS schools had high enough competencies and resources to offset the negative effects of context, while others found more difficulty in tackling their problems.

In the more advantaged catchment areas, one school involved in the HRS project provides an illustration of how rigorous implementation was critical to success. Four Square Comprehensive School entered the project above the national average for 5 or more A*–C GCSEs. Given its well-to-do and comfortable socio-economic base, ability to gain and hold strong teachers and substantial support from the parents, this was a well-positioned school.

Yet over the years, Four Square did not improve greatly, rather it gradually slipped downwards towards the average for the country. Close examination of records, discussions with teachers and administrators, and reviews of HRS audits suggests much less than the necessary commitment to improve. Firstly, Four Square refused to clearly select and hold a few central goals focused around student success. The school often looked at the range of activities for students, the linkages with parents and the happiness of the staff as additional measures for success. As often communicated by the HRS co-ordinator, Four Square School found the HRS focus too narrow, the efforts too labour intensive and the work with lower performing students of little interest to the staff, who valued the academic students to the exclusion of those who were not doing as well. Little effort was made to bring students up to speed if they fell behind. There was little done to create an atmosphere supportive to all students and the efforts of the HRS staff to train or organise teachers to examine their own teaching was met with hostility from the administration, and regarded also as intrusive.

How schools were able to lift themselves beyond their historic level of performance regardless of their starting point is of particular interest. Another school, Chateau School, was another 'leafy suburb' school with a competent staff and solid parental support. The Chateau School began above the national average and made ongoing gains that well exceeded national performance, leaving the school comfortably ahead of other schools.

When the school entered the HRS programme, they determined that the performance of their pupils on GCSE was critical to their improvement and the Head determined he wanted to create a data-rich environment to track the individual performance of students to assure that they reached their potential.

Examining the performance of students over time against their predicted performance did this. When students did not perform at expected levels, he delivered resources to the class or student to assure success. A side value of this strategy permitted the Head to compare the performance of departments against one another. There was no expectation that each student would receive the same number of high grade GCSEs, rather the question was asked, are there departments who do remarkably well with students and some departments that are particularly unsuccessful? This permitted the Headteacher to adjust teaching loads, deliver additional resources where necessary and focus attention on certain areas of the school. The level of consistency rose between departments as well as the number of high grade GCSEs for each pupil across departments. By the end of the third year, gains were significantly higher than comparable schools in the district.

The most dramatic change in performance was in a school in a highly deprived area with originally approximately 10% of the students gaining scores of five or more A$\star$–C's on the GCSE tests. Claymound School appeared defeated and unable to determine how it might survive. Even its physical plant was in dire need of repair. Broken windows, water-stained walls and filthy halls were the norm. No one seemed prepared to take the effort to lead the school. A new Head was appointed to the school who seemed committed to the HRS process and pulled together staff for a meeting. In a large faculty hall, HRS consultants suggested the staff choose a simple task as a first step in the process of setting goals and directions for the school. Since the idea of improved GCSE performance seemed impossible, the commitment of the school to the short-term goal of respect for the school environment – even the simple cleaning of halls and repair of windows – could be a worthwhile first step, it was argued.

The new Head stood up at the end of a meeting and said he wanted to make this commitment and through a good clean-up would bring about a new beginning for the school and the pupils. There was a positive buzz in the hall as teachers nodded yes: then from the back of the room came a staff member's voice saying, 'This is all well and good, but I am sure we will run afoul of the public health regulations'. At this point, the room exploded with anger as the staff with a single voice shouted down this dissent. This was the turning point for the school.

From this day forward, Claymound believed it could turn around its image and performance. There has been no looking back. Over time its results have continued to move from below 10 through the teens and twenties into the 40% levels, an astounding set of gains over a short time. While the commitment and spark of its first HRS year has carried this school, there have been enormous positive changes in the quality of leadership and instruction. The Head worked with three other talented Heads to help develop Standard Operating Procedures. The teachers worked together to focus instruction on clear outcome goals for the school. The school used data systems to determine their improvement in these areas and focused on year by year improvement as well as some long-term goals. As basic problems have been solved through better feedback, Standard Operating Procedures and improvement of teaching performance, the leadership team has been able to work on more specific needs of Departments that could not be cleared up with general strategies. The efforts of the school are now focused on specific programmes and teachers to reduce within school variation to enhance the ongoing positive movement of the school.

Conclusions

We began this chapter by outlining the bodies of knowledge that pointed us towards attempting a new kind of school improvement initiative. Work in fields as diverse as educational policy analysis, school effectiveness and teacher effectiveness pointed us towards the importance of reliability in organisational processes, a concept which itself was further developed from the early 1990s by a number of schools and researchers working outside of educational settings.

We have shown in our work with schools that a programme of school improvement in schools, co-constructed with school personnel and based upon insights from the knowledge bases in high reliability research, school effectiveness and school improvement, is linked with the school's enhanced 'added value' to pupil achievement. We have also shown that individual aspects of the HRS 'technology of practice' are differentially associated with these gains, with 'maintenance of the school environment', 'mutual monitoring of staff' and 'data richness to improve the processes of the organisation' being particularly important determinants of the degree of gain over time.

We are now analysing our full datasets and attempting to explain the variation that exists between areas and individual schools, hoping to emerge with case studies of what contextual and school factors are present in those schools that have improved most. We have also further data on academic achievement results for the 2000/1 and 2001/2 school years, plus a wide range of further performance data on other pupil outcomes such as attendance rate and the specific goals that were chosen by individual schools.

Although our analysis is still ongoing, we would conclude that our results show that the achievement of what have been historically regarded as highly ambitious goals is indeed possible if the optimum combination of local contextual factors and school factors is obtained. Whilst much remains to be learned, it is clear that secondary schools can be transformed by an improvement programme like ours that:

- improves the quality of decision making by generating and using high quality performance evaluation data;
- reduces unreliability by insisting on the following of Standard Operating Procedures for core organisational functions;
- restricts the focus of effort to a small number of finite goals, on which very high targets are set;
- systematically recruits staff and trains and re-trains them through benchmarking against internal and external best practice;
- commits to high quality in terms of the functioning and upkeep of site and equipment.

Acknowledgement

First published as D. Reynolds, S. Stringfield and E. Schaffer (2006) 'The High Reliability Schools Project', in A. Harris and J. Chrispeels (Eds) *Improving Schools and Educational Systems*, London: Routledge. Reprinted here with permission from Taylor & Francis.

9

The remit and methods of the Numeracy Task Force

Introduction

1. One of the first acts of the new Labour government was to announce national targets for literacy and numeracy. These are:

- for 80% of 11 year olds, by 2002, to achieve the standards expected for their age in English, i.e. Level 4 in the National Curriculum tests; and
- for 75% of 11 year olds, by 2002, to achieve the standards expected for their age in mathematics.

2. The Numeracy Task Force was established by David Blunkett, Secretary of State for Education and Employment, in May 1997. It was asked to develop a national strategy to raise standards of numeracy in order to reach the national numeracy target by 2002. Our recommendations therefore inevitably focus on numeracy in primary schools. The Task Force was asked to take into account relevant national and international evidence, including evidence about wider educational and social factors affecting performance. We have also taken into account comments about numeracy offered in response to the government's White Paper, *Excellence in Schools*, and comments offered to the Task Force during its work, both those volunteered to us and those from people with an interest in numeracy whom we specifically consulted.

Structure of this report

3. The first three chapters of the report set out the Task Force's views about this evidence. After each section, desired outcomes for a National Numeracy Strategy are proposed in the light of the evidence. Chapter 4 explains how the Task Force moved from these desired outcomes to recommendations. Chapter 5 sets out the preliminary recommendations themselves, and lists a number of questions for consultation. We should particularly welcome responses to these questions, as well as any comments on other aspects of the report. (See Numeracy Task Force, 1998.)

4. We are consulting a wide range of people about this preliminary report, including teachers, teacher organisations, teacher trainers, LEAs, organisations with an interest in mathematics, parents and employers. The Task Force's final report to the Secretary of State will take into account the views received during consultation. It will be published in time to feed into decisions about the grants that will come from the DFEE's Standards Fund in 1999–2000, through which the implementation of the National Numeracy Strategy will be funded. The implementation of the National Literacy Strategy begins in 1998/99. The implementation of both strategies will be overseen by the Literacy and Numeracy Strategy Group established by the DFEE's Standards and Effectiveness Unit. The group includes experienced educators and representatives of OFSTED, QCA, TTA and the Basic Skills Agency. One of its key tasks will be to ensure that the strategies together are seen as coherent in schools and do not overload teachers. The Task Force has also borne this need in mind in framing its recommendations.

Why numeracy matters

5. Numeracy and literacy are both important in enabling children to access the full curriculum, and, later, to play a full part in adult working and social life. But a failure to be numerate is often seen to be somehow more acceptable than a corresponding failure to be literate. Society also tends to underestimate the extent to which a lack of numeracy skills holds people back. One quarter of the adults taking part in a Basic Skills Agency survey in 1997 had numeracy skills that would make it difficult to complete everyday tasks successfully; 9% of these people recognised or acknowledged their difficulty, as compared with 19% of people with poor literacy skills (Bynner and Parsons, 1997).

6. People find life much easier if they can answer basic numerical questions, e.g. "What is the discount worth if it is 10% of £24.95?", "How much are 50 stamps at 26p each?". A good grasp of numeracy is also needed to manage personal financial affairs. This is increasingly important as more and more people assume responsibility for long-term financial obligations such as hire purchase, mortgages, student loans and pensions. People need to be numerate, too, to interpret statements in the news about changes in unemployment figures or interest rates, or to interpret data in graphs or tables, such as weather charts or illustrations of insurance benefits.

We hope that one of the effects of the Task Force's report, and the wide consultation on it, will be that more people understand the importance of numeracy as an essential life skill.

7. Early work in mathematics must begin to lay the foundations for the skills and insights children will use in later life. A solid grounding in numeracy at primary school will also help children with the mathematical skills needed in other subjects, and later, to develop the higher order mathematical skills that are indispensable for large areas of higher education and future employment, such as engineering, science, business, computing, economics and teaching.

8. The Task Force believes strongly that being fully numerate is an entitlement for all children. Reaching the national target for numeracy will be an excellent achievement, but it will nonetheless mean that some children have not attained this basic level of numeracy. A few children may be unable to reach the Level 4 target because of special educational needs, but these children, too, need to have the opportunity to reach whatever their full potential may be. In drawing up our recommendations, we have therefore looked towards a time when virtually all 11 year olds achieve the standard expected for their age.

What is numeracy?

9. Numeracy is an important part of mathematics, and a major aim of mathematics in primary schools is to teach children to be numerate. Primary schools teach National Curriculum mathematics as a whole subject, and numeracy should not be separated from it. Therefore, the government's national target for 2002, while focusing on numeracy, aims to raise standards of mathematics as a whole. The target offers an important goal for children's attainment in the National Curriculum tests in mathematics, but does not, in itself, explain what numeracy actually is. The Task Force therefore felt it important to have a clear definition of numeracy, in addition to the national target, to inform its work and responses to the consultation.

10. We adopted as our definition the one used in the National Numeracy Project:

> Numeracy means knowing about numbers and number operations. More than this, it requires an ability and inclination to solve numerical problems, including those involving money or measures. It also demands familiarity with the ways in which numerical information is gathered by counting and measuring, and is presented in graphs, charts and tables.

11. The Project goes on to say that numerate primary pupils should:

- have a sense of the size of a number and where it fits into the number system;
- know by heart number facts such as number bonds, multiplication tables, doubles and halves;

- use what they know by heart to figure out answers mentally;
- calculate accurately, both mentally and with pencil and paper, drawing on a range of calculation strategies;
- recognise when it is not appropriate to use a calculator;
- make sense of number problems, including non-routine problems, and recognise the operations needed to solve them;
- have strategies for checking their answers to judge whether they are reasonable;
- explain their methods and reasoning using correct mathematical terms;
- suggest suitable units for measuring, and making sensible estimates of measurements; and
- explain and make predictions from the numbers in graphs, charts and tables.

The national numeracy target

12. The national targets of 75% of 11 year olds achieving the standard expected for their age in mathematics by 2002 is ambitious. The Task Force is convinced that it is achievable, for three main reasons:

- The government has committed itself to an extensive programme of educational reform to address the problem of underachievement generally. These general reforms will have some impact on the specific problem of mathematics.
- Primary schools are improving their results quite rapidly. The percentage of 11 year olds achieving Level 4 or better in Key Stage 2 mathematics tests was 62% in 1997, an improvement of 18 percentage points since 1995. Evidence suggests that this improvement may be due to a number of factors, including teachers' growing familiarity with the requirements of the National Curriculum and an increasing emphasis on pupils acquiring essential mathematical knowledge and skills. Progress at this rate may be difficult to sustain, but is certainly very encouraging.
- It is now possible to point with some confidence to teaching methods, ways of organising classrooms and other specific factors that are more effective than others in raising standards of numeracy. It is these factors in particular that the Task Force has set out to identify, and then to spread widely through its recommendations.

13. As noted above, it is important that the national target is used as a milestone on the route to achieving numeracy for virtually all pupils, rather than as an end in itself. It is therefore vital that schools do not only invest energy in helping the children currently closest to Level 4 to reach it. A national strategy should also help children who would otherwise achieve below Level 3 to improve their performance, and those already achieving Level 4 to reach their full potential, which may be well above the Level 4 threshold. This suggests that it might be helpful for schools to demonstrate publicly the improvements that all pupils are making.

14. At present, primary school performance tables show only the numbers of pupils achieving Level 4 or better. Schools are already required to report to parents the numbers of pupils achieving each level in the Key Stage 2 test, and we should be interested in views about whether this more detailed information should be publicly available in performance tables. We should also welcome comments on whether it is desirable to summarise more simply the information currently given to parents — whether or not this is made public — such as showing the average level achieved by all pupils in a given year. The QCA's recent consultation on target setting found widespread support for the use of average levels and this information will be available in the QCA's benchmark tables. The Task Force recognises that the reporting and publication of performance data is a sensitive issue for schools, which will need careful consideration by those responding to this consultation.

Achievement in numeracy

15. Studies comparing England's performance in mathematics with other countries show this country to be performing relatively poorly in comparison with others. For example, evidence from the Third International Mathematics and Science Survey (TIMSS) indicates that our Year 5 pupils (aged nine and ten) are amongst the lowest performers in key areas of number out of nine countries with similar social and cultural backgrounds (Harris et al., 1997). Other data from TIMSS suggest, however, that we also have areas of strength related to numeracy. For example, English pupils are comparatively very successful at applying mathematical procedures to solve practical problems, and have a positive attitude to mathematics as a subject.

These are important aspects to preserve while we attempt to raise standards. It is important to raise standards both for the sake of the life chances of individual children, and for our international competitiveness.

Attitudes and expectations

16. English pupils tend to show greater confidence in their mathematical ability than pupils in many countries, despite the fact that levels of attainment in number tend to be low. This may be because although English pupils met the expectations of their teachers, the expectations are themselves comparatively low. Pupils in some of the countries where expectations, and corresponding levels of attainment, are high tend to have less confidence in their ability and a more negative attitude to mathematics. The challenge for teachers in England is to maintain pupils' positive attitudes, but to raise expectations, and the standards of numeracy. Effective teachers have high expectations of all pupils. They believe that all of them can acquire numeracy skills, even though some may take longer than others, and continually seek to move pupils' understanding forward.

17. Teachers who are confident about the mathematics they teach and are enthusiastic and effective, stimulate pupils' interest in the subject. Good initial teacher training, in-service training and support within the school can help. These allow teachers to deepen their mathematical knowledge and connect different elements of it together, by using research and other evidence to focus on and discuss different ways of tackling problems, and giving opportunities to share experiences and exchange ideas about classroom teaching. Targeted and structured activities of this sort can allow teachers whose attainment is initially modest, and who have a negative attitude to the subject, to identify their needs and gain mathematical knowledge and understanding. They can thus become enthusiastic and effective in the classroom, and take on a leadership role in mathematics in school.

18. With all this in mind, the Task Force has aimed for a strategy to ensure that teachers teach mathematics effectively and pupils achieve high standards of numeracy. We also want teachers and pupils to be confident and positive towards the subject, and keen to use and develop their mathematical knowledge. We want teachers to have high expectations of their pupils, and constantly try to move them forward, especially in their mental capabilities. High expectations are regularly identified by OFSTED and the QCA as a key factor in achieving high standards of mathematics. If teachers expect pupils to do well, pupils themselves will expect to succeed. This means pitching work at a high standard, setting a good pace to learning, and maintaining challenging, direct, active teaching.

The guiding principles of this report

19. Five key principles have guided the Task Force in preparing this report. These are:

- Looking at the evidence. Our aim has been to focus on evidence from research, inspection and practice about the problems with mathematics, and the methods that tackle these problems most effectively. We are of course aware that the content of mathematics in schools, in particular, has been the subject of vigorous debate in the past, but we have not set out to take part in detailed debate about the content of the National Curriculum. These matters will be for the QCA to consider in their review of the curriculum. Outside this area, our overriding objective has been to set out our collective view of the evidence, particularly about effective teaching, and, in the light of this, to make practical proposals to raise standards of numeracy. We plan to make available a review of the research material we have taken into account during our work, when our final report is published.
- Building on existing best practice. The Task Force does not believe that any single "wonder drug" can solve all the problems of teaching mathematics. Criticism of mathematics achievement in the past has sometimes led people to advocate a complete change in the way it is taught. The problem with root and

branch changes of this sort, however well-intentioned, is that they tend to eliminate not just the worst of what has been done before, but the best as well. The changes suggested have sometimes not yet been fully evaluated themselves, or may only have been seen to work well in a very different education system in a different country. Our aim has been to build on the existing teaching practices that work, whilst making clear those that do not, and recommending that these are replaced with different, more successful, practice.

- The best of both worlds. We believe that in the increasingly international perspective to discussions about education in all countries, successful countries attempt to get the best of both worlds. This means recognising and promoting what one's own country does well, but also attempting to learn from the achievements (and mistakes) of others. In this report, we have tried to benchmark against our own best practice, and propose ways of making that practice even better, by looking at the emphases, structures and organisations of other countries where appropriate.
- The importance of both school and home environments. Teachers have a vital and immensely challenging job. Teachers, as well as the children they teach, need the support of parents and the wider community if they are to succeed in raising standards generally, and standards of numeracy in particular. We have therefore considered both school and external influences on a child's educational progress, and made recommendations that address both.
- Other developments in education. The recommendations of the Task Force are offered in the context of a number of other important developments and contributions, including the impending review of the National Curriculum, the work of OFSTED, the new national curriculum for initial teacher training, the new mandatory headship qualification, and existing programmes that aim to improve the quality of mathematics education, such as the National Numeracy Project. All these impact on the work of primary school teachers to a greater or lesser extent. We have tried to ensure that our recommendations work with the grain of what is already taking place in education, and focus on things that will help teachers, rather than merely imposing further burdens on them.

Acknowledgement

First published in Department for Education and Employment (1998) *Numeracy Matters: The Preliminary Report of the Numeracy Task Force*. London: HMSO for DfEE. Reprinted here with permission from HMSO.

10

School improvement for schools facing challenging circumstances
A review of research and practice

Introduction

In this report we outline what we have found out from the research literature, and the reports of practitioners, about 'what works' to improve schools that face challenging circumstances. We concentrate upon the 'universals' of what seems to work across the very varied settings that this group of schools inhabit, but are very aware that the literature suggests that although many of the principles governing improvement are universals, some are 'context specific' and must be tailored to the individual circumstances of each school.

For this reason, we propose to undertake a programme of visits to schools in different contexts in the first few weeks of the Summer Term 2001, and will report fully on what our ideas about school improvement are, additional to those reported here.

We should help the reader to begin with by outlining the various phases or stages that the school improvement community of researchers and practitioners has passed through over the last fifteen years, as a context to the literature that we concentrate upon in this publication, which mostly comes from the 'third age' of school improvement that has only been in existence for the last five or six years.

Although the intellectual background to school improvement can be traced back to Kurt Lewin, it was in the first phase in the late 1970s and early 1980s that the field took shape as a distinct body of approaches and scholars/practitioners. This first phase was epitomised by the OECD's *International School Improvement Project* (ISIP) (Hopkins 1987), but unfortunately many of the initiatives associated with this first phase of school improvement were 'free floating', rather than representing a systematic, programmatic and coherent approach to school change. There was correspondingly, in this phase, an emphasis upon organisational change, school self evaluation and the 'ownership of change' by individual schools and teachers, but these initiatives were loosely connected to student learning outcomes, both conceptually and practically, were variable and fragmented in conception and application, and consequently in the eyes of most school improvers and practices struggled to impact upon classroom practice (Hopkins 2001; Reynolds 1999).

The second phase of the development of school improvement began in the early 1990s and resulted from the interaction between school improvement and the school effectiveness communities. Early voices calling for a merger of approaches and insights (Reynolds, Hopkins and Stoll 1993; Hopkins *et al.* 1994; Gray *et al.* 1996) were followed by a 'synergy' of perspectives in which both effectiveness and improvement researchers and practitioners made contributions to a merged perspective (see for example the contributions of Hopkins, Reynolds and Stoll in Gray *et al.* 1996). School effectiveness brought to this new, merged intellectual enterprise such contributions as the value-added methodology for judging school effectiveness and for disaggregating schools into their component parts of departments and teachers. It also brought a large scale, known-to-be valid knowledge base about 'what works' at school level to potentiate student outcomes (Teddlie and Reynolds 2000).

Third age school improvement practice and philosophy attempts to draw the lessons from these apparently limited achievements of existing improvements and reforms. It is in evidence in a number of improvement programmes in the United Kingdom such as the Improving the Quality of Education for All (IQEA) Project, the High Reliability Schools (HRS) Project and many of the projects associated with the London Institute of Education National School Improvement Network (NSIN). In Canada, it has been in evidence in the various phases of work conducted in the Halton Board of Education; in the Netherlands in the Dutch National School Improvement Project (further details on these programmes are available in Reynolds *et al.* 1996; Teddlie and Reynolds 2000; Hopkins, Ainscow and West 1994; and Hopkins 2001). There are course variations between these various programmes that make any global assessment difficult. Nevertheless, if one were to look at these exemplars of third wave school improvement as a group, it is clear that:

- There has been an enhanced focus upon the importance of pupil outcomes. Instead of the earlier emphasis upon changing the processes of schools, the focus is now upon seeing if these changes are powerful enough to affect pupil outcomes.
- The learning level and the instructional behaviours of teachers have been increasingly targeted for explicit attention, as well as the school level.
- There has been the creation of an infrastructure to enable the knowledge base, both 'best practice' and research findings, to be utilised. This has involved an internal focus on collaborative patterns of staff development that enable teachers

to enquire into practice, and has involved external strategies for dissemination and networking.

• There has been an increasing consciousness of the importance of 'capacity building'. This includes not only staff development, but also medium term strategic planning, change strategies that utilise 'pressure and support', as well as the intelligent use of external support agencies.

• There has been an adoption of a 'mixed' methodological orientation, in which bodies of quantitative data plus qualitative data are used to measure educational quality, and variation in that quality. This includes an audit of existing classroom and school processes and outcomes, and comparison with desired end states, in particular the education experiences of different pupil groups.

• There has been an increased emphasis upon the importance of ensuring reliability or 'fidelity' in programme implementation across all organisational members within schools, a marked contrast with the past when improvement programmes did not have to be organisationally 'tight'.

• There has been an appreciation of the importance of cultural change in order to embed and sustain school improvement. There has been a focus on a careful balance between 'vision building' and the adapting of structures to support those aspirations.

• There has been also an increased concern to ensure that the improvement programmes relate to, and impact upon, practitioners and practices through using increasingly sophisticated training, coaching and development programmes.

Findings from the literature: effective schools, improving schools and less successful schools

We've looked at a wide range of studies to get a handle on 'what works' and what schools facing challenging circumstances could do in their drive for improvement, including:

• studies of schools that improved rapidly over time;
• studies of 'effective schools';
• studies of schools that were less successful, and those who had serious long term difficulties;
• accounts of exemplary headteachers who 'turned round' schools.

Some projects were aimed at whole school improvement, some at improving student performance. Some are based upon one school – others are district or nationally based.

School improvement describes a set of processes, managed from within the school (Stoll and Fink 1996), targeted both at pupil achievement and the school's ability to manage change (Ainscow et al. 1994) – a simultaneous focus on process and outcome. All authors stress the self-managing nature of the improving school (Southworth 2000: schools are self-managing and self-improving organisations 'aided from time to time by external support'), apparently taking control of an externally determined agenda – controlling, rather than the objects of, change. This paper adopts the tighter definitions of effectiveness and improvement used by Gray *et al.* (1999: 5): if effectiveness describes above-expectation pupil academic performance, improvement is a sustained upward trend in effectiveness. An improving school is thus one which increases its effectiveness over time – the value-added it generates for pupils rises for successive cohorts.

Certain features of improvement programmes flow necessarily from this concept of improvement:

* *vision*: without a concept of where we are trying to get to, the verb 'to improve' has no meaning;
* *monitoring*: we must know where we are now in relation to the vision;
* *planning*: how will we get from where we are towards where we want to be?
* *performance indicators*: to track progress over time in respect of the aspects we monitor.

Thus a focus on the quantitative review of trends in pupils' academic performance is inevitable.

Schools which succeeded 'against the odds' in improving against a background of significant pupil and community disadvantage (Maden and Hillman 1996) shared the following characteristics:

* a leadership stance which embodies (in its leadership team) and builds a team approach;
* a vision of success couched in academic terms and including a view of how to improve;
* careful use of targets;
* improvement of the physical environment;
* common expectations about behaviour and success;
* investment in good relations with parents and the community.

Internal pre-conditions for successful improvement (amalgamated from Gray *et al.* 1999; Ainscow *et al.* 1994) include:

* transformational leadership in the leadership team, offering the possibility of change;
* school-wide emphasis on teaching and learning;
* commitment to staff development and training;
* use of performance data to guide decisions, targets and tactics;
* teamwork both within staff groups (collaborative planning, effective communication) and with stakeholders (involvement of teachers, pupils, parents in decision-making);
* time and resources for reflection and research.

Characteristics of less successful schools (especially from Reynolds in Stoll and Myers 1998, Stoll in ditto, Teddlie and Stringfield 1993) have been argued to be:
At whole-school, including leadership, level:

- lack of the competences needed to improve;
- unwillingness to accept evidence of failure;
- blaming others – pupils, parents, LEA . . . ;
- fear of change and of outsiders who embody it;
- belief that change is for other people;
- controlled by change rather than in control of it;
- dysfunctional relationships, with cliques;
- goals are not plausible or relevant;
- lack of academic focus;
- principals who take no interest in curriculum and attainment;
- passive about recruitment and training;
- school does not build longitudinal databases on pupils' progress – not outcomes-oriented;
- valid improvement strategies are adopted but not carried through;
- governing body may be passive, lack knowledge or have factions (may be political or ethnic).

At classroom level:

- timetable not an accurate guide to academic time usage;
- inconsistency, including some high-quality teaching;
- low expectations;
- emphasis on supervision and routines;
- low levels of teacher/pupil interaction about work;
- pupils perceive teachers as not caring, praising, etc.;
- high noise levels and lots of non-work-related movement;
- lots of negative feedback from teachers.

Problems may be mutually reinforcing: since the agencies of effective change are synergistic (Hopkins and Harris 1997), so is their absence. The scale and intractability of problems in the long-term, serious difficulty school cannot be ignored; these schools may have:

- lost public support;
- been vilified in the press;
- suffered multiple staff changes, including at SMT (senior management team) level;
- 'enjoyed' false dawns;
- lost numbers and therefore have had to take other schools' excludees;
- a very challenging pupil population, with extremely high SEN demands of all kinds;

- huge budget problems;
- a community of extreme poverty and deprivation;
- a migrant population, many of whom have low literacy and/or EAL issues;
- a significant number of 'ghost' pupils who take up excessive amounts of time and who depress exam and attendance statistics;
- a history of factionalisation and industrial unrest;
- a crumbling physical environment.

(Drawn especially from reports of schools in very serious difficulties in Hackney and Hammersmith; see especially O'Connor *et al.* 1999.)

Turning round schools in serious difficulties

A persistent failure to improve argues that these schools cannot achieve the school improvement processes we noted above, since these are self-managed. There is a competence line below which the school cannot use normal processes to avert decline or sustain improvement. The processes and intentions of conventional support programmes and the activities of school improvement projects provide appropriate help for schools that are functioning 'normally'.

By definition therefore schools in long-term, serious difficulty need major programmes of intervention. Hopkins and Harris (1997) describe this as a 'Type 1' school – a failing school in which the intervenors are taking basic actions to establish minimum levels of effectiveness – involving high levels of external support and a clear and direct focus on a limited number of organisational and curricular issues. Most frequently, such programmes are provided or led by the LEA; LEAs have both *de facto* (such as in the judgements made in OFSTED inspections of LEAs) and *de jure* (in the regulations governing Education Development Plans in successive Education Acts including 1998 – formal warnings, etc.) responsibility for schools causing concern. In some cases, the failings of the LEA are major factors in the failings of the school, and other support agencies are involved. If the school cannot manage improvement alone with normal levels of support, the activities of an intervention body must lie in a combination of:

- changing the chemistry by changing the people;
- training and supporting the new team – appropriate to the school context.

The intervention team withdraws in a planned way as the level of on-site competence rises.

The principles of effective intervention (especially Fullan 1992; Hopkins and Harris 1997; Stringfield in Stoll and Myers 1998) are:

- early and determined action;
- resources are needed – lots of them – but will not work without strong management in place;

- simultaneous action at whole-school (leadership), teacher and classroom levels;
- balance of support and pressure;
- internal and external processes, top-down and bottom-up, must be co-ordinated.

Accounts of turning schools round written by their headteachers stress the importance of:

- managing the tension between a focus on a few things and the need to change everything;
- political wrangles at governor and LEA level;
- making tangible environmental improvements;
- using literacy as a Trojan horse of curriculum/teaching improvement.

The stages of recovery are described (Stark in Stoll and Myers, 1998) as:

- acknowledge failure, face up to problems, prepare an action plan which is aimed at regaining commitment as well as re-establishing basic competence [three months];
- implement action plan: restore leadership, re-establish sound management, improve teaching and learning [18 months], within which period morale and self-esteem are re-established by early success with e.g. environment, behaviour;
- 'progress towards excellence'.

One key finding in the work of many authors, but most clearly expressed by Stringfield (in Stoll and Myers 1998 and elsewhere), is that gain in scores varied more within projects due to level of implementation than between projects – in other words, given that most projects are sensibly predicated, schools achieve greater gain by pursuing a project thoroughly than by choosing project (a) rather than (b). The originators of American improvement projects (see especially Slavin's 'Success for All') talk about 'fidelity of implementation'. A senior officer of an English LEA, reflecting on a school in persistent serious difficulty, says that everyone knew what was wrong and what needed to be done, but they didn't do it consistently.

The common challenging issues for managing improvement projects and programmes which span a number of schools are (summarised here from Stoll describing the Lewisham Project, in Barber and Dann 1996: 113–115):

- what to do with non-volunteer schools which need to but do not want to take part (of the 50 projects listed in 'Raising Education Standards in the Inner Cities', pp. 193–4, 8% were identified by need and a further 16% comprised all the schools in a disadvantaged area, while 40% were self-selected);
- managing the tension between ownership and accountability: how much action is 'done to' a school which cannot do it to itself, how and when to enable the school to resume local decision-making;
- the complexity of evaluation: attributability – how to assess what worked when everything is changing; poor base-lining or success criteria in many projects;

- avoiding the project as bolt-on rather than bloodstream, event rather than process; projects which are linked to funding which dwindle or die when the funding runs out;
- concurrent agendas – e.g. development paralysis caused by OFSTED inspection in some schools;
- getting a school moving – how to start to move schools.

Findings from the literature as a basis for supporting schools facing challenging circumstances

The aim of the initiative to support schools facing challenging circumstances is to support the improvement of the lowest-performing secondary schools, as defined by a single measure – those in which 25% or under of pupils achieved five or more grades A*–C at GCSE in 1999 and/or 2000. PRUs, special and primary schools are not included. This also includes a number of schools which achieve above the 25% floor target, but where over 35% of their pupils are receiving free school meals (fsm).

The schools vary considerably, they are numerous and diverse, including low-achieving, underachieving and failing schools – and some which are already highly effective schools. It is therefore expected that each school will design an improvement strategy to fit its specific circumstances.

In formulating this improvement strategy, schools are encouraged to learn from the research into effective school improvement programmes. These have/are/do the following:

- a multi-level approach but with the stated improvement focus on the classroom and on academic achievement;
- securing strong leadership at headteacher level, before . . .
- . . . building an effective leadership team, before . . .
- . . . gaining staff commitment, before . . .
- . . . a large input of resources;
- securing the understanding of, and, preferably, the involvement of, the community, especially parents;
- adopting the characteristics of high-reliability organisations:
  - i   clarity of mission: a small number of clear, agreed and inflexible goals, with ambitious targets for pupils' academic achievement at their heart;
  - ii careful monitoring of key systems to avoid cascading error;
  - iii data richness, with good benchmarking and openness about performance data;
  - iv Standard Operating Procedures (SOPs), including an agreed model of teaching and consistent implementation of agreed actions in teaching, managing learning behaviour, attendance etc.;
  - v   a focus on pupils at risk of failure;

   vi   pro-active, extensive recruitment and targeted training, including the delivery of the agreed teaching methods;

   vii rigorous performance evaluation to ascertain the rapid, early and continuous impact of initiatives;

   viii maintenance of equipment in the highest working order.

- a 'club' structure with support, networks – a learning network which may involve HEI (higher education institution)/LEA/other schools/consultants; working with a multi-skilled support team which provides pressure as well as support; fidelity of implementation;
- strong rules and processes at the start of the programme (and recognising that fulfilling the rules is more important than the rules themselves!), with the school making greater input as confidence increases and the school begins to turn;
- seeking a sense of early achievement through a clean-up campaign and some improvements to fabric.

We have sought to develop a two-stage approach:

Stage 1
Devise a programme which is built on the following core values:

- every school can improve;
- improvement must ultimately be assessed in terms of improved pupil outcomes;
- every individual in the school has a contribution to make to the improvement;
- start from where the school is but help staff to set high goals;
- help schools help themselves and guard against creating dependency;
- model good practice;
- help heads/staff raise their expectations of what is possible and to see beyond the school.

Stage 2
Encouraging schools to work with partners to:

- take early, firm intervention to secure effective management and leadership;
- help the school identify its core issues through:
  - surveys of staff and student opinion;
  - gathering, analysing and presenting data on student achievement;
  - using these data to identify good practice.
- gain staff commitment through working with those staff unable or unwilling to change;
- introduce models of leadership and teaching quality:
  - building a leadership team, with appropriate contribution from the head;
  - introducing experienced new blood in the classroom.
- focus on dealing with issues in a phased manner in order to achieve a track record of success whilst recognising the importance of:
  - addressing any OFSTED key issues;

- improving the cleanliness of the environment;
- developing pride and self-esteem;
- emphasising attendance/punctuality/uniform.
AND
- focus on teaching and learning:
  - establishing a set of core values and an agreed teaching model;
  - re-skilling teams of teachers in a limited repertoire of teaching styles;
  - firm and consistent policy on behaviour (around the site as well as in classrooms);
  - supporting and building on models of excellent teaching.

Acknowledgement

First published as part of D. Reynolds, D. Hopkins, D. Potter and C. Chapman (2001) *School Improvement for Schools Facing Challenging Circumstances*. London: HMSO for DfES. Reprinted here with permission from HMSO.

11

What leaders need to know about teacher effectiveness

Introduction

Teaching is the most important thing that teachers do. It is the most important thing that goes on in schools – in fact, all the research evidence suggests that the teacher at the learning level has three to four times more influence over how students perform than the organisation of the school (the school level).

Yet the amount of research in the United Kingdom into what makes teachers effective in adding value to students' academic and social development is very small. The micro-political problems of talking about variation between individual teachers, the absence of data in key areas such as social development and the need for highly complex work to observe and understand what teachers actually do in their classrooms have all been mentioned as possible explanations. This is why we will be looking at material from the United States also.

In this short article, we look at the evidence that we have on this topic, review it from its United States and United Kingdom sources, outline the more recent thinking about advanced teacher effectiveness, and talk about directions research needs to move in and the important issues still to be properly understood.

The American knowledge base

There is an extensive body of knowledge from the United States concerning the behaviours of teachers who add value to pupils' achievements. This evidence is produced by the use of pre-tests and post-tests of reading and other skills, together with the study of the relationship between observed teacher behaviours in the classroom, and the pupils' achievement scores over, usually, an academic year.

One of the factors that most consistently and most strongly affects pupils' achievement is opportunity to learn or learning time, whether it is measured as the amount of the curriculum covered or the percentage of test items taught. Opportunity to learn is clearly related to such factors as the length of the school day and year, and the hours of teaching within them. It is, however, also related to the quality of teachers' classroom management in maximising engaged time and especially to what is known as time on task (i.e. the amount of time children are actively engaged in learning activities, in the classroom). Opportunity to learn is also clearly related to the use of homework, which expands available learning time.

Another highly important factor which distinguishes effective teachers from less effective, a factor that is also connected to children's time on task, is a teacher's academic orientation. Effective teachers emphasise academic instruction and see learning as the main classroom goal. This means that they spend most of their time on curriculum-based learning activities and create a task-oriented, business-like, but also relaxed and supportive environment.

Obviously, the achievement levels of the children are strongly influenced by teachers' classroom management. Effective teachers are able to organise and manage classrooms as effective learning environments in which academic activities run smoothly, transitions (between lesson segments) are brief, and little time is spent getting organised or dealing with inattention or resistance. For this to happen, good prior preparation of the classroom and the installation of clear rules and procedures (before or at the start of the school year) are essential. All in all, effective teachers manage to create a well-organised classroom with minimal disruption and mis-behaviour.

Teacher expectations are also very important. Effective teachers show they believe that all children can master the curriculum (not just a percentage of children). They emphasise the positive (e.g. if a child is not so good in one area, he or she might be good in another), and these positive expectations are transmitted to children. Effective teachers emphasise the importance of effort, clarifying the relationship between effort and outcomes, and helping pupils gain an internal locus of control by constantly pointing out the importance of their own work in getting things right.

Research has also found that children learn more in classes where they spend time being taught by their teacher rather than working on their own, the so-called "active teacher" model. In such classes, teachers spend most of their time presenting information through lecture and demonstration. Teacher-led discussion, as opposed to individual work, dominates. This is not to say that all individual work is negative, since of course individual practice is necessary and important, but many teachers have been found to rely too much on pupils working on their own, at the expense of lecture-demonstration and class discussion.

Research has found that classrooms where more time is spent teaching the whole class, rather than on letting individual pupils work by themselves (e.g. with worksheets), see higher pupil achievement gains. This is mainly because teachers in these classrooms provide more thoughtful and thorough presentations, spend less time on classroom management, enhance time on task and make more child contacts. Teachers giving this whole-class instruction have also been found to spend more time monitoring children's achievement. There were also likely to be fewer child disruptions with this method, thus again increasing time on task. The effective teacher carries the content personally to the student rather than relying on curriculum material or textbooks to do so.

This focus on the teacher presenting material in an active way to students should, however, not be equated to a traditional lecturing-and-drill approach in which the students remain passive. Active teachers ask a lot of questions (more than other teachers) and involve students in class discussion. In this way students are kept involved in the lesson and the teacher has the chance to monitor children's understanding of the concepts taught. Individual work is only assigned after the teacher has made sure children have grasped the material sufficiently to be ready for it. In general, effective teachers have been found to teach a concept, then ask questions to test children's understanding, and if the material did not seem well understood, to re-teach the concept and follow this with more monitoring. Overall, it is clear that effective teaching is not only active, but interactive as well.

The British knowledge base

This, by contrast to the American, is a highly restricted one. Early research attempts to relate pupils' achievement gains to the broad educational philosophies and practices of teachers rated as progressive or traditional, of course, generated rather little success and were widely criticised. While progressive teachers had lower gains, interestingly teachers with what could be called structured, consistent progressivism as a philosophy or practice generated the highest learning gain. In any case, the amount of variation in achievement explained by variation in teaching style was small.

Later came the notable ORACLE study, which involved a process–product orientation similar to that of the American teacher effectiveness material above and which found that the "class enquirer" category of teachers, who utilised a high proportion of whole-class teaching, was more effective in developing gains in mathematics and language, but that this did not apply in reading.

The major British study of teacher effectiveness is, of course, the Junior School Project (JSP) of Mortimore et al. (1988), which reported the following factors as important in terms of teacher effectiveness across all achievement areas.

- Consistency among teachers: continuity of staffing has positive effects, but pupils also performed better when the approach to teaching was consistent.
- Structured sessions: children performed better when their school day was structured in some way. In effective schools, students' work was proactively organised by the teacher, who ensured there was plenty for them to do, yet

allowed them some freedom, within the structure. Negative effects were noted when children were given unlimited responsibility for a long list of tasks.

- Intellectually challenging teaching: student progress was greater where teachers were stimulating and enthusiastic. The incidence of higher-order questions and statements and teachers frequently making children use powers of problem-solving were seen to be vital.
- A work-centred environment: this was characterised by a high level of student industry, with children enjoying their work and being eager to start new tasks. The noise level was low, and movement around the classroom was usually work-related and not excessive.
- A limited focus within sessions: children progressed when teachers devoted their energies to one particular subject area and sometimes two. Student progress was marred when three or more subjects were running concurrently in the classroom.
- Maximum communication between teachers and students: children performed better, the more communication they had with their teacher about the content of their work. Most teachers devoted most of their time to individuals, so each child could expect only a small number of contacts a day. Teachers who used opportunities to talk to the whole class generated higher progress.
- Record keeping: the value of monitoring student progress was important in the Headteacher's role, but it was also an important aspect of teachers' planning and assessment.
- Parental involvement: schools with an informal open-door policy which encouraged parents to get involved in reading at home, helping in the classroom and on educational visits tended to be more effective.

More advanced teaching skills

While behaviours in a direct instruction or active teaching model are effective in improving achievement in basic skills, doubt has been cast on whether this approach is sufficient for teaching higher-order problem-solving or thinking skills, the importance of which has received increasing emphasis in recent years. While direct instruction focusing on basic skills may be a necessary condition for being able to develop higher-order thinking and problem-solving skills, it is not sufficient. A number of additional classroom processes may be needed to enhance higher-order thinking: a focus on meaning and understanding, direct teaching of higher-level cognitive strategies and problem solving, and co-operative small-group work, the most powerful approach, which we deal with here.

The advantages of co-operative small-group work to developing problem-solving skills lie partly in the scaffolding process, whereby pupils help each other learn in the "zone of proximal development". Giving and receiving help and explanation may develop children's thinking skills, as well as helping them to verbalise and structure their thoughts. By co-operating in small groups, children can share their own ways of thinking and reflect on them and on the thinking and ideas of others.

This exchange may encourage students to engage in more higher-order thinking. Pupils thus provide assistance and support to one another. Co-operative small groups force the accommodation of the opinions of various members, and students must therefore search, engage in problem-solving and take one another's perspective. In this way students can develop an enhanced understanding of self and others, and learn that others possess both strengths and weaknesses.

This may help students who are less able problem-solvers to overcome their insecurity about problem-solving because they can see more able peers struggling over difficult problems. The fact that a group contains more knowledge than an individual means that problem-solving strategies can be more powerful. This may help students see the importance of co-operation. Group members may serve as models to one another, which thus enhances learning-to-learn skills. Students also receive practice in collaboration, a skill they will require in real life.

A number of people have pointed to possible problems with this method, however. Shared student misconceptions can be reinforced by group work. Furthermore, students might be tempted to engage in off-task social interaction. Students may also receive differentiated status in groups. Some may start to perceive themselves as having little to contribute to the group or may find that their contributions are not greatly valued. This may lead them to become passive in the group. Small-group work may then advantage high-ability students over lower-ability ones. Studies have found low-ability students to be less active in small groups, in part because they understand the task less well and in part because student talk can also express low expectations of certain other students. One of the main problems with small-group work is the fact that small groups require far more classroom management skills from the teacher. If not well prepared, small-group work can significantly increase the time the teacher spends on direction, transition and managerial activities. To be effective, teachers also need to have access to a large number of problems, which further exacerbates the difficulties involved with group work. All in all, small-group work requires a lot of preparation time for the teacher.

While the benefits of co-operative small-group work for enhancing students' problem-solving skills seems important, it is clear that for group work to be effective it is insufficient to put students into groups and let them get on with it. A number of conditions need to be met. The most important of these are group goals and individual accountability. Group goals are essential to motivate students to work co-operatively and thus help their group's learning.

Individual accountability increases the engagement of individual students and decreases the probability of "free-rider" effects, whereby certain students choose to remain passive while letting other group members do all the work.

Overall, it is clear that effective small-group work is a structured activity that requires a lot of teacher effort. If the subject worked on requires higher-order thinking and problem-solving skills, and is used under the conditions described above, the effort will be worth it, however, in terms of learning gains in higher-order areas.

In no sense, though, is the development of higher-order skills to be seen as unrelated to that of basic skills, since performance on the two sets of skills is related.

What is required for an optimal level of achievement across a range of skills is both whole-class interactive, and collaborative group-based, teaching.

Some unresolved important issues

We know a lot about what the effective methods are, but are still working on four unresolved issues.

First, there is a growing evidence of context specificity in the precise factors associated with learning gains, originally shown at the school level in interesting research from California, where highly effective schools in poor catchment areas pursued policies discouraging parental involvement in the school, in contrast to the effective schools in more advantaged catchment areas that encouraged the practice. While some factors apply across classrooms in all social contexts (such as having high expectations of what children can achieve or lesson structure), it may be that certain factors apply only in certain contexts. An example might be that teachers proceeding in small steps is important for all children learning new knowledge in all contexts, while in the contexts inhabited by lower-social class or lower-attaining children, it may be necessary to use small steps for teaching all knowledge.

Effective practices within low socio-economic status contexts seem to involve the teacher behaviours of:

- generating a warm and supportive affect by letting children know help is available;
- getting a response, any response, before moving on to the next bit of new material;
- presenting material in small bits, with a chance to practise before moving on;
- emphasising knowledge and applications before abstraction, putting the concrete first;
- giving immediate help (through use of peers perhaps);
- generating strong structure, ground flow and well planned transitions;
- using the experience of pupils.

Effective practices within middle socio-economic status contexts seem to involve the behaviours of:

- requiring extended reasoning;
- posing questions that require associations and generalisations;
- giving difficult material;
- using projects that require independent judgement, discovery, problem-solving and the use of original information;
- encouraging learners to take responsibility for their own learning;
- very rich verbalising.

A wide range of possible contextual factors may determine the precise nature of what generates effectiveness in classrooms:

- the socio-economic status of the catchment area;
- the level of effectiveness of the school;
- the trajectory of effectiveness of the school (i.e. improving, static, declining);
- the region of the school;
- the urban or rural status of the school;
- the religiosity of the school;
- the culture and history of the school;
- the primary or secondary status of the school.

Secondly, it may be that we have not yet developed policies that are strong enough to maximise teacher effectiveness. The great majority of the policy levers being pulled are at the school level, such as school development plans and target-setting, and at a local education authority (LEA) level, such as LEA development plans. The problems with the mostly school-orientation of contemporary policy are:

- Within-school variation by department within secondary school and by teacher within primary school is much greater than the variation between schools in their mean levels of achievement or value-added effectiveness.
- The effect of the classroom level in those multi-level analyses that have been undertaken since the introduction of this technique in the mid 1980s is probably three to four times greater than that of the school level.

Simply, the most important determinant of children's outcomes, the nature of their classroom experiences, is being targeted less than are their school and their LEAs. It may be, though, that a classroom or learning-level orientation would be more productive of achievement gains for the following reasons:

- The departmental level in a secondary school, or year level in a primary school, is closer to the classroom level than is the school level, which opens up the possibility of generating greater change in classrooms.
- Teachers in general, and those teachers in less effective settings in particular, may be more influenced by classroom-level policies that are close to their focal concerns of teaching and the curriculum than by the policies that are managerial and orientated to the school level.

It is also important to note that the most powerful intervention strategies we have – Reading Recovery and the Success for All programme – have a pronounced focus upon pulling the lever of the instructional level as well as ensuring school-level conditions are conducive. Indeed, in these programmes, which generate both the highest levels of achievement gain ever seen in educational research and achievement gains that are (most unusually) higher amongst initially low-scoring children, the school lever is seen as merely setting the conditions for effective learning to take place at the classroom or instructional level.

While it is clear that a focus upon teaching rather than schooling needs to permeate the range of educational policies, quite what these policies need to be is unclear, other than that they need to involve exemplary professionals within peer-observation or buddying systems of some kind.

Thirdly, we need to investigate how different subjects require different kinds of effective practice from teachers. Individualised methods appear to have particularly negative effects in mathematics, but not in all other subjects. In reading, a climate of rich verbal elaboration appears to be important, and one-to-one peer tutoring to be effective. There are whole subject areas like art, music, physical education and, for that matter, the vexed area of information and communications technology (ICT) that need attention.

Lastly, the great majority of the knowledge we have is about effective teaching in academic, not social areas. We live in a world where learning-to-learn skills and the motivation to be a life-long learner are viewed as essential, but the kinds of experiences in classrooms and behaviours by teachers that can deliver these educational outcomes are unknown.

There is still clearly much to do to understand what makes for effective teaching and how to make learning effective.

Acknowledgement

First published as D. Reynolds (2006) 'What leaders need to know about teacher effectiveness' in National College for School Leadership, *Teaching Texts*. Nottingham: NCSL. Reprinted here with permission from NCSL.

12

Schools learning from their best
The Within School Variation (WSV) Project

Introduction

Trying to improve schools has been the core mantra of educational policy and practice for virtually two decades now. There have been national programmes based on areas (e.g. Education Action Zones, Excellence in Cities), programmes across all schools like the National Primary and Secondary Strategies, and programmes in which individual schools, Headteachers and teachers attempt to improve school organisation and ethos, and improve student learning and teachers' teaching, either by self-inventing various effectiveness and improvement initiatives or by bringing ones to their schools that have been taken 'off the shelf'.

Overall, the effects of all these attempts can be probably judged as somewhat disappointing. National standards of education judged by test and examination results have been increasing, but not at a rate to hit the optimistic targets of governments. There is still variation between schools, between teachers within schools and of course very substantial variation between students from different backgrounds, all of which may have been only marginally affected by educational reform.

This report focuses upon the results of what is a novel way of improving school quality, in which the system of schools itself learns from its own best people and practices rather than being encouraged to mimic central guidance, central policy or central advice. This project is beyond the focus of much present educational policy upon 'schools helping other schools' through Federations, twinned schools and the use of 'superheads' from one school to 'turn around' whole groups of them, and instead focuses on what an individual school can do to learn from itself. Moving on from 'school to school', this report focuses on the practicality of a 'within school' perspective and associated policies.

Most schools in England have in recent years been made aware of what variation lies within them by a whole range of educational policies that have emerged related to:

- provision of more data on the academic outcomes of schools, often related to subject subdivisions within schools;
- the opening up of the classroom to others such as parents, helpers, assistants, other teachers and student teachers, who now may see what goes on inside the educational 'black box' in ways unusual before;
- the routine use of classroom observation, pupil voice surveys, and indeed much school-based in-service education;
- the increased attention given to the views of educational consumers, like parents and pupils, who are often very sensitive to variation in their interaction with different teachers within their schools, or their pupil's schools.

But it is one thing to recognise that the variation is there, and another thing to use it in ways that can promote educational improvement. Some individual schools have managed this but thus far there has been no 'route map' that tells schools what may 'work' in this area, what may not and what are the foundations on which school practice could be built.

Finding out if these foundations could be established, and seeing if success could be built in this most sensitive and interpersonally difficult of areas, has been the aim of this project.

Within school variation (WSV): the extent

Variation within schools, rather than between them, has been occasionally re-marked upon over the last two or three decades, but has only recently come into major focus. Fitz-Gibbon (1985) reported on differences between Mathematics Departments that were large even after value added estimates were made, and indeed her own philosophy of empowering teachers with quality data had the learning from, and reduction in, WSV at its heart.

However, it took the announcement of the Programme for International Student Assessment (PISA) results published by the Organisation for Economic Co-operation and Development (OECD) to fully bring this issue into the professional spotlight. In PISA, 80% of the variation between the pupils in their achievement lay *within* schools, fully four times as much as lay *between* them (20%), a finding that was markedly different to many OECD societies' results, and which put the UK towards the very top of the 'within school variation' table. Some societies, like Germany for example, had a very small amount of variance within schools, and the greater number lay between them.

Quite what the explanation of the UK performance was is still unclear. In a comprehensive system like that of the UK, there are no selective types of schools which, as in Germany, would inflate the 'between school' statistics. Perhaps the strong influence of social class in the UK would minimise the effect of 'school' differences, and maximise the effects 'within a school', any school.

It is also possible that there might be some 'structural looseness' in the UK system by comparison with those of other countries. This 'unreliability' or 'variability' is shown by Table 12.1 below – compare the variance at school level shown in the column looking at seven-year-old pupils' intake scores to later scores (marked 'C') in the UK, USA and Taiwan for example, which shows that the school 'level' in these analyses is more constant and less variable in Taiwan than those of the UK and USA.

It is also possible that the historic relative autonomy of schools from society, local authorities (LAs) from state control, schools from local education authorities and teachers/departments from school management control, created a system of 'multiple autonomies' and unreliability that might explain the UK results.

Contemporary data certainly suggest that WSV continues to be large. Using unpublished data from the Fischer Family Trust, and looking at the 65–75% of secondary schools where pupils' progress in Key Stage Three is roughly in line with national expectations, then if one takes six groups of pupils (boys/girls in the three core subjects), then:

- 80% of all schools show value added significantly higher than might be expected for one or more groups;
- over a three-year period 50% of schools have at least one subject in which progress would put them in the top 20% nationally in the subject concerned (see Reynolds, 2004 for further details).

Our own research on primary schools also shows the power of within school factors. Table 12.2 shows the variance in pupil mathematics scores that is explained

Table 12.1 Percentages of variance in mathematics achievement to be explained at school level before and after correction for student background variables, for selected countries

	Intake end Year 1 A1 unconditional model	Intake end Year 1 B1 with background covariates	End Year 1 End Year 2 A2 unconditional model	End Year 1 End Year 2 B2 with background covariates	Intake End Year 2 C
	A1	B1	A2	B2	C
USA	0.35	0.29	0.37	0.20	0.25
UK	0.21	0.11	0.22	0.07	0.10
Taiwan	0.03	0.02	0.07	0.04	0.04

Source: Reynolds et al., 2002.

Table 12.2 Variance at the school, classroom and pupil levels on mathematics achievement

	School	Class	Individual pupil
Year 1	9.9	14.1	76.0
Year 2	5.6	18.0	76.4
Year 3	4.8	28.8	66.4
Year 4	5.7	22.4	71.9

Note
Year above is the year of the study itself.

by individual background factors (the customary 75–80%) and by educational organisations and processes (in this case a slightly higher 20–30% of total variance than is usually seen in such studies, perhaps explicable by the use of mathematics as the outcome factor, on which educational effects are much higher than reading ability).

The class 'level' related to the practices of individual teachers explains considerably more variation than the school 'level', a very similar picture of WSV to the secondary departmental data (for full data see Muijs and Reynolds, 2003).

WSV: the causes

The factors responsible for this variation in performance within both primary and secondary schools would seem to be the following:

- individual variation in teacher competence that is not sufficiently reduced by initial training or subsequent Continuing Professional Development (CPD);
- unreliable implementation of national strategies, school improvement programmes and the like in which the gap between the 'floor' of less competent teachers and the 'ceiling' of more competent teachers widens as the programmes tend to maximise pre-existing variation;
- the effects of recent increased pressures in education leading to enhanced difficulties in 'coping' for the less competent teachers, whilst the more competent 'thrive on chaos', generating enhanced differentiation between professionals.

Interestingly, the school effectiveness knowledge base suggests that the schools that are consistent outperformers are intolerant of large negatives, reduce variation in teacher performance and are reliable and consistent. It is more ineffective schools which show the largest range of within school variation.

Interestingly also, the school improvement knowledge base suggests that gains vary more within improvement projects than between them, and that schools achieve greater gain by pursuing any project thoroughly rather than by choosing one project rather than another, the 'fidelity of implementation' issue.

WSV: the problems in addressing it

Our historical barriers to dealing with within school variation may be the following:

- weak school management that finds it hard to confront the issue and to develop mechanisms to learn from best practice;
- false modesty on the part of effective teachers/departments, perhaps associated with a misplaced egalitarianism that does not reward helping other practitioners who are less effective because this would mean marking out the less effective and labelling them;
- small schools in which the range of excellence between teachers may be less and therefore more difficult to use, and the one-/two-person departments that may make performance evaluation by subject a highly personal activity;
- the absence of systems to 'buddy' the less good with the better, because of the difficulty of the intense micro-political issues in this area;
- budget/time constraints that make it difficult to create these skill sharing systems since they require time, space and buy out of teaching for observation/debriefing, etc.;
- the difficulty of separating out the *personal* reasons for some teachers'/departments' more effective practice from the *methods* that are being used, since all factors appear confounded with each other;
- the difficulty in secondary schools of getting departments to see any utility in swapping practice when the subject cultures of departments are so strong (it's not like that in art);
- the practice of using exceptional individuals to be the models for others when the exceptional may be often idiosyncratic and utilising their character as much as any distinctive methods. The exceptional may also be so far in advance of the remainder of the staff in a school that they cannot be imitated.

In spite of these difficulties that would be inevitable in attempting to learn from WSV, this is exactly what we did.

The chronology of the project

WSV had emerged as of interest to national educational policymakers in 2001, due to the PISA results noted earlier. David Miliband, the Minister for School Standards, asked officials within the Department for Education and Skills (DfES as was) what was known on the subject, and became even more interested when they reported that little work was ongoing.

David Reynolds, interested in WSV because of its links with unreliability of school organisation that were the opposite side of the coin of High Reliability Schools, presented the most recent data showing the importance of teacher variation in primary schools from the Gatsby-funded Mathematics research and the evidence on secondary WSV, to a number of internal DfES committees and the decision was taken to form a joint project between the DfES (through The Innovation Unit) and the National College for School Leadership (NCSL), overseen by a Steering Group of DfES and NCSL representation, with David Reynolds in a consultancy role.

The project began with schools that were already working with the NCSL's Leadership Network, a group of mostly high achieving schools (in raw results terms) and extremely able Headteachers who were engaged in high quality, interactive networking that had created a high quality network of practitioners. Put simply, the network was helping good schools to get better, although the network itself was attempting to broaden its constituency.

These schools comprised about two-thirds of the first group of schools that became known as 'Phase One' schools, that ran the project in their school for the school years 2003/4, 2004/5 and 2005/6, although the 2003/4 school year was one of preparation and design for the project rather than action, as we will see later. These schools, though, were joined by a number of others that were in 'Challenging Circumstances', with more disadvantaged intakes and in some but not all cases a history of special measures, fractured leadership, high levels of staff turnover and poor results. In most cases, these additional schools came into the project based upon the arrival of new, mostly highly competent Headteachers whose job it was to turn these schools around. These new Heads came into the Leadership Network mostly sponsored by already existing Heads, who knew the quality of the new recruits. Others of the Phase Two schools were not in such circumstances.

These two rather different kinds of schools created a 'bi-polar distribution' of schools of both excellence and challenge, but on key indicators such as free school meal rates and even on 'raw' pupil results, the schools as a group were very close to the national average for all schools. Phase One secondaries, for example, had a mean free school meal rate of 21%, compared with a national average of about 18%, and the percentage of pupils gaining five or more passes at GCSE, grades A* to C was in 2003 53%, exactly the same as the national rate.

Also, whereas the Leadership Network schools were volunteers attracted by an open invitation to all schools in the Network to become involved in the project if they were interested in WSV, and were in many cases already doing WSV-related work, some of the other schools did not appear to be doing much school improvement at all historically, let alone WSV work.

The sample of 'volunteers attracted because they had already started work on WSV', and 'schools with no interest in WSV historically but probably possessing a lot of it', again despite its bipolar nature, was probably not far different from the average 'improvement readiness' as it were of the total English school population.

Phase One began with an opening conference in September 2003, and with only halting progress initially. WSV was the new educational kid on the block, and whereas in such areas as school effectiveness research or school improvement designs more generally, there are bodies of knowledge that exist to guide practitioners and researchers about 'what works', in the case of WSV there was no such guide.

There was no alternative but to openly say to schools that the first year of the project, 2003/4, was to be used to 'let a thousand flowers bloom', and schools were encouraged to search for ideas, try things out and, in a phrase, design the WSV project 'in flight'.

The individual school-based, innovative designs for WSV interventions that were developed soon became a foundation for all schools, as a number of initial project conferences were held (in December 2003 and July 2004) to share emerging ideas about those things which seemed to be working. But the planning year 2003/4 in general showed:

- a low level of understanding of WSV as a concept, and practically;
- a very slow start in many schools, not unrelated to competing pressures;
- a lack of clarity about exactly what the focus of the interventions should be;
- a confusion of WSV initiatives with general school improvement work, and also an absence of clarity about exactly how these two things might have differed;
- a difficulty in getting into WSV at all, because of the absence of WSV initiatives in 2003/4 development plans, the pressure of already existing activities that were in the development plans, etc.

Some schools never really recovered from this first year paralysis, an inevitable consequence of letting schools go without a clear route map. In some, WSV was merely an *event* when it needed to be a *programme* if it were to have impact.

But, in general, from Spring 2004 the pace of the project quickened for the 16 secondary and 9 primary schools, and most schools picked up momentum greatly. This was maintained by National Project meetings for all the schools, the exemplary work of the National and Regional Co-ordinators of the NCSL Leadership Network, and special meetings of regional groups of schools in Summer Term 2004 and Summer Term 2005, involving in the case of the latter the schools of 'Phase Two' for the first time.

The Steering Group also met three or four times per year in school years 2003/4, 2004/5 and 2005/6, and the Research Group of the NCSL gave exemplary leadership and support.

The project was further widened in scope in 2005 with the addition of a further 28 Phase Two primary and secondary schools, each to be partnered by one of the Phase One schools that were by Autumn 2005 moving into their second action year of the project. The aim was to 'double test' the ideas that would be emerging from Phase One about the factors 'that worked' in reducing WSV and upping pupil achievement, and also to further test whether there were any factors in the nature of the working arrangements between Phase One and Phase Two schools that could be seen as 'working'.

For the new Phase Two schools and the Phase One schools there were national conferences in school year 2005/6, regional events in Spring 2006, continued visits from Regional Co-ordinators and also the beginning of the activities whereby Phase One brought on Phase Two. Phase One schools formally finished the project with the 2006 public examinations taken in Summer 2006 although WSV actions continued. For Phase Two schools, these examination results were their first to be taken while in the project.

The project results: outcome changes

There are of course many objectives that are given to schools for them to aim for in terms of the development of their pupils. Social outcomes like positive self-esteem, or economic productivity, are both goals that have been extensively emphasised in recent years, and of course in the *Every Child Matters* agenda.

However, in this project, we made the academic achievement of pupils the prime focus of our attention for a number of reasons. Academic outcomes were those where we had the best data – across schools in the project, and to compare our schools with the national totality of schools. Academic outcomes are of primary importance in determining the trajectory of children's lives. And, of course, since we wanted to explore the relevance of WSV for the national educational policy-making agenda, we wanted to focus on what policy-makers would pay some attention to, and on what was the focus of national policies.

We commissioned therefore an evaluation of the 'project's effects' by an outsider with no project connections to obtain a totally unbiased and 'neutral' perspective, though this only began with the Summer 2005 examination cycle, and concluded with the Summer 2006 results that became available in 2007.

Note that a number of analyses are available:

- for primary schools, progress between KS1 and KS2;
- for secondary schools, progress in KS3;
- for secondary schools, progress in KS2/KS4;
- for secondary schools, progress in KS3/KS4.

All these analyses have been undertaken on a 'value added' basis, with the gain over time of individual pupils looked at and the existing differences between schools or Years in schools stripped out or 'controlled for'. In all four groups above, we focus on VA (whether academic outcomes have improved) and WSV (whether there is a reduced variation between subjects in the value added). Put simply, we are interested in excellence (VA) and equity (WSV), and the 'raising the bar' of excellence and the 'reducing the range' of equity.

The results for Phase One schools in the 2005 data, when they had been participating in the project for one planning year (2003/4) and one action year (2004/5), were disappointing, although given the trajectory shown for other school improvement interventions not surprising. For the primary schools, five out of ten schools showed an increase in VA (albeit small in most cases), and half an increase in WSV, with an overall small positive effect in both cases. For secondaries, in KS3 the results were similar with seven out of 15 schools showing value added gain and five out of 15 schools a reduction in within school variation.

For KS3 to KS4, a majority (9/14) of schools showed an *increase* in WSV and half (7/14) a reduction in VA pupil progress, a disappointing finding. For KS2 to KS4 though, more schools (7/12) showed a reduction in WSV than not but also more showed a reduction in VA pupil progress (9/12) than not. Again, these findings were disappointing.

Two further analyses were undertaken, which had little effect on the overall picture. For KS3 to KS4, an analysis was done that did not measure the mean difference between 'actual' and 'expected' scores but instead looked at the difference related to the total numbers of pupils taking the subject. For KS2 to KS4, and KS3 on its own, an analysis was done that looked not at the range between the best and the worst subject scores but at the maximum negative difference from the mean value added score. Neither of these alternative measures made any material difference to the original conclusions.

The 2006 examination data were released in Spring 2007 and showed a more promising picture. For the primary schools, looking from 2003 to 2006 about half the schools had shown a decrease in WSV scores and about two-thirds an improvement in VA scores. There was little difference between Phase One and Phase Two schools.

For the secondary schools, the results were considerably more encouraging. At KS3 a large number (8/10) of Phase One schools reduced WSV and half (5/10) improved VA. For KS2 to KS4, a large number (8/10) of Phase One schools showed a reduction in WSV between the start and the end of the project, and a majority (6/10) an increase in VA scores. For KS3 to KS4, 7 out of 12 Phase One schools reduced WSV and 9 out of 12 improved VA. For the Phase Two schools, neither in KS2 to KS4, nor in KS3 to KS4, nor in KS3, was there comparable evidence of effect on WSV or VA.

For the data for 2003/2006, covering two/three years of the project, we thought it was appropriate to employ limited statistical methods to test out the findings in the datasets. This involved making an estimate of the probability of our obtaining our mostly positive results by chance, a standard statistical procedure. The conventional measure that is used to calculate that the result could not have been achieved by chance is a probability of 0.5 or less (the 'significance level').

If we apply these statistical methods to the data from the secondary schools of Phase One, then we get the following picture:

	Value added	Within school variation
KS3:	5/10 not significant;	8/10 significant
KS3/4:	9/12 close to significant;	7/12 not significant
KS2/4:	6/10 not significant;	8/10 significant

Note that, using the most stringent tests, many changes are *statistically* significant, in addition to the *practically* significant and *educationally* significant scale of the results as expressed in terms of the proportion of schools improving.

Note also that the 'key' or 'foundational' KS2/4 indicator, which most schools focused upon and which encompass the KS3 and KS3/4 indicators, is positive. And note also that for the secondary schools of Phase One, no performance data has ever been negative overall, whereby a majority of a group of schools does worse at the end of the project. The worst result for our schools is for half to improve: the best results are for 75–80% to improve, looking at both value added improvements and reduction in within school variation.

Some further analysis was undertaken to see if there was indeed a relationship between the VA and WSV changes. If not, than any improvement in excellence (VA) could not be related to a reduction in difference (WSV), and could therefore clearly not relate to any possible WSV programme effects.

The hypothesis was that there should be a negative relationship between schools' changes over time in that reducing WSV would be expected to generate increasing VA. The linear correlations are as follows, for the whole sample of primary and secondary schools in both Phases, given that it is a whole sample issue:

KS2:   −0.62
KS3:   0.19
KS2/4: −0.63
KS3/4: −0.20

The pattern of the data across the four age Phases strongly suggests that there *is* a relationship between WSV and VA change and that when there is movement of outcomes it is in the expected direction. The WSV and VA changes are linked, and therefore reducing within school variation will be associated with an improvement in value added outcomes.

What worked: the project levers

The results above show a picture that is quite encouraging, even though it might have been somewhat predictable. The primary schools achieved less than the secondaries in terms of increasing VA and reducing WSV – this may be due to:

- the absence in these schools of building blocks of more than one (unlike departments in secondary schools);
- the consequent conflation of WSV initiatives with individual teachers' performance and development issues;
- an absence of a focus on subject variation beyond the three 'core' subjects, in marked contrast to the secondary sector, who had been publishing (and in some cases evaluating and acting upon) multiple subject performance data in the annual reports to parents made compulsory in the Conservative Government's educational reforms of the 1990s;

- an historically 'liberal' educational orientation that preferred to see the staff of a school as a collective group who should not be marked out as different, or variable, from each other;
- the presence of an average staff size (10–15 in most cases) that meant it was difficult to fragment it, or treat it, or analyse it in any differentiated way, unlike a secondary school of on average 70 to 80 teachers.

But for a particular group of Phase One secondaries, something had clearly happened to make the project work. Originally it had been intended to rate or rank what each of the schools in this group had achieved on a number of dimensions, such as the particular area of the project they had impacted most upon, or the phasing of the initiative in terms of which area of the project they had impacted upon first.

  But reading of the case study material that had been provided by schools (a three foot high pile!) suggested that differences between schools were less evident than a quite standard use of a technology of reducing WSV and raising VA that applied across all schools. It is with this that we deal here, looking at six areas of activity in these schools.

School ethos and culture

Attention to this was seen as critical across the group of schools, since attempting to do work upon WSV that necessarily involved collaboration, within an educational setting that did not foster it, would have been impossible, and possibly educationally dangerous. Schools specifically attempted to:

- start small but quickly scale up by either using one or two departments to start things off, or with one issue across all departments;
- use within school training events to build a coalition for support of the project;
- use re-titling (such as Departments becoming 'Attainment Teams') to symbolise change;
- use participation in project events and meetings with other schools in the project to build networks across individual schools that would give esteem to participating;
- using able, or aspirant, staff in schools as the pioneers, given that this would maximise the chance of success;
- use the national scale and potential international significance of the project to motivate participation;
- ensure very full provision of knowledge about the project within schools;
- use off site events that ensured staff were free from the 'furniture' of the school, given that WSV is part of any school furniture.

Data usage

The project did provide the group of schools with more data on their academic achievement outcomes in the value added format provided by the Fischer Family Trust, although many schools had been getting this data before. This data went to schools in both Spring 2005 and Spring 2006.

Additionally, some schools added further data from indicator systems that they heard of from other schools in the project. However, the great majority of schools sought to improve the *use* of existing data by more specifically developing it into useful management information that would benefit pupils and the school. This involved:

- encouraging the sharing of data between and within departments, and from any feeder schools;
- developing clarity about what data should be used for;
- monitoring at the point of outcomes, involving sampling pupils' work;
- using data to build a 'coalition for change' in the schools and to build morale through showing improvement;
- using data to track pupils against expectations;
- using data to identify the 'excellent' departments (and for that matter 'the less excellent') who could be used in whole school work;
- developing better systems of prediction of grades and performance, identification of grades and underperformance, etc.;
- analysing data at Year level in addition to cross-Year Departmental level, for all Years;
- collecting data on new areas in addition to that of academic achievement, such as pupil attitudes and valuing qualitative as well as quantitative data;
- more informed use of existing national data sources;
- collecting data from new constituencies (e.g. parents and employers).

Teaching and learning

The focus of the project upon a level closer to the classroom than that of the school clearly encouraged a focus on teaching and learning issues in these schools. This showed in:

- the development of high quality observational systems, used by peers with peers, that gathered high quality data on teaching behaviours, pupil behaviours, classroom processes, learning and the climate in different classrooms;
- encouraging pupils to feed back their opinions on their own learning-related issues as well as on their teaching;
- attempting to specify within and across subjects what might be the 'core' classroom related teacher behaviours;
- encouraging discussion of teaching in departments and across the school;

- attempting to enrich teaching through use of new curriculum developments;
- attempting greater consistency in teaching behaviours and especially in the expectations of pupils, within and across departments;
- encouraging, using effective 'lead' departments, the use of novel methods of teaching and learning;
- encouragement of a common language for the description of teaching and learning across departments;
- developing academic tutoring within pastoral teams.

Middle management training

Virtually every one of these secondary schools launched initiatives with their Departmental Heads. In most schools, these roles had been historically poorly resourced and indeed sometimes regarded as an infliction upon the people holding them rather than as a 'management' tier offering opportunity for personal and professional development. These initiatives were specifically:

- changing philosophy from being purely middle managers to being middle leaders;
- training of middle managers, particularly in areas such as coaching/mentoring, data usage, classroom observation, etc., not just using exceptional individuals as the models but using all middle managers on the sound basis that all had learned one good piece of professional practice to share;
- 'buddying' or 'matching' of middle managers with others specially chosen to permit transfer of skills, attitudes and behaviours rapidly;
- using exemplary middle managers in whole school training days;
- using key personnel – Heads of Department respected by the wider staff group – to start the ball rolling;
- extending the focus to Heads of Year, or Heads of House, and ensuring the same programmes were created for them as for Heads of Department;
- disaggregating data to subject level to permit fine-grained analysis;
- inspection of pupil performance and its variation across subjects.

Pupil voice

The involvement of pupils in furnishing data on learning in these schools is a further example of what happens when the 'lever' of the Department, or the individual teacher, or the pastoral/tutoring team is being addressed rather than that of the school, given the closeness of these levers to teaching and learning. Specific initiatives involved:

- greater involvement of pupils in planning for their future achievement;
- pupil-based surveys of learning styles;
- pupil-based surveys of teaching.

Standard operating procedures

As schools explored the variation in their gains across different Departments and Years shown by their use of data systems, and attempted to focus upon training of middle managers and their Departments, many of them moved towards tighter specification of systems, procedures and responses to pupil needs in an attempt to iron out WSV.

The experience of the work on data that most schools began with was that there was huge variation in what were regarded as the normal procedures in what happened to the data, what was meant by data-related words and indeed what 'data' was. Most schools used in-service sessions, based on a cascade from the Departments or parts of the pastoral structure that were exemplary in their use of data, to ensure that there was 'reliability' and 'consistency' in these issues and most schools gained remarkable improvements, with limited efforts and limited time. This encouraged a broader focus on other areas:

- on ensuring all Departments and Year Teams had consistency in other areas in their expectations and procedures;
- reducing the isolation of staff by promoting team approaches and networking;
- on ensuring at school level that there were clear expectations of what was expected from pupils in their commitment to school (e.g. timekeeping, bringing the right equipment, getting work in on time, ensuring work is properly presented).

The process of change

The description of the levers of change that the successful Phase One secondary schools employed should not delude us into thinking that getting these 'levers' in place was unproblematic. The process of change is a complex one, more complex within today's schools than at any other time in educational history because of the speed of technological change and the historic absence of any proven principles of managing educational change other than the simple. Our group of schools varied – rightly – in how they handled change in accordance with their own culture, context and catchment area.

But a number of clear principles of how to handle change in the complex, potentially fraught and delicate area of within school variation are clear:

- The introduction of WSV-related change requires a systematic 'audit' of individual schools' presenting cultures, organisational factors, past attempts (if any) to deal with the issue and indeed the present scale of WSV itself.
- Change should be contextually specific to each school, which will each have their own 'entry points' into the WSV area and issues. These could be micro (the issue of variation in coursework marking standards, say) or macro (Departmental/ Academic Year variation in pupil outcomes), according to context.

- The core issue in managing change is to hold on to the necessary collegiality which is needed to collaboratively generate change, whilst at the same time recognising the variation within schools by individuals and departments that is necessary to generate professional learning.
- Holding on to that collegiality, and maintaining enthusiasm for WSV activities, is best shown when *existing* training days and resources are utilised, rather than the imposition of an additional burden through special, additional sessions. Besides, the argument that WSV, and reducing it, is a 'core' mainstream issue can only be sustained if the training activities related to it are themselves 'mainstreamed' rather than 'bolted on'.
- Change may be bitty, messy and chaotic at first, and progress will come in bursts and fits and starts, but the vision of learning from WSV and not being afraid of it needs to be held on to. Only Headteachers and, to an extent, middle management leadership can do that.
- Clarity about what change related to WSV means is essential to avoid WSV-related issues being seen as part of general school improvement activities, when in fact they are anything but.
- Close attention needs to be given to ensuring schools possess a culture of openness, collaboration and collegiality *before* any WSV work is begun, given the sensitivity of the WSV issues.
- Whilst each school is different, there is much sense in beginning the WSV work by ensuring that data about WSV, of the highest quality, is available to begin the professional conversation within schools, and to identify the sources of strength to be benchmarked against.
- Relatedly, WSV needs to be seen as a programme of interacting factors and not a series of unconnected 'one offs'. This necessitates more than badging and labelling of activities to get professional support and understanding, and requires a level of conceptual understanding within the senior management of schools getting into WSV.
- School underachievement may be the 'peg' on which WSV can be hung in many schools but in schools which are already overachieving, other hooks (accelerated learning for example) may be needed.
- Schools are likely to need multiple sources of support from external agencies (other schools, Higher Education, local authorities) to enable WSV initiatives to take place successfully, given their novelty.
- In an area where our knowledge of what to do is still incomplete, 'short cycle innovation' that involves a large number of initiatives that are tested, and destructed if necessary, should be used, involving prior thinking, action evaluation of results and re-design in cycles of months rather than years.

Conclusions and policy implications

Overall, much was learned within the WSV Project that can act as a foundation for further work in this area. We now have a 'toolkit' of successful approaches to learning from WSV that could be used by all schools. It is important that the work of the primary schools in the project is better understood and that the experience of Phase Two schools is also charted in detail so that knowledge can be further advanced as these schools participate for as long as Phase One schools did. It is also important that wide dissemination of our results is undertaken to a number of constituencies:

- to policymakers, who will be interested in the relevance of WSV work to the personalisation agenda, itself disaggregating pupils' within-school experience substantially;
- to practitioners, who will be interested in the examples of practices that appear to be associated with 'raising the bar' and 'reducing the range'.

In conclusion, what we have found was that across all our schools any reduction in WSV is linked with an improvement in VA, so schools embarking on the journey of reducing WSV can be certain that it will be productive of results. We also found a group of secondary schools that, in three years, had developed approaches which, judged by their data viewed overall, were impacting upon VA and WSV successfully. For a group of schools resourced by only additional resources of £1,500 per school per year, on top of whatever they and Leadership Network were able to contribute in time and in kind as it were, this was an extraordinarily valuable achievement, of national and international significance.

The 'micro-level' educational policy implications of the work are important for practice in that:

- while it might not be possible to have policies for what happens in individual classrooms, this might be feasible at the subject Departmental level or Academic Year level in a secondary school or the 'Year' level in a primary school. Targeting these means that policy can get far closer to what ought to be the real focus, the classroom level, than if it only addresses the school level;
- while not every school is effective, all schools will have within themselves some practice that is relatively more effective than elsewhere in the school. Every school can therefore look for generally applicable good practice from within its own internal conditions;
- it might well be that one limitation to whole-school self-evaluation and improvement is that Headteachers are often overloaded, because of having to deal with problems that should fall to middle managers and so lack the time to think strategically. Targeting sub-groups within the school could get round that;
- within-school units of policy intervention such as years or subjects are smaller and, therefore, potentially more open to being changed than those at 'whole school' level;
- teachers in general, and those teachers in less effective schools in particular, seem to be more influenced by classroom-based policies that are close to their focal concerns of teaching and curriculum and less by policies that are 'managerial' and orientated to the school level.

The WSV Project hopefully moves us closer to a world where no school needs to wait for another school to help it out, since it can help itself by looking at its own best people and learning from them. This world is one where a school's Departments and teachers cannot use excuses such as 'it's the pupils' for their performance, since they have generally the same pupils. This world is one where excellence is regarded not as something to be hidden, but something to be learned from, for the benefit of all. This world could be attained, quickly.

More generally, the work on WSV has 'macro-level' implications both for educational policies and for public policy reform. In the case of educational policies, the last decades have seen a number of attempts to improve schools through different kinds of programmes. Firstly, there was the influence of the school effectiveness movement in the 1990s, which provided to practitioners in schools the famous checklists of eight, ten, fifteen or twenty things that the 'effective' or 'high added value' schools do, from having effective management to generating a climate of high expectations.

This phase, although useful, had a number of limitations, though. It was based upon giving schools, from outside as it were, ideas about what to do and there was subsequently no 'ownership' by the school and its teachers. And as more and more schools now do what the knowledge suggests they should be doing – from ensuring the entrance hall displays the details of the languages spoken in the school to ensuring that there are formal organisational structures to involve parents – the prospects of any future 'return' on further concern with these issues is limited.

The next two phases of educational reform were limited in their effectiveness too. The specification of what schools should be doing by the State – in the prescriptive practices outlined in the Literacy, Numeracy and Secondary strategies – gives perhaps a short-term boost to teaching skills and test scores, but does not provide for the long term development of the profession. The use of 'school to school' methods is likewise probably not in the long term hugely powerful – schools can be geographically far apart, are often psychologically distant from each other, with different cultures, and often used to employing excuses as to why they shouldn't take up the methods of operation of the school down the road ('they would say that with their catchment area, wouldn't they!').

Likewise, the potential for networking between schools, school federations and the like is probably slightly difficult to deliver if schools are competing against each other in educational markets.

However, no one would suggest that 'school to school' is not useful. At the level of subject specialisms, contact between departments in the same subject in different schools can be really powerful, indeed sometimes transformative. And there are many examples of schools picking up useful ideas they would not have thought of themselves from their collaborations with other schools.

Within school variation is very much the new child on the block that may – or may not – develop into producing its own 'phase'. Perhaps it might be sensible to propose a continuation of 'school-to-school' to give subject support in secondary schools at the same time as schools start investigating their own conditions internally. Perhaps there is a case for differentiated models whereby some schools begin with WSV, some with school-to-school collaboration and some do both at once right from the start, the precise 'mix' and 'phasing' to depend on the particular state that individual schools are at.

At the very least, it would be sensible to see if WSV might, with profit, influence national publication of information upon schools' results, with perhaps a 'dispersal' or 'range' measure being introduced alongside the customary measures, which would be applied to the GCSE 3 subject 'core' and at other stages as appropriate. Further promotion of WSV activities could move beyond this, to generation of toolkits to enable schools to focus on the issues, and learn constructively.

More generally, there may be lessons from the WSV Project for the direction of public sector reform. This has involved a focus upon trying to improve service delivery through improved pre-service, initial training across many professions, but has been less sure-footed when it comes to maximising knowledge transfer of 'good practice' subsequently.

Organisation-to-organisation transfer is thought to have been maximised by varying the external contingencies within which state welfare works, as with the use of the private sector to lever up standards in the public sector, or the use of performance information and public choice to expose poor performance.

Yet while such policies may encourage welfare organisations and professionals to work *harder*, they may not generate *smarter* working unless the persons and organisations have more effective 'technologies of practice' as it were on which to draw. Getting *these* to move between schools, or hospitals, or prisons when all organisations have relatively impermeable cultures, boundaries and defences is the problem.

Fortunately, we now are beginning to have the understandings of how to achieve *smarter* working. It involves resourcing organisations with performance data on their sub-units or individuals to enable benchmarking against their best people. It involves systematic attempts to transfer knowledge between professionals at the point of impact of the individual concerned upon service delivery, the front line as it were. It involves making available to individuals and organisations the 'fundamental' knowledge of good practice that has accumulated since their pre-service education, using the IT systems that now make this much easier than before.

It involves charting the views of consumers directly, gathered at the point of service delivery. And finally, it involves attempting to *use* the naturally occurring variation that exists within organisations for the benefit of the organisation's effectiveness by not sweeping it under the carpet, but by creating an engine of improvement that operates independently of outside organisations.

That 'engine' can operate at local level, within each organisation and within each workforce, without any need for national 'top-down' strategies that dis-empower. It may just be the 'wave' or 'phase' of the future to restore disappointed hopes of public sector reform.

Acknowledgement

First published in an extended version as *Schools Learning From Their Best – The Within School Variation (WSV) Project*. National College for School Leadership (2007) Nottingham: NCSL. Reprinted here with permission from NCSL.

13

The future agenda for school effectiveness research

Introduction

Several authors have speculated upon the future of school effectiveness research (e.g. Bosker and Scheerens, 1997; Good and Brophy, 1986; Mortimore, 1991; Reynolds and Cuttance, 1992; Teddlie and Stringfield, 1993) over the past decade. However, due to rapid developments in the field, in terms of both methodology and substantive findings, the areas identified as in need of further research ten years ago or even five years ago either are no longer relevant, or have been significantly reconceptualised.

The following chapter contains a summary of eleven issues that we have identified as being on the 'cutting edge' of school effectiveness research as we approach the twenty-first century. These issues emerged as we reviewed the substantial body of the world's research findings presented in the previous eleven chapters of this Handbook. Some of these issues are simply embodiments of repetitive themes in the literature (e.g. the need for multiple outcome measures to judge school effects and the importance of context issues), while others have only emerged in the past one or two years (e.g. the study of the relational aspects of schooling and the study of the possibly additive effects of school and family).

Before examining each of these issues, we will briefly review some criticisms of SER and speculate on the general health of the field.

The current criticisms of SER

It has been somewhat fashionable in certain educational circles to criticise SER, with assaults being launched on the earliest work (e.g. Acton, 1980; Cuttance, 1982; Goldstein, 1980; Musgrove, 1981; Ralph and Fennessey, 1983; Rowan, 1984; Rowan, Bossert and Dwyer, 1983) and through to the present (e.g. Elliott, 1996). The reasons for these criticisms have been part political, part methodological and part theoretical.

SER will always be politically controversial, since it concerns 'the nature and purposes of schooling' (e.g. Elliott, 1996), but it is interesting that SER has been criticised politically on contradictory grounds. For instance, much of the scathing early criticism of effective schools research in the USA (e.g. Ralph and Fennessey, 1983; Rowan, 1984) concerned the researchers' embrace of well defined political goals (i.e. equity in schooling outcomes for the disadvantaged and ethnic minorities), which critics believed blocked the researchers' use of appropriate scientific research methods. Critics believed that these effective schools' researchers were liberal reformers more interested in improving the lot of the children of the poor than in conducting good science.

In the UK, on the other hand, much recent criticism (e.g. Elliott, 1996) of SER has come from 'progressive' educators. These critics portray SER as being underpinned by an ideology of social control and SER researchers as having an overly 'mechanistic' view of the organisation of educational processes. Critics from the UK perceive SER as giving credence and legitimisation to a conservative ideology. As Elliott stated:

> The findings of school effectiveness research have indeed been music in the ears of politicians and government officials. Currently, for example, they are being used to politically justify a refusal to respond to teachers' anxieties about the increasing size of the classes that they teach, the use of traditional teaching methods, such as whole class instruction, and a tendency to blame headteachers for 'failing schools' on the grounds that they lack a capacity for strong leadership.
>
> (1996, p. 199)

Political criticism is probably always going to be a part of the literature associated with SER. It seems safe to conclude that as long as the researchers in the field are accused at the same time of supporting *both* conservative *and* liberal causes, these criticisms can be accepted as simply an unwarranted part of the territory in which we work.

Methodological criticisms have been a part of SER since its beginnings. Much of the history of SER, as outlined in Chapter 1, has been a reaction to these methodological criticisms. With the advent of the methodological advances described in Chapter 3, many of these criticisms have now become muted. In fact, a sign of the health of the field is that we now have a set of generally agreed prescriptions for conducting methodologically correct studies, including the following:

- School effects studies should be designed to tap sufficient 'natural variance' in school and classroom characteristics.
- School effects studies should have units of analysis (child, class, school) that allow for data analysis with sufficient discriminative power.
- School effects studies should use adequate operationalisations and measures of the school and classroom process variables, preferably including direct observations of process variables, and a mixture of quantitative and qualitative approaches.
- School effects studies should use adequate techniques for data analysis, which involves multilevel models in most cases.
- School effects studies should use longitudinal cohort-based data, collected on individual children.
- School effects studies should adequately adjust outcome measures for any intake differences between schools.

Not only do we now know how to design methodologically correct studies, we also know how to conduct the kind of studies that will be more likely to demonstrate relatively larger school effects. Based on our review of the literature from Chapters 3 and 5, we can conclude, in general, that school effects will be *larger* in SER studies:

- that involve a variety of socio-economic status (SES) contexts, rather than a sample of schools with homogeneous student SES backgrounds;
- that examine the elementary (or junior) school level;
- that examine schools from a wide variety of community types and in which types of community truly vary among themselves;
- that examine schools that have more control of their academic operations;
- from a country that has more variance in its educational system processes;
- that use mathematics as the dependent variable; and
- that involve the gathering of process variables that relate to measures of teachers' behaviour rather than their other attributes.

Similarly, we can conclude that school effects will be *smaller* in studies of schools:

- that have similar SES contexts;
- that examine the secondary level;
- that examine community types that are homogeneous in terms of economics, economic structure and culture;
- that have less control of their academic operations;
- from a country that has less variance in its educational system factors;
- that use reading as the dependent variable; and
- that do not involve the gathering of process variables such as in-class measures of teacher behaviour.

SER has also been criticised as having little or no theoretical basis. This criticism still has some validity, but evidence presented in Chapter 10 indicates that researchers and theoreticians are busily working to address this perennial problem and appear to be making some headway, at least in terms of the development of heuristic midrange theories, and in the illumination of some of the possible theoretical explanations between various school and classroom factors, by interrogating existing studies with the predictions of 'meta' or 'grand' theories such as contingency theory or public choice theory (e.g. Scheerens and Bosker, 1997).

We now move beyond issues of criticism, and responses to our eleven 'cutting edge' areas where the future of the discipline lies:

* the need for multiple outcome measures in SER;
* the need for the study of the third relational dimension of school (relationship patterns);
* the need to expand the study of context variables;
* the need to analyse range within schools and classrooms;
* the need to study the possibly additive nature of school and family;
* the need to explore the interface between levels in schooling;
* the need to study naturally occurring experiments;
* the need to expand variation at the school level;
* the need to study school failure/dysfunctionality;
* the need to recognise the salience of issues to do with curriculum and assessment;
* the benefits of multilevel structural equation modelling.

The need for multiple outcomes measures in SER

This issue has been discussed by many since the 1970s (e.g. Good and Brophy, 1986; Levine and Lezotte, 1990; Rutter, 1983; Rutter et al., 1979; Sammons, Mortimore and Thomas, 1996), with most commenting that multiple criteria for school effectiveness are needed. Critics have noted that schools may *not* have consistent effects across different criteria, and that to use one criterion (typically academic achievement) is not adequate for ascertaining the true effectiveness status of a school. This issue was discussed in Chapter 3 under the scientific properties of consistency and differential effectiveness. It is also now widely recognised that multiple outcomes force the development of more sensitive explorations than are likely with restructured measures, since the pattern of why school and teacher factors are associated with some outcomes but not others (as in Mortimore et al., 1988 for example) is exactly the kind of scientific dissonance that is needed for creative theorising.

Within the past decade, researchers have been making progress in this area as follows:

* More sophisticated studies of consistency across different achievement scores have emerged, especially from the USA (e.g. Crone et al., 1994; Crone and Teddlie, 1995; Lang, 1991; Lang, Teddlie and Oescher, 1992; Teddlie, Lang and Oescher, 1995). These studies have utilised more statistically appropriate measures of consistency across achievement scores (e.g. kappa coefficients), have

compared consistency ratings generated by composite and by component scores and have compared consistency ratings across very different types of academic achievement tests (e.g. criterion-referenced tests versus norm-referenced tests, or different public examination boards in the United Kingdom).

- Studies from the UK have continued to compare different criteria for school effectiveness beyond academic achievement scores. These comparisons have included academic versus affective/social, different measures of attitudes, different measures of behaviour and different measures of self-concept (Sammons, Thomas and Mortimore, 1996).

- Recent research utilising composite academic achievement scores have yielded higher estimates of consistency, thus indicating the value of constructing such scores (e.g. Crone et al., 1994; Crone and Teddlie, 1995). Additionally, Kochan, Tashakkori and Teddlie (1996) have explored the use of composite scores measuring student participation rates (including student attendance, drop-out and suspension data) at the high school level in the USA. Results from a comparison of two composite school effectiveness indices from this study (one based on academic achievement scores and the other on student participation rates) indicated moderate agreement between them (Kochan, Tashakkori and Teddlie, 1996).

- Teddlie and Stringfield (1993, p. 84–85) utilised a matrix approach to classifying schools in a longitudinal study of school effects. In this study, seven different indicators of school effectiveness (two concerning academic achievement, four behavioural and one attitudinal) were compared to determine the current effectiveness status of matched pairs of schools that were being studied longitudinally. The resulting classification of school effectiveness status was multidimensional, involving achievement, behavioural and attitudinal SEIs.

These results point the way toward designing SER that utilises multiple criteria in the determination of school effectiveness status. Guidelines as to 'good practice' include the following:

- Use varied measures of the effectiveness of schooling, including academic achievement, attitudes (toward self, and towards others), and behaviour.
- Use measures that are sensitive to the mission of schools in the twenty-first century. For instance, measures of perceived racism may be important indicators of the effectiveness of schooling in some contexts (e.g. Fitz-Gibbon, 1996). Equal opportunities concerns are important in schools in many countries, yet equal opportunities orientated behaviours and attitudes are rarely used to assess school effectiveness. 'Learning to learn' or 'knowledge acquisition' skills are widely argued to be essential in the information age, yet the achievement tests used continue to emphasise student ability to recapitulate existing knowledge.
- Use composite variables where possible, since they present a better overall picture of a school's effectiveness.
- Use where possible multidimensional matrices to assess the effectiveness of schools.

- Use measures of student behaviour wherever possible, since it is behaviours that are likely to be crucial in determining the nature of the future society that young people inhabit.

The need for study of the third dimension of schooling (relationship patterns)

A new area of study has emerged in SER over the past few years: the study of the relationship patterns that exist within staff and within student groups. This relational component constitutes the third dimension of schooling, joining the more frequently studied organisational and cultural components (Reynolds and Packer, 1992). There are three reasons why the relational component of schooling has *not* been featured much in SER until now:

- The relational patterns of faculties and teachers of students are difficult to measure, since questionnaires and interviews regarding school relationships may constitute 'reactive' instruments susceptible to socially desirable responses (e.g. Webb *et al.*, 1981). By contrast, sociograms are relatively non-reactive instruments designed to measure the social structure of a group and to assess the social status of each individual in the group (e.g. Borg and Gall, 1989; Moreno, 1953). The study of Teddlie and Kochan (1991) was the first within SER to use sociograms to assess the types of relationships that exist among faculty members, although, of course, many researchers have used sociograms to measure student peer relationships in classes and schools (e.g. Asher and Dodge, 1986; Tyne and Geary, 1980), including individuals working within the SER paradigm (e.g. Reynolds, 1976a; Reynolds, Sullivan and Murgatroyd, 1987). It is also important to note that in many cultures (such as probably the Netherlands, Scandinavia and the countries of the Pacific Rim) it would be regarded as an unwarranted intrusion into aspects of teachers' lives to even ask them the sorts of questions that are needed to evoke analysable data (e.g. 'Which three of your colleagues would you approach for help if you had a professional problem?').
- The interpersonal relations of teachers and of students has been difficult to conceptualise and analyse due to the complexity of interactions within such social groups. The analytic technique that has been used in the handful of studies in the area is network analysis, utilising data gleaned from the administration of sociograms to staff members. Social network analysis is a relatively new field, begun in the late 1970s and early 1980s (e.g. Rogers and Kincaid, 1980) that appears to provide the requisite analytical and modelling tools for analysing school generated sociograms. The recent work of Durland (e.g. Durland, 1996; Durland and Teddlie, 1996) is the first in SER to utilise network analysis to model and analyse data from sociograms administered to faculty members in schools.
- There is a common perception that interpersonal relations within a school, especially among staff members, are very difficult to change, so researchers in

the school improvement area have not been particularly interested in studying these patterns of relationships until recently.

The recent realisation of the importance of the relational dimension, especially in the case of interpersonal relations among staff members (Reynolds, 1991, 1996a; Reynolds and Packer, 1992), has been due to three factors:

- Empirical work in the USA noted above (e.g. Durland, 1996; Durland and Teddlie, 1996; Teddlie and Kochan, 1991) that has successfully linked the effectiveness levels of schools with their different patterns of interpersonal relations among staff members.
- More speculative work done in both the school effectiveness and the school improvement traditions in the UK and the USA that has linked ineffective schools with the presence of dysfunctional relations among staff members (e.g. Reynolds and Packer, 1992; Stoll, 1995; Stoll, Myers and Reynolds, 1996; Stoll and Fink, 1996; Teddlie and Stringfield, 1993). Reynolds (1996b) has characterised these 'grossly dysfunctional relationships' in such schools as follows:

  The presence of numerous personality clashes, feuds, personal agendas and fractured interpersonal relationships within the staff group, which operate . . . to make rational decision-making a very difficult process.

  (p. 154)

  These dysfunctional relationships arise through the unique social-psychological history of the school (Teddlie and Stringfield, 1993) and have a tendency to continue unless drastic changes (planned or not) occur. Often these relationships manifest themselves in the generation of sharply delineated subcultures (Stoll and Fink, 1996) or cliques within the school.
- Some of those in the school improvement tradition have found that the existence of relational 'shadows' or 'ghosts' of the past has had a considerable influence in affecting the progress of attempts at staff professional development (Hopkins, Ainscow and West, 1994).

Recent interesting work in this field has been done by Durland and Teddlie (1996), who posit the Centrality-Cohesiveness Model of Differentially Effective Schools, which was briefly described in Chapter 11. This model postulates that differentially effective schools can be distinguished by how cohesive the faculty is (measured in network analysis as network density) and how central the principal (or surrogate) is within the organisation (measured by group centralisation, or betweenness centralisation in network analysis terminology).

Sociograms generated by network analysis can be utilised to detect the presence of cliques, such as those that occur in dysfunctional schools. Durland and Teddlie (1996) have presented some suggestive preliminary results utilising network analysis to analyse the differences between effective (described as 'well webbed') and ineffective (characterised by cliques and/or 'stringy' structures) schools, but this area of research is obviously still in its infancy.

If relational patterns do relate to effectiveness levels, then clearly they require more intensive study, particularly since school improvement is likely to have to influence these factors as well as school organisation and culture if schools are to be changed.

Further research in this area could develop in several ways:

- More work needs to be done on more refined descriptions of effective and ineffective schools in terms of sociometric indices and sociograms. Hopefully, this work will lead us to sets of prototypical sociometric indices and sociograms for differentially effective schools.
- Longitudinal studies of sociometric indices and sociograms should prove useful in describing how social relations change over time (e.g. setting the sociograms in 'motion' over time) and whether or not those changes are associated with changes in effectiveness status.
- Sociometric indices and sociograms should also be developed for students within classrooms. These data may be considered as additional school effectiveness indicators, if one assumes that effective schools should be fostering positive relationships among students. It may also be that there are different *student* relational patterns in more effective classes and schools than in less effective.

The need to expand the study of context variables

The introduction of context variables into SER has had a large impact on all three strands within the field (school effects, effective schools, school improvement), as described earlier in Chapter 5. The consideration of contextual variation in SER has also led to increased sophistication in theory development (e.g. Creemers and Scheerens, 1994; Scheerens, 1992, 1993; Scheerens and Creemers, 1989; Slater and Teddlie, 1992; Wimpelberg, Teddlie and Stringfield, 1989) as theorists have explicitly taken into account the impact that different levels of a context variable can have on school effects and processes associated with them. These contextually 'sensitive' theories of school effectiveness have incorporated tenets of contingency theory (e.g. Mintzberg, 1979; Owens, 1987) as a framework from which to interpret results from SER.

Contingency theory purports to explain why certain school effectiveness variables 'travel' across levels of context, while others do not. For instance, the failure of the well known principal leadership effect on student achievement in the Netherlands (e.g. van de Grift, 1989, 1990) is a good illustration of a school effectiveness variable that did not 'travel' from one country to another due to the differences in country contexts.

The study of context in SER is also beginning to have an impact on theories of school improvement, because school improvers realise now that there aren't 'silver bullets' that always lead to school improvement. Instead, as we noted in Chapter 7, contextually sensitive models for school improvement with 'multiple levers' have emerged as studies have demonstrated that what works to change processes can vary to a large degree by context factors such as SES of catchment area, school effectiveness level or schools improvement 'trend line'.

Our review in Chapter 5 indicates that several context variables (i.e. SES of student body, community type, grade phase, and governance structure) have a 'main effect' upon school effects and the processes that accompany them. Perhaps even more interesting, however, are the 'interactions' between context variables that have emerged periodically in the literature, including the following:

- *Community type by school size*: Hannaway and Talbert (1993) reported that school size had a positive effect on teacher community in suburban schools and a negative effect on teacher community in urban schools: as the size of school increased in suburban schools, so did indicators of a positive teacher community, whereas when size of school increased in urban schools, indicators of a positive teacher community decreased.
- *Community type by country*: An interaction also appears to be occurring between country and community type across some of the USA and UK studies. Community type does not play as significant a contextual role in the UK as it does in the USA, primarily because there is less variance in the UK on this variable. Rural schools in the UK are generally closer geographically and culturally to urban areas than they are in the USA, and this mitigates the effect of the community type variable in the UK.

While the impact of context variables in SER is now well established, there are several research areas where additional work would be useful:

- The variation in context should be expanded by the enhanced use of 'nation' as a context variable. However, the enhanced range of educational factors and cultural contexts that this produces may be potentially damaging if study leads to the simplistic, direct import of 'what works' without analysis of cultural differences. The study of the interaction between context variables is clearly of considerable importance.
- Researchers should enhance the variation in context factors where possible. Considering international studies, it would be very beneficial to have more developing societies in comparative studies of SER. It would be interesting to determine the magnitude of school effects for these countries compared to First World countries using a common methodology, and it would be also interesting to expand further our knowledge of the 'context specificity' of effectiveness factors that was mentioned in Chapter 1.
- Other, new context variables should be added to SER designs. For instance, the region of a country could have a large impact in some countries. In the USA, for instance, it could be argued that school effects and the processes associated with them may be quite different in the North-east, the Midwest, the South, and the West. In the UK, there are considerable historical differences and cultural differences between regions, such as the tradition of sons following their fathers into mining or industrial employment in the North-east, compared with

the Welsh tradition of encouraging the 'escape' of children from the prospects of such employment, both of which differential contextual responses to disadvantage could be argued to have considerable implications for 'what works' within schools. Another example concerns grade level: pre-school and college could be added as additional levels of this context variable.

- In general, as the study of context in SER matures, there should be more levels of the context variables and more range across the variables.

The need to analyse range within schools and classrooms

There are some interesting hints in the recent literature that the *range* or variation in school and teacher factors may be important determinants of outcomes and effectiveness additionally to the *average* levels scored on the factors themselves. The Louisiana School Effectiveness Studies mentioned earlier in this Handbook noted the reduced range evident in effective schools and in their teachers' within lesson behaviours (Teddlie and Stringfield, 1993), as did the study of Crone and Teddlie (1995). (See Table 13.1.)

The International School Effectiveness Research Project (ISERP) (Creemers *et al.*, 1996; Reynolds *et al.*, 2002) also found both that successful and educationally effective countries possessed a more homogeneous set of teachers and schools, and that effective schools in all of the nine countries participating evidenced predictability and consistency in their organisational processes both over time and between organisational members at a point in time. Interesting speculations about consistency, constancy and cohesion, and the power of these factors to socially control young people, have been offered by Creemers (1994) and Reynolds (1996a). In a similar way, Murphy (1992) has talked about the symbolic, cultural and organisational 'tightness' of effective school organisations and, by implication, the looseness and range of ineffective organisations.

And from school improvement, as we noted in Chapter 7, has come a recognition that reliability or fidelity of implementation (i.e. lack of range) is necessary to ensure improved educational outcomes from school improvement programmes. Indeed, the growing recognition that school improvement can generate enhanced range (and lower its potential effectiveness) because the educational ceiling of competent persons/schools improves much faster than the floor of less competent persons/schools, seems to be a powerful face valid exploration for the consistently disappointing effects of school improvement that has been unconcerned with 'range', viewing it as a necessary part of teacher professional development.

Such ideas are not surprising – the literature upon family socialisation has always indicated parental consistency in rule enforcement as of crucial importance to healthy child development, and erratic and inconsistent discipline, role enforcement and goal setting has long been seen as a cause of disturbed and dysfunctional individual behaviour.

It is arguable, though, that the influence of the range of school and teacher factors may have become more important of late, since many of the more historically

Table 13.1 Comparison of variance in scores on teacher behaviour for effective versus ineffective schools

Teachers in effective schools (n=25)

Variable	Lowest score	Highest score	Range	Coefficient of variation
Time-on-task (interactive)	0.15	0.85	0.71	31.22
Time-on-task (overall)	0.55	0.90	0.36	10.39
Management	2.37	5.00	2.64	11.78
Instruction 1	2.74	4.61	1.88	12.28
Instruction 2	2.75	4.88	2.14	12.42
Climate 1	2.60	4.90	2.31	12.71
Climate 2	2.33	5.00	2.68	17.88

Teaching in ineffective schools (n=30)

Variable	Lowest score	Highest score	Range	Coefficient of variation
Time-on-task (interactive)	0.08	0.75	0.68	34.45
Time-on-task (overall)	0.48	0.96	0.49	19.01
Management	2.10	4.60	2.51	18.86
Instruction 1	1.28	4.30	3.03	23.74
Instruction 2	1.38	4.38	3.01	22.04
Climate 1	2.30	4.80	2.51	16.97
Climate 2	1.50	4.67	3.18	22.07

Note

The coefficient of variation is computed by dividing the standard deviation by the mean and multiplying by 100.

Source: Crone and Teddlie, 1995.

consistent influences upon child development such as the family, the community, the mass media and the wider society have all become more heterogeneous and varied. The past possibility that inconsistent schooling, with a wide range in goals and means, might have been outweighed in any possible negative influences by consistency emanating from non-educational sources seems to have been reduced by social changes of the last 30 years.

All this suggests that we need further research to establish the importance of 'range', 'variance' and variation in such areas as:

- teacher behaviours in lessons, looking at differences between teachers at a point in time, and at individual teacher consistency over time;
- the goals of education as perceived and practised by school members;
- consistency in the relationship between classroom factors, school factors, district level factors and societal factors.

Ensuring that SER always presents the standard deviations for all variables (and other measures of variation), as well as the more conventionally used means, would seem to be axiomatic if these speculations are to be further developed.

The need to study the possibly additive nature of school and family

There are now a number of datasets across a variety of national contexts which suggest that family background and school quality may be related, with consequent considerable importance both for children affected and for educational policy in general. Work in London by Mortimore and Byford (1981), in Sweden by Grosin (1993) and in the United States by Teddlie (1996) shows that even after one has controlled out the effects of individual pupil background factors and/or achievement levels, there is a tendency for schools in low SES areas to do worse than one would have predicted and for schools in middle class areas to do better. Particularly marked is the existence of a group of schools 'below the regression line' in disadvantaged communities, even though such schools have often been the source of additional financial resources to help them improve and even though they have often attracted considerable attention from educational reformers.

What may be happening, then, is that school and home have additive effects, a possibility also suggested by an intriguing study of male delinquency by Farrington (1980), in which schools acted to increase the levels of delinquency when the prediction was already for a high rate, and to lower it below prediction when that prediction was for a low rate. From within recent writing on dysfunctional schools noted earlier (Reynolds, 1991, 1996b; Stoll, Myers and Reynolds, 1996) has also come an appreciation of the depth of problems that schools in this category can face, an appreciation now increasingly shared by those school improvers who are attempting to unravel the complexities of such schools (Hopkins, 1996).

The 'additive' idea is an important one, since it might explain that most persistent finding of all post-war educational reform attempts – that social class inequality in access to educational qualifications has been largely unchanged by educational 'improvement' on both quantity and quality dimensions. It also integrates two literatures which have appeared to be at cross purposes, much to the detriment of the mutual understanding of the scholars working in the two fields – that from the sociology of education, which stresses the influence of social structure, and that from school effectiveness, which stresses the independent effects of schools. Schools do make a difference in this formulation, but that difference acts to reinforce pre-existing differences in the structure of society.

We still need to know, of course, why there is this tendency for the less effective schools to be in more disadvantaged areas. Differential quality in schools' teacher supply may be a factor, given the likelihood of a greater number of applications for jobs going to schools in advantaged areas. The 'drift' of good people to more socially advantaged settings, offering expanding job prospects because of population growth and a less stressful environment, may also be a factor, as may the tendency for high stress situations such as the education of the disadvantaged to find 'flaws' and 'weaknesses' in organisational arrangements and personnel that would not occur in the absence of the 'stressors' that are associated with disadvantage.

The need to explore the interface between levels in schooling

The recent popularity of multilevel methodology has clearly created a need for reconceptualisation of the process data that has historically been collected, since the use of the individual, class, school and potentially outside school factors (such as district or even possibly country) has clearly created multiple levels where formerly in the early years of SER there was only one (a group of pupils generating a school mean).

At present, we have very little understanding of the 'interactions' or 'transactions' between levels, either at the more commonly used focus of classrooms nested in schools (class/school) or the more rarely used schools nested in districts (school/district), although Scheerens and Bosker (1997) have begun to explore this issue. The growing recognition of the importance of 'range' or variation noted above propels us urgently in this direction also, given that the management interface between school and classroom generates enormous variation in classroom effectiveness in some settings, but not in others (e.g. Teddlie and Stringfield, 1993).

What might the focus of investigation be, for example, of the classroom/school interface? Possible areas of interest might include:

- the selection of teachers;
- monitoring of the teachers' performance by the principal (at the school level);
- the schools' use of mechanisms to ensure homogeneity of teachers' goal orientation;
- the use made of performance data to detect 'unusual' or 'outlier' teacher performance;
- the constancy of personnel at the two levels, and the relational patterns between them.

Other interactions take place at other levels, with perhaps the interaction between the school and the District level being of considerable importance. Areas of interest here include:

- school variation in what is evoked from district level advisers, inspectors and personnel;
- district differential allocation of staff to different schools (in the case of schools in the USA where this is a possibility);

The pupil/class interface would also be an interesting one to explore further, with interesting areas here including:

- the extent to which there are well managed transitions between teachers across grades/years;
- the coordination of various distinctive pupil level programmes for children with special needs perhaps, or for children of high ability.

The need to study naturally occurring experiments

All societies, and perhaps especially Anglo-Saxon ones, currently show considerable experimentation with their educational systems, involving both national macro level policy changes and more micro level classroom and school changes in organisation, curriculum, governance, assessment and much else.

Experimental studies have, of course, considerable advantages for the study of school effectiveness, with the methodological 'gold standard' (Fitz-Gibbon, 1996) being the random allocation of some educational factor to a 'treatment' group of children and the use of other children as an untouched 'control'. However, various considerations have greatly held back the utilisation of experiments, namely:

- ethical problems concerning the difficulty of denying any control group the factors that were being given to some children in the 'treatment' group;
- contamination between the experimental and the control groups if the random allocation is within a school, or if the schools being used are geographically close together in a district.

The use then of experiments of nature could be of considerable potential use within the field since this involves the utilisation of *already existing* experiments to generate knowledge, with schools or classes or children that are being given educational factors being studied by contrast with those similar schools or classes or children that are not being given the educational novelties. If the groups compared are similar in the background factors that may affect educational outcomes, then any differences in educational outcomes can be attributed to the effects of educational factors.

This method has the benefit of avoiding (by the separating out of home and school effects) the problems of multicollinearity that we noted in Chapter 3 have bedevilled the field since its inception, given the well researched tendency for more able children to be educated in more highly performing schools. Inevitably the study of experiments of nature is likely to involve a long-term and often cohort-based design, given the tendency of the experiments to be long term themselves.

However, the problems involved in utilisation of this methodology of educational research cannot be overlooked either – experiments of nature are sometimes themselves changed over time, and are sometimes taking place where *multiple* factors are changing, as is the case currently with educational reform in Britain that involves teacher training, school organisation, school curriculum and teaching methods. Attempting to unravel the effects of some of the component parts of the 'experiment' from the general effects of the experiments may be difficult, and in the long term the problem of multicollinearity may return, given that the already advantaged students from already advantaged homes often seem able to find the schools that are showing the most promise in their utilisation of new programmes.

However, the considerable advantages offered by experiments of nature to generate a more rigorous and robust knowledge base in SER seem to heavily outweigh any disadvantages. We would hope that SER researchers would be increasingly drawn to the 'quasi experiment', particularly since virtually all countries are conducting multiple experiments of nature at the present time and are thereby providing multiple opportunities for study (e.g. Cook and Campbell, 1979).

The need to expand variation at the school level

Everything that we have read in our field is strongly suggestive of the view that the 'class' level or 'learning level' is a more powerful influence over children's levels of development and their rate of development than the 'school' level, which is in turn a more powerful level than that of the District or Local Education Authority (see Chapter 3). Until the development of various forms of multilevel methodology, variance at the classroom level was 'hidden', by the exclusive use of school level 'averages'. Now the classroom variance within schools is clearly exposed. As Stringfield (1994) rather nicely puts it, 'Children don't learn at the Principal's knee – they learn in classrooms', although if one examined SER historically one would see much greater concentration upon the Principal's knee than the classroom context. The teacher and classroom are the 'proximal variables'.

We have been insistent throughout this Handbook, however, on the need to continue and develop the study of the school. The school and its processes are the unit of policy analysis and of policy intervention, as discussed in Chapter 4. Schools have their own effects separate from those of classrooms or departments. School influence at the level of 'culture' or 'ethos' is more than the influence of the summation of their component parts, as Rutter *et al.* (1979) originally noted.

Part of the reason for the inability of researchers to show much 'strength' or 'power' at school level has been that they have been operating with highly constricted variance in the 'school' factor itself, since samples have been taken from within countries and cultures that already possess schools that are quite similar because of the influence of national traditions. As an example, British schools for the primary age range vary from the smallest of perhaps 15 pupils to the largest of perhaps 750 pupils, so within Britain sampling will generate a range. However, in Taiwan the smallest schools (in the rural areas) are of restricted size, perhaps 60, whilst the largest is perhaps of 8,000 pupils. Sampling cross-culturally and across national boundaries would therefore be likely to generate much greater variation than sampling within country.

Classroom variation is unlikely to increase as much as school variation if sampling were to be cross-national. To take size as a factor, class sizes within the United Kingdom range perhaps from 17/18 up to a maximum 40. Sampling across the globe would only increase the variation probably to 12/13 at the lower end and perhaps 60/70 in some developing societies at the top end.

The hugely enhanced range, and likely enhanced explanatory power of the school, if one deliberately seeks to maximise its range rather than minimise it by within nation sampling, is also likely to be found in terms of school *quality* factors, not just *quantity* factors. As an example, within Britain there would be a degree of variation in the leadership styles of Headteachers, ranging from the moderately lateral or involving/participatory, to the moderately centralised and dominating. Looking outside the United Kingdom context, one could see apparently totally autocratic, non-participatory leadership Pacific Rim societies such as Taiwan, and also apparently virtually totally 'lateral' decision making within the primary schools of Denmark, where school policy is generated by teachers.

We would argue, then, that our existing estimates as to the size of school effects noted in Chapter 3 and reflected throughout this Handbook are an artefact of researchers' unwillingness to explore the full range of variation on the 'school variable'. Cross-national research would expand variation on the school level by much more than on the classroom level – since classrooms are more alike internationally than are schools – and is essential if a more valid picture of school/classroom influence is to be generated.

The need to study school failure/dysfunctionality

SER has historically taken a very different disciplinary route to that of many other 'applied' disciplines such as medicine and dentistry, in that it has studied schools that are 'well' or effective, rather than those that are 'sick' or ineffective. Indeed, with notable exceptions in SER (Reynolds, 1996b; Stoll and Myers, 1998) and in school improvement (Sarason, 1981) the dominant paradigm has been to study those already effective or well and to simply propose the adoption of the characteristics of the former organisations as the goal for the less effective.

In medicine by contrast, research and study focuses upon the sick person and on their symptoms, the causes of their sickness and on the needed interventions that may be appropriate to generate health. The study of medicine does not attempt to combat illness through the study of good health, as does school effectiveness: it studies illness to combat illness.

It is, of course, easy to see why school effectiveness has studied the already 'well' or effective schools. The failure of the experiments of social engineering in the 1970s (Reynolds, Sullivan and Murgatroyd, 1987), combined with the research and advocacy that suggested that schools make no difference (Coleman et al., 1966; Jencks et al., 1972; Bernstein, 1968), led to a defensiveness within the field of school effectiveness and to an unwillingness to explore the 'trailing edge' of 'sick' schools for fear of giving the educational system an even poorer public image. Access to sick schools additionally has always been more difficult than to well or effective schools, given the well-known tendency of such ineffective schools to want to isolate themselves from potential sources of criticism from the world outside. The routine involvements of professional life in education have also tended to be between the good schools and the researchers, who tend to prefer to involve themselves in the successful schools, rather than to put up with the toxicity, problems and organisational trauma that is the day to day life of the ineffective school.

The problems for SER because it has concentrated upon the effective rather than the ineffective schools are numerous. Because the effective schools have already become effective, we do not know what factors *made* them effective over time. There may be whole areas of schooling which are central to educational life in non-effective schools that simply cannot be seen in effective schools, such as staff groups that possess 'cliques' or interpersonal conflict between staff members for example. Dropping into the context of the ineffective school these factors that exist in the effective school may be to generate simply unreachable goals for the ineffective school, since the distance between the practice of one setting from the practice of the other may be too great to be easily eradicated.

If SER were to reorientate itself towards the study of the sick, then a number of likely events would follow. Given that these schools are likely to increasingly be the site for numerous interventions to improve them, then there will be naturally occurring experiments going on that are much more rare in the 'steady state' effective schools. The study of sickness usually necessitates a clinical audit to see which aspects of the patient are abnormal – an educational audit can perform the same function, which of course is not necessary in an effective school because there is no concern about organisational functioning.

We believe that SER has been fundamentally misguided in its belief that the way to understand and combat sickness is through the study of the already well. The sooner that the discipline reorientates itself to the study of sickness, ineffectiveness, dysfunctionality and failure the better.

Curriculum and assessment

It will be obvious that the study of curricular variation within and between schools has not been a focus at all over the last three decades of SER. The explanations for this are simple:

- The orientation of researchers has been towards a behavioural, technicist approach in which the vessel of the school is studied rather than the contents.
- SER has often possessed a conservative political orientation in which schooling was seen as a 'good' which SER was to encourage more children to take up. In such a formulation any evaluation of the 'most effective curriculum' in terms of desired knowledge produced was superfluous, and less important than cascading existing knowledge at more children.
- SER was in many ways a reaction against those educationalists who generated a discourse within educational research that concentrated upon discussion of value judgements about what ought to be and what ought to be the goals of education. SER therefore accepted existing goals, accepted the pattern of exist- ing curricular knowledge that existed to orientate children towards those goals and concentrated upon discussion as to the most appropriate school organisa- tional means that were appropriate to achieving them.
- SER has been well aware of the immense difficulties involved in measuring the variable 'curriculum'. Time allocated to curricular knowledge in general has not been difficult to measure, likewise the time allocation to different subject groups (see for example the results of international surveys reported in Reynolds and Farrell, 1996).

However, attempts to move further and develop typologies of curriculum content and organisation, along continua such as 'open/closed', 'traditional/new', or 'culturally relevant/culturally elitist', have resulted in the expenditure of considerable effort for very little reward! Indeed, perhaps the best-known attempt to organise and analyse curriculum as *knowledge*, that of Bernstein (1968), was systematically destroyed by the work of King (1983), who noted that there were in practice only perhaps a tenth of relationships between curricular variables that were in the direction predicted by Bernstein's theory of classification and training.

Whilst the neglect of curricular issues is not surprising, there is now the possibility that such neglect may be damaging the field. Partly this is because the reluctance to think about curricular issues cuts the field off from the very widespread discussions now in progress about the most appropriate bodies of knowledge that should be in the schools of a 'post-modern age' or an 'information economy and society'. (Also, the reluctance to discuss curriculum matters and participate in the debates about whether 'new' bodies of knowledge may be more effective than the 'old' ones encourages the discipline to continue with what can only be labelled as a strikingly traditional range of outcomes, rather than diversify towards new and more broadly conceptualised ones.)

As an example, metacognitive skills are currently receiving a considerable amount of attention, in which learning is seen as an active process in which students construct knowledge and skills by working with the content (Resnick and Resnick, 1992). The new metacognitive theories differ considerably from the traditional views that are on offer historically within SER, in which teacher instruction generates the possibility of a student mastering the task, with the knowledge being mainly declarative (how it works) and procedural (how to do it). With metacognitive theorising the focus is more upon conditional knowledge (how to decide what to do and when to do it). The old model of instruction that SER represents aims mainly at the direct transfer and the reproduction of the existing knowledge as it is defined by schools and teachers in curricula, while the new model of instruction takes the learning of strategies by students as the centre of attention. These new models see a consequent need to change the role of the teacher, since the student being responsible for his or her own learning means that the teacher is no longer the person who instructs but the one who now teaches the techniques and strategies that students need to use to construct their own knowledge.

SER and its conservative curricular and outcome orientation is, therefore, not engaging with, and learning from, the new paradigms in the field of learning instruction. Additionally, it is not learning from or debating with those who argue for a new range of social or affective outcomes to be introduced relevant to the highly stressed, fast-moving world of the 1990s, except through some of the interesting speculations of Stoll and Fink (1996).

The SER of the present may, because of its reluctance to debate issues of values that are incorporated in discussions of the curriculum, and because of its reluctance to countenance new outcomes measures that are appropriate to the future rather than to the past, be in danger of being left behind by those who are actively exploring these issues. Will the new outcomes that an information age requires such as 'students' capacity to handle and access and construct information' be generated by the schools that are 'effective' that we have characterised in this book? Will the schools successful in generating conventional academic, and occasionally social, excellence through their predictability, cohesion, consistency and structure be the schools to generate the new social outcomes of 'coping' and 'psychosocial resilience' that are needed for today's youth?

We fear the answers to both these questions are 'no'.

Multilevel structural equation modelling

The great success of multilevel modelling has been largely due to the fact that such models more adequately depict the process of schooling, as we currently envision it, than does regression analysis. It is possible that multilevel structural equation modelling (SEM) will eclipse multilevel modelling in the future for the same reason.

Several authors (e.g. Hallinger and Heck, 1996; Bosker and Scheerens, 1997) have speculated that the effects of the school on the student are indirect, largely through the mediating level of the class. Recent advances in multilevel SEM, discussed in Chapter 6, make it possible to model statistically the indirect effects of school variables on student achievement using the multilevel approach. Given the tremendous enthusiasm that has been associated with multilevel modelling among the 'scientists' studying SER, the emergence of multilevel SEM is likely to generate much high quality theoretical and statistical work over the next few years.

Conclusions: understanding the research base

Over the 12 chapters of this Handbook we have ranged broadly over the field of SER, and into the related fields of school improvement, indicator research and comparative education. We have found a remarkable degree of consistency across cultures in our findings in such areas as the processes associated with school effectiveness, the size of school effects and their scientific properties. We have also found evidence of the importance of national and local context in determining the knowledge base, as we have made clear in numerous areas above.

It is clear that some of these differences between contexts reflect differences in the methodological structure of the research enterprise in different countries such as the tendency of research in the USA to not use prior achievement measures as input variables, and the commonplace use of these measures in European research. Likewise, the choice of elementary schools for the research sites of SER in the USA by comparison with the customary choice of secondary schools in the United Kingdom (reflecting the availability of routine assessment data in the case of the USA and secondary school examinations in the case of the UK) may also have influenced the pattern of results. In our opinion, after having undertaken this compendious review, it is absolutely essential that researchers make themselves far more aware than hitherto as to the methodological strategies employed in different national contexts to avoid the possibility of methodological variation passing itself off as substantive variation in knowledge.

Acknowledgements

First published as D. Reynolds and C. Teddlie (2000) 'The future agenda for school effectiveness research', in C. Teddlie and D. Reynolds (Eds) *The International Handbook of School Effectiveness Research*. London: Falmer Press. Reprinted here with permission from Taylor & Francis.

14

How can recent research in school effectiveness and school improvement inform our thinking about educational policies?

Introduction

The purpose of this short paper is to examine how the research evidence on school and teacher effectiveness and school improvement can inform the development of current schools policy. In particular, the paper considers what the research findings suggest for two initiatives: the 'New Relationship with Schools' and the proposals that teaching should be far more customised to the needs and preferences of individual pupils as a means of ensuring all reach their potential. This is sometimes referred to as 'Personalised Learning', although the rather resonant US term 'No Child Left Behind' also captures the spirit of these ideas.

The effectiveness and improvement research

The three fields of school effectiveness, school improvement and teacher (or, in US parlance, 'instructional') effectiveness have been in existence now for 30 years or more. They have also experienced rapid expansion with perhaps 1,500 to 2,000 relevant publications (Teddlie and Reynolds, 2000). Indeed, there are so many studies that there are now also many literature reviews and indeed reviews of the reviews!

About half of these studies have appeared in the last seven or eight years as the research ideas spread from the USA, the UK and the Netherlands to making a presence in perhaps 50 countries now. Many of the studies can be found on the

'High Reliability Schools' website (www.highreliabilityschools.co.uk). At the same time, the specifically UK or, more precisely, given the institutional differences, English schools research is not plentiful and the world literature is largely from the US.

The studies have attracted controversy and considerable criticisms (e.g. Thrupp, 2002) as well as robust defence (Teddlie and Reynolds, 2000), and indeed one of the most prominent arguments of the critics is that the very notion of school and teacher effectiveness implies a far too close embrace by researchers of the aims and values of policy makers.

Whatever the suspicions, it is very debatable how far policy in the past has consciously followed the research evidence or indeed even sought retrospective validation from this. (There have been various policy evaluations but these have tended to be ad hoc and specific both in their methods and aims.) Though whether serendipity, tacit use or permeation of research findings into the practical debate, there is some consistency – and it is certainly not the case that policy in general contradicts what the research would suggest.

School effectiveness
The strengths of the school effectiveness research are:

- the 'check lists' about school process characteristics of effective schools;
- its beneficial educational effects in persuading teachers that they can make a difference by showing that essentially similar groups of pupils, taught by different teachers, make substantially different rates of progress – as close as educationalists can normally get to the classic controlled experiment used in medical research;
- its emphasis on measuring pupil progress by 'value added' – i.e. a measure of the extra pupil attainment attributed to good schools – correcting for differing school intakes in terms of prior pupil attainment levels.

However, it also has significant weaknesses, which are:

- its predominant focus upon effectiveness of academic achievement, rather than embracing broader educational goals, e.g. vocational skills and attitudes towards learning;
- its lack of much information about the characteristics of effective teaching and learning in classrooms;
- its inability so far to successfully transfer its insights to 'practitioners' – teachers, Heads, teacher trainers;
- its 'one size fits all' orientation, born out of tending to focus on the disadvantaged 'schools in high poverty communities', which then fails to take account of different school contexts and neighbourhoods and how they might affect what is needed to 'work';
- its 'cross-sectional' or 'steady state' concern which focuses upon schools that ʰᵉcame effective. (Such longitudinal studies are far more time consuming and ᵢce costly.)

School improvement

The strengths of the improvement field include:

- its clear understanding of the importance of school culture;
- its emphasis on the importance of Heads, teachers and pupils needing to accept and embrace – to 'own' – the reforms;
- its focus on the professional 'deep cultures' of values, beliefs and socialisation that can affect the ability and/or willingness of teachers in schools to change in the way that researchers and policy makers might want them to.

But again, this field – like school effectiveness – is characterised by 'one size fits all' solutions, by a lack of evidence about the effect of its interventions and by a noticeable absence of any focus upon the process of teaching. And there is an irony here, because much school improvement research stems from a desire to raise the quality and hence the efficacy of teaching.

Teacher effectiveness

Teacher effectiveness, or 'instructional effectiveness', as it is called in the US, is much less well developed in the UK. Yet given the clear evidence, albeit from just a few studies, that teachers in classrooms are more important determinants of how students do than anything else (Muijs and Reynolds, 2001), the neglect of these issues over time in the UK has been particularly impoverishing. Indeed, it might be partially responsible for the emphasis of most national policies on the school level (Reynolds, 1999), though the current and novel DfES-funded four-year longitudinal study of teacher effectiveness which reports later in 2005 (CUITAD) should help redress this.

The strengths of the teacher effectiveness field are:

- its focus on the 'alterable teacher behaviours' that affect pupils' achievement, and in particular on the description of what makes for effective 'whole-class' and 'pupil-interactive' teaching;
- the description of the collaborative pupil group work settings that can promote the development of 'higher order' thinking.

The weaknesses are:

- the limited range of subjects studied (mostly Maths and English);
- the concentration upon socially disadvantaged pupils (for the same reasons as school effectiveness), which limits the scope for generalising the findings. There is, though, at least the compensating advantage that the findings, while narrowly based, are relatively robust because they have been frequently replicated;
- the limited understanding of pupil learning, particularly important given the contemporary interest within the teaching profession into the ways pupils learn and into pedagogical approaches designed to improve pupils' thinking and reasoning skills. As noted earlier, this area of research has also not yet succeeded

in offering useful insights into teacher professional development, although the National Strategies (Literacy and Numeracy and Key Stage Three) are an exception to this.

What do we mean by the 'school' and 'teacher' effect?

School and teacher effects, as used by researchers, refer to the extra pupil attainment that is attributable to the actions of a given school or a given teacher relative to an average, such as all schools in England or in an LEA. The effect can be positive or negative and is expressed as a definite number, e.g. 1.3 GCSE A–Cs.

How do researchers measure school effects?

The typical method is to take a sample of schools and relate, using a mathematical model, the pupil academic outcomes to the 'inputs' from the school and the pupil. A simple and crude model would take a measure of pupil disadvantage, e.g. free school meals, which is known to be correlated with attainment for this. Some schools tend to do better than expected, given their level of pupil disadvantage, others do worse and many will do as expected. These differences are between actual and expected attainment.

It is important to realise that these effects refer to the differences between schools; they cannot address the question of what difference schools make in absolute terms – if there was no education. That is because in a country such as England almost everyone goes to school and does so for at least 11 years. School (and teacher) differences are important because in principle they suggest that there are avoidable differences in the effectiveness of schools that can be remedied. However, the absence of any school effect does not mean that there is then no role for education policy! It could be that all schools were equally good (or bad) but all could still improve. Indeed, this is one of the reasons for taking part in the international comparisons, to see whether the levels of attainment that we have in one country are the best that there can be.

Measuring school effect by value added

It is demanding on research resources to undertake good school and teacher effectiveness studies and they are still quite scarce. Thus it is far better to measure pupil attainment by means of value added – because schools differ in the attainment levels of their intakes and because initial attainment also influences progression. Yet it is only recently that we have had such data for all schools. Teacher-level studies are still more difficult because they require value-added results for individual classes of pupils and a means of linking them to specific teachers who have taught those classes. At present, that linking is not possible with national data so that the only research results come from ad hoc studies, and even those are scarce.

So, to say that the school effect is small is to say that, taking the actual difference in attainment between pupils – the part attributed to variation between schools is about a tenth (and it is higher for primary than secondary schools, and higher in some school subjects than others). The school effect, for example, is higher in Maths and Science because pupils are probably more dependent on their teachers for these, whereas in English, family experiences tend to be important. The effects can still be worthwhile, though. In one study (Muijs and Reynolds, 2001) the difference between the most effective and least effective teachers over the course of a school year was over 20 points' difference on a standard Mathematics achievement test. In another study (Mortimore *et al.*, 1988), the best schools in working class communities succeeded in catching their pupils up with the average schools in middle class areas.

Pupil background factors

It might be thought that pupil social and economic factors (family income in particular) are the most important influences on attainment, and, certainly, if we simply link school average attainment to average pupil family income or social class, there is a strong relationship; still more so if we add pupil gender and ethnicity. However, if we look at any one of these measures on its own, say social class – perhaps the most 'obvious' non-school measure – the impact is very small, around 3% of the difference between pupils in their attainment, and adjusting for prior attainment (value added) tends to make this even lower. Now even 3% is educationally significant but what this is saying is that pupil attainment is not mechanically determined on the basis of unalterable characteristics. Coming from a disadvantaged background does not mean that a child has to do less well than their schoolfellows. Individual attitudes and aptitudes also matter. Equally, on our present knowledge, much of the difference in pupil attainment that we see remains unexplained, or seems to come down to previous attainment, which simply raises the question: what then determined that?

The implications of the research findings for educational policy

Despite a fairly hefty set of reservations about the quality of the research base across the three areas, there are significant insights from the effectiveness and improvement research which are useful in assessing current policy. A few examples make the point:

- There is a long-standing debate about just how far schools and teachers are either *the*, or *a*, prime determinant(s) of pupil attainment. At the least, we can say that family background factors, socio-economic conditions and behavioural factors are sufficiently important that significant educational reform is more likely to occur when school and home are jointly addressed. So, *do current policies sufficiently reflect this evidence?*
- Such evidence as there is suggests that teacher effects and the effects of 'the learning level' can be three to four times more important than the school level (Teddlie and Reynolds, 2000). Furthermore, some studies also suggest that these teacher-level factors are more related to teachers' behaviours than attitudes or personality. Thus, they are the result of the influence of a large number (about 30) of relatively independent key behaviours and are an 'alterable variable'.

Moreover, they can be modified by appropriate training as, for example, in the case of those school improvement models that begin with a theory of effective instruction and then look at practical behaviours to achieve this (Hopkins and Reynolds, 2001). *Do current policies adequately recognise the salience and importance of 'teaching' and its connection to learning?*

- In the early years of school effectiveness research, the educational ('cognitive') and other ('affective') outcomes of schools were seen as highly intercorrelated, so that a school 'good' in areas such as academic achievement was also seen as good in encouraging pupils' self esteem (Reynolds, 1976a; Rutter *et al.*, 1979). Yet in more recent research reviews (Teddlie and Reynolds, 2000, Chapter 3), some of the intercorrelations shown between academic and social/affective areas go as low as 0.3 or 0.4. *If it is the case that schools 'good' in one area of educational development may not be 'good' in others, then will current policies that are aiming to expand the supply and use of performance data on academic 'outcomes' distort the 'market' and flood it with contradictory judgements?*

- In comprehensive school systems, within-school variation in pupil attainment seems to be much greater than between-school variation, a finding that has considerable implications for educational policies. An unpublished DfES study of 2003 data showed that in value added terms, Key Stage 2 (KS2) within-school variance is five times greater than between-school variance, for KS3 it is 11 times greater and for KS4 it is 14 times greater. This makes the use of within-school variation for school improvement a potentially important policy target, for a number of reasons.

  (a) While it might not be possible to have policies for what happens in individual classrooms, this might be feasible at the subject departmental level in a secondary school or the 'year' level in a primary school. Targeting these means that policy can get far closer to what ought to be the real focus, the classroom level, than if it only addresses the school level.

  (b) While not every school is effective, most schools will have within themselves some practice that is relatively more effective than elsewhere in the school. Every school can therefore look for generally applicable good practice from within its own internal conditions.

  (c) It might well be that one limitation to whole-school self-evaluation and improvement is that headteachers are often overloaded, because of having to deal with problems that should fall to middle managers, and so lack the time to think strategically. Targeting sub-groups within the school could get round that.

  (d) Within-school units of policy intervention such as years or subjects are smaller and, therefore, potentially more open to being changed than those at whole school level. For example, at the whole school level, each part can blame the rest for shortcomings and take the credit for strengths.

  (e) Teachers in general, and those teachers in less effective schools, seem to be more influenced by classroom-based policies that are close to their focal concerns of teaching and curriculum and less by policies that are 'managerial' and orientated to the school level.

To sum up: do national policies reflect this opportunity to generate powerful within-school levers?

- There is considerable evidence that *'context matters'* in the precise factors that are needed to support effective learning in different circumstances. There are classic studies in the school effectiveness work to show that schools in disadvantaged areas (low pupil socio-economic status (SES)) create effectiveness by tending to isolate and 'buffer' themselves from their communities. But effective schools in better-off areas tend to be closely involved with their local communities (Teddlie and Reynolds, 2000). Again, research on teacher effectiveness shows that teachers of disadvantaged pupils need to pay more attention to classroom climate, classroom management, rapid reinforcement and positive expectations to get the best out of pupils. Also, relatively unsophisticated measures based upon tight, centralised, top down management can work in the short term in relatively disadvantaged catchment areas. In better off areas, however, approaches based upon pedagogy, learning and classroom methods seem to work better (Gray *et al.*, 1999). The existing range of policies does of course include some that are targeted at certain areas, notably, Excellence in Cities, and these are 'specific', for example in terms of a greater focus upon schools and/or Headteachers that need more support. *But do national policies or the OFSTED Inspection Framework give due weight to the finding that running a school, or being a teacher, effectively in disadvantaged areas, requires significantly different behaviours, attitudes and processes from other areas?*

- Recent research evidence suggests that the *effects of home and school* are additive, in that children from less well-off families are doubly disadvantaged since they attend less effective schools and also come from less rich educational environments at home (Teddlie and Reynolds, 2000). The reasons for the school effects in this 'double dose' are unclear but are likely to involve their difficulty in recruitment of the more effective teachers, who will be attracted to the more advantaged catchment areas, and not attracted to the 'stresses' that teaching in these poorer areas generates. *There is certainly a range of policies aimed at the catchment areas of schools in deprived areas, and the Government is attempting to 'join up' its range of educational, economic, social and environmental policies. But does national policy adequately reflect this 'double dose' effect?*

- There is much evidence to show that the *school and teacher effects on attainment become less important as pupils get older*. So the biggest estimated impact in the research is in early years schooling and the smallest is in secondary. Indeed, the biggest 'school effect' ever seen in the worldwide literature was that of almost 50% of variance in achievement being due to school (as against the customary 10–12%) shown in the Tymms, Merrill and Henderson (1997) study of early years. Spending on early years provision is, though, lower than that on later years, and more generally the policy emphasis has been on primary education (from 1997 to 2002) and secondary education (since about 2001 to date) rather than with early years. This of course reflects strategic and indeed political considerations of the need for quick attainment gains and it is important to ad that the Government's Sure Start Programme has also acted to shift the balance to early years. *Is national policy appropriate in its balance of allocation of resources and quality of policy thinking for the early years phase, given its importance?*

The implications of research for contemporary policies

To sum up: it is clearly salutary to see the somewhat sharp contrast between what the research suggests and what policy makers do. Thus:

- Educational institutions have quite a small effect compared to pupil background, parental income, health, etc. Education policy to date has tended only to focus on schools and teachers and historically there has been a lack of co-ordination across policy areas. However, the expanded role for the DfES, to include the children's services and specifically the development of 'Every Child Matters', means that children's education and well being are being considered together for the first time.
- The evidence shows it is at the individual teacher level that education has its main effect; school effectiveness and improvement policy focus on schools.
- Variation in effectiveness within schools far exceeds that between schools; policy tends to treat schools as single entities.
- Policies should give due regard to context (the local demographics, for example) but largely ignore this.
- Education institutions seem to have their greatest impact in the early years; until very recently, policies have focused on the primary and secondary years.

It is hard to say whether there is a greater disjunction between policy and research now than previously. There is also the difficulty, of course, that research tends to lag behind new policies and it is generally only possible retrospectively to study the relevant factors or 'levers'. It is therefore difficult to appraise new policies and their likely effectiveness; still more so at a time of great dynamism as there has been in recent years in English schooling. Of course, equally, this points to a greater need to evaluate policies, during, as well as after, their implementation. And certainly 'boldly going where no policy has gone before' and trying out policies, without adequate testing and on a national scale, can be costly, as many US reform efforts have discovered. At the least, we can try to use the general findings of research to analyse present policies, even if we cannot evaluate them in their specifics.

The New Relationship with Schools (NRwS)

Among the valuable features of NRwS are its rationalisation of an elaborate set of policies, the decentralised delivery system and its phased implementation.

Perhaps its most valuable feature is the principle of differentiated help for schools, differentiated both in its content and in its targeting, and schools themselves will be in charge. Except where there are clear concerns about a school's capacity, the school will map out its own calls on support. But one element will be provided for all schools: help in shifting them from being 'data rich' to being 'information rich'. For many schools at present, it is not clear that their substantial capacity to collect data is matched to their capacity to analyse and use it.

As NRwS goes forward, schools will need to ensure their efforts in development planning are well focused on tackling their real needs, and followed up with effective action for improvement. Development planning can go badly awry if it is not appropriately targeted. A sobering anecdote here – and maybe, that is all it is – is that one study found, for a sample of schools, the greater the attention given to improvement planning, the lower the improvement in individual school results over time! (Gray et al., 1999).

The commitment to lateral 'networks' of schools collaborating to raise attainment might be misplaced if schools do not have the competences to give and receive knowledge, which is highlighted in recent projects, e.g. Fielding et al. (2005). This might be, for example, because they have not developed these internally, in their own individual day-to-day school life. If that is so, then it suggests that there might be a need for there to be simultaneous 'within school' and 'between school' transfer of knowledge. As noted before, policy still seems to reflect the historic focus with the school rather than realising that it is the teacher in the classroom who is the most powerful 'lever' of change. On the other hand, the DfES has embarked on an extensive suite of policies for the reform and restructuring of school staff. Indeed, the new terminology of 'school workforce' is meant to convey a very different approach to the deployment of teachers and other staff in the school, implying a greater flexibility and willingness to rethink roles.

Meeting the needs of all pupils: personalised learning, individualised learning

Looking at this and remembering the earlier caveats about using research from the past to analyse policies from the present, the Department's commitment to 'assessment for learning' rightly recognises a potentially very powerful lever for raising pupil attainment. However, it might well be that the training needs of teachers to implement this successfully are greater than current policy allows for.

Personalisation – a more individually determined curriculum that reflects the 'pathways' that children are on – could increase achievement through greater motivation but could also increase inequality if children from some social and economic backgrounds choose pathways which will encourage them to remain in those circumstances.

Individualisation – increasing the amount of independent pupil learning (often, but not inevitably, by use of ICT) – might well be sensible in that an 'information age' requires these skills to be developed in our students. However, it is possible that this too could increase the range of attainment between children, as they will bring varying abilities to this 'independent learning', and the potentially balancing 'constant' of the teacher will become less important.

There are other possible concerns about customising learning through personalisation or individualisation. Thus, the former risks having a target setting regime, but *without* the intense pressure to improve standards that would ensure high achievement for all, but with instead individual targets that reflect children's social background. The latter continues to place a lot of the faith seen in earlier initiatives in ICT and risks returning to pupils being isolated as individualised learners (though this might be offset through the use of more collaborative group work).

Conclusions: knowledge transfer is the key

An underlying problem with all present policies, and indeed with policies in education historically, is that of exactly how we 'skill the system up', whatever the policies that might be pursued. Schools as a system remain highly variable, in which there are important variations in effectiveness between schools taking similar intakes of pupils, and still more so between departments and teachers within the same school. It is notable here that discussions of how to transfer knowledge are themselves usually characterised by thickets of jargon that make knowledge transfer to the reader, let alone to the teaching profession, most unlikely! (See Hargreaves, 2004 for a better attempt, while Fielding *et al.*, 2005, report the results of some recent DfES-funded research into the practice of knowledge transfer across schools.)

All this is rather surprising, since there is a fair amount of evidence, admittedly mainly based on experience, about what might 'work' in this area. So we know that:

- Teachers prefer 'practical' rather than 'intellectual' knowledge, since they see it as relevant to their concerns, although it is clear that they need the provision of 'theory' also in the sense of understanding the underlying reasons why some practices work better than others and how far what works for some pupils generalises to all.
- Teachers need knowledge not in the abstract, but related to the particular contexts within which they work.
- Teachers need a common language to ensure that they mean the same thing when they attempt to describe their practice or observe each other teach. The decision underpinning the National Strategies to give only a fraction of the total knowledge there is on effective teaching practices has probably made the obtaining of this common language more difficult (though a taxonomy of teaching and learning – currently being developed – should help here).
- Teachers need high quality systems to ensure that observations of their teaching and their pupils in classrooms focus on the key behaviours that affect learning (the MECORS system of Muijs and Reynolds (2001), for example, has 57 behaviour categories) and also relate to the learning experiences of pupils in

classrooms. Here it is extraordinary – indeed ridiculous – that the optional observation framework for the teacher Performance Management System still does not involve gathering data about pupils' 'time on task' or other aspects of their learning!

- There are other barriers that restrict transfer of practice: the historic culture of individualism in the profession, the reluctance to differentiate between teachers in their 'effectiveness' or 'competences', and sometimes the strange reluctance of outstanding professionals to let their good practice go to others because it might be seen as demeaning to those who might be expected to receive it. Teachers are strangely reluctant to be taught!

In all these topics, there is much work for researchers in the three areas of school effectiveness, school improvement and teacher effectiveness to do if the promising efforts of the last 20 years are to have the major effects on policy and practice that they deserve.

Acknowledgements

First printed in D. Hopkins, D. Reynolds and J. Gray (2005) *School Improvement: Lessons from Research*. London: HMSO for DfES. Reprinted here with permission from HMSO.

15

What do we want our educational system of the future to look like? What do we need to do to make it happen?

Introduction

It is difficult to avoid being anything other than quite impressed by the direction of travel set out in the existing *21st Century Schools* consultation document and the associated material such as that on *Excellence and Fairness: Achieving World Class Public Services* (Cabinet Office, 2008).

The thesis being advanced seems sensible:

- Societal change worldwide is creating a demand for new skills and attributes.
- Society itself may have changed in its capacity to engender these, leading to pressure on the education/welfare system to do more.
- The means within education/welfare need to be differentiated more and 'personalised' to meet more individually determined needs.
- State provision itself needs to link better with the 'outside education system' determinants of learning – the family and the community.

However, there are two notable omissions in the characteristics seen to be necessary in Twenty-first Century Schools. Firstly, IT is barely mentioned, save occasionally as a means to achieve some of the other goals that are discussed. It is very much the policy dog that no longer barks, yet 'IT literacy' is a likely future educational attribute as necessary as conventional reading, writing and maths are held to be.

The use of IT has moved beyond the simple 'access to knowledge' that characterised early use, and now knowledge can be created in IT-enabled learning communities across distance, organisational boundaries and cultures. Mobile technologies bring new possibilities for learning and, crucially, for the possibility – given their universality – for truly listening to 'student voice' and involving young people in their learning. IT now – through Facebook for example – is creating new communities.

The Twenty-first Century School needs to harness IT – not be afraid of it, or unsure about it because policy-makers have backed off it due to past impact disappointments.

The second notable omission from discussion is that of 'schooling for sustainability'. Interestingly, there are close relationships between 'schooling for sustainability', by which we mean addressing issues of global economic sustainability in formal school settings, and 'choice schooling', which is the international trend to give parents and students enhanced freedom to choose public schools free from state or local government constraint (Kelly, 2009). Increasingly, school choice is the preferred and irreversible mechanism by which governments are responding to the individualisation of responsibility for economic prosperity and well being, and it is also well recognised that it is through this individualisation of responsibility that global sustainability is best addressed in terms of long term effects.

However, the practices that may be necessary to develop 'eco literacy' in addition to the IT literacy noted above may be unclear. Little is done to connect students to ideas that see them as humans on an interconnected planet. We have a sense that five areas are important (Clarke, 2009):

- *principles*: if we took seriously that all education is environmental education, the crisis may be seen as *of* education, not *in* education;
- *purpose*: we need young people to understand how human systems interrelate with natural systems so we can build resilient communities and ecologically literate economies:
- *priorities*: living systems provide us with the insights that they have adequate capacities to create life together, and communicating: these have implications for our educational designs too;
- *practice*: we need a renaissance of practical, simple ideas that connect persons and environments;
- *presence*: as used by Senge (2006), we can use nature as a guide and teacher and learn that sustainability is a community practice.

But if the 'direction of travel' and destination seems sensible other than these omissions – indeed, it is squarely on the lines of some of the more radical definitions of the goals of the education system outlined by thinkers like Leadbetter (2008) – the problems involved in getting to the destination are legion. We now turn to look at these for the remainder of the paper.

The problems of new outcome measures

Firstly, the educational system is being required to respond to the *Every Child Matters* outcomes – be healthy, stay safe, enjoy and achieve, make a positive contribution, and achieve economic well-being. However, the volume of evidence about what educational practices generate the four 'new' goals is a fraction of what exists in the conventional 'enjoy and achieve' outcome area (although here it must also be admitted that 'enjoyment' has been researched much less than 'achievement') (Mortimore *et al.*, 1988; Sammons, Mortimore and Thomas, 1996). As is the case currently with the social or affective outcome areas by comparison with the academic (Teddlie and Reynolds, 2000), it may also be the case that educational system effects are less in these new outcome areas, leaving us to attain goals where we have little educational leverage.

Where is the knowledge about the new 'stretched' educational mission to come from? There are no existing plans for the major research and development work required to generate this. In the absence of this, no doubt the 'Pathfinder' or exemplary institutions and their personnel will be used to model and transmit good practice, but these 'early adopters' of new practices are likely to be very different kinds of institutions to those more 'in the circle' (Fullan, 1991). Besides, policy-maker use of these outliers is likely to continue to focus more on the persons creating them than on their methodologies – and indeed with continued likely use of one-off case studies that conflate persons and their methods in ways that multisite work does not.

Further problems may also lie in:

- the likely relative independence of the new outcome measures from each other, which will be masked if any 'overall' rating through the traffic light system is utilised. Indeed, the 'overall' rating is exactly what, in a rational world, would be happening less with the multiple 'new' measures than the more limited existing ones;
- the inadequate development of measurement of the 'new' outcome areas;
- the absence of proposals to 'value add' the new outcome measures, which would be essential if schools in disadvantaged areas are not to be unfairly judged (this would clearly require 'input' measures in the value added equation as well as 'outcome' ones);
- the absence of any attempt to prioritise academic achievement outcomes, since there is abundant evidence that although there is a loose relationship between academic outcomes and social/affective/other outcomes, it is the academic outcomes that are causal of the social/affective rather than the other way around (Muijs and Reynolds, 2000a, 2000b, 2003, 2005).

Pulling weak levers: the neglect of teaching/classrooms

But, secondly, if we want to develop the talents of our young people fully in Twenty-first Century Schools, it is the basic discourse of our discussion about education that needs to change. Put simply, policy in the UK has historically been obsessed with 'the school' as the unit of measurement, accountability, policy change and improvement. Although in the future it is currently acknowledged in general policy discourse that education will take place across multiple settings additional to schools, these settings are still seen in terms of their macro-level organisational provision and features, rather than their micro-level teaching and learning processes. However:

- Young people do not learn in schools or other organisations. They learn in classrooms and in other face to face locations with their teachers. If we are truly interested in meeting their needs, we need to have educational perspectives and policies that look upward from their (probably highly variegated) experiences, rather than down from their school or 'organisational level'. We need a focus on education as *experienced*, not as *intended* by policy, two very different things.
- It is the teacher or educator in the classroom or learning setting that is the biggest source of influence over children, not the level of the school. Indeed, in virtually all multilevel analyses conducted to date, in whichever country or sector, teacher or classroom effects on achievement outcomes are four to five times greater than school effects (again, see Muijs and Reynolds, 2000a, 2000b, 2003, 2005).
- School-level organisational factors do not appear to be very powerful determinants of anything at all, whether they are size, formal designation, type of school or any other school-level variables. Yet if one reads the number of references to 'the school' in policy documents, it is much greater than the references to the classroom. This is something that appears to be greatest in Anglo-Saxon countries rather than others, perhaps related to the way in which 'education' in these societies has become intensely politicised and the repository of simplistic political solutions. In most societies of the world – including the high scoring Pacific Rim and Finnish ones – discussions about education are usually about teaching and curriculum rather than about the school unit. They are therefore linked to the most powerful 'levers'.

All this is a pity, since teaching as a research area is endlessly fascinating. There seem to be about 60 behaviours associated with student outcomes, most of which are weakly intercorrelated and with an absence of strong correlations, suggesting that good teaching is not about getting a few 'big things' right but a large number of 'little things' right. There is a relationship between the beliefs that teachers have – about themselves, their efficacy – and their students' progress, but their behaviours influence their attitudes as well as vice versa. Teaching can be modified, e. effectively (Hopkins and Reynolds, 2001; Slavin, 1996), which makes o. cerned about the popularity of the 'teacher supply' arguments – often using as an exemplar – which now strangely emanate from those who spent a decade operating within the established paradigm that teaching was an 'alterable variable'!

Given the centrality of teaching and learning, existing limited attempts to develop its study and potential would have no place in the Twenty-first Century School, or in the other institutions that will be involved in skill development and socialisation. It is sad therefore that there is currently very limited additional attention to following up teaching-related factors in the PISA cycle. Japanese methods of 'collaborative instructional renewal' are not prevalent in England (Stigler and Hiebert, 1999), and CPD/inset seems to focus on school-level issues more than on pedagogy.

The concentration upon 'the school' is not solely the fault of the politicians and policy-makers. From the beginning, the school effectiveness movement (Teddlie and Reynolds, 2000) researched and celebrated the 'school' rather than the classroom, leading to knowledge bases that were much depleted when it came to effective teaching behaviours, although this has changed somewhat in the past ten years.

But – whoever's fault it is – the twenty-first century educational provision of all kinds that we need to see will not be generated by further focus on schools, their leadership or their management. Such managerial focus means that many teachers will simply not identify with the policies, since their focal concerns are much more likely to be teaching and subject related. Such a focus would also mean that policy in the Twenty-first Century School will pull 'weak' levers rather than 'strong' ones at the learning level.

The need to focus on within school variation (WSV)

Our present managerial 'whole school' focus also means, thirdly, that we are neglecting a potential policy area – within school variation – that could transform our schools of the future if it were focused upon, particularly if it was part of a range of 'disaggregated' school policies.

Interestingly, there is no mention of WSV in the Consultation Document, which maintains the historical obsessions with the school level.

WSV is much larger than school-against-school variation, not surprisingly since school averages are an aggregation of multiple persons/Departments. In the PISA 2006 study, England had amongst the highest levels of WSV in the participating countries. Only half (approximately) of WSV was explicable by prior attainment and background characteristics, leaving the remainder to be explained in all likelihood by variable teacher quality, and other factors.

In existing Research and Development programmes for NCSL (2003–2007), and TDA (2008 to date), schools have shown that the reduction of WSV is linked to rises in Value Added. Additionally, a range of interventions proven to be successful have been codified into a programme designed to help schools learn from their best *within the school* and to make *their best practice their standard practice* (see NCSL, 2006; Reynolds, 2007). These involve attention to:

- ensuring school culture can support what is potentially difficult inter-professional collaboration to learn more from each other;
- high quality data systems to ensure best practice is recognised;
- using student voice to inform discussions of what different departments and individuals can learn from each other (often delivered with shocking clarity);
- using Standard Operating Procedures to minimise variability, without sacrificing creativity;
- focusing upon teaching and learning, not school-level organisational matters;
- turning the middle leaders' 'level' into an engine of improvement, rather than merely of administration and management.

The Twenty-first Century School needs therefore to be a disaggregated one – in its organisation, conceptualisation and functioning. Individuals (in the case of primary schools) and departments (in the case of secondary schools) are closer to the real business of education – teaching and learning. They are smaller and more malleable, additionally, than entire school staff groups. Learning from one's own colleagues is quicker than waiting for the arrival of the school-to-school transfer of persons and knowledge. It is also devoid of an excuse-making culture, since in the case of core subjects in secondary schools, and many others too, largely the same students will be studying each one, meaning that differences will reflect how students are educated rather than the variation between them.

Whilst the Twenty-first Century School clearly needs to connect more with other sources of valuable learning and experiences outside itself, it also needs to connect better with 'itself', as it were. Conceptualising it and organising itself in smaller units would seem to be axiomatic here.

The opportunities provided by cognitive neuroscience

But the greatest omission, fourthly, from the Consultation Document – and indeed from discussion generally in education – is the prospects for education offered by the cognitive neuroscience revolution now gathering pace. In its neglect of the importance of this for the future of schooling, DCSF is in good company – in British educational circles generally there has been a muted response to some of the emerging findings. Educationalists seem to need to believe in improvement through the systems of education (linked with us) rather than remediation through involvement directly with the human physiology or genotype. The latter approaches cut against the grain of our discipline because there are widespread misunderstandings that the brain is a static, self-contained unit that begins the process of learning from a pre-determined, immutable set of attributes with high genetic heritability. In fact, the brain is at certain ages highly 'plastic' and billions of neurones in the brain are capable of connecting with each other or not (what is referred to as the 'wiring'). It is inherently social also and learners need opportunities to clarify, discuss and question to enhance memory and retrieval.

The extent to which a person feels they belong to a group profoundly influences their ability to focus, remember, respond and mature intellectually, socially, emotionally and cognitively. Interestingly, given the very positive effects for formative assessment approaches, the brain is self-referencing and so relies heavily on feedback to develop. What have we learned, and what are the implications for the Twenty-first Century School?

The first set of insights concerns the neglected role of the cerebellum. We know that skill acquisition occurs in several stages – one is the 'declarative' stage in which a person learns what to do; another is the 'procedural' stage in which a person learns how to do it, and then there is the 'automatic' stage where the skill is exercised without conscious control.

The cognitive neuroscience revolution has demonstrated that there are two circuits in the brain – one for declarative learning (the frontal lobe and hippocampus) and the other for procedural learning (the frontal lobe, cerebellum and motor areas). The cerebellum functions for physical skill and mental skill, and is central to language acquisition, temporal processing and with clear connectivity to the frontal cognitive regions.

Nicolson, Fawcett and Dean (2001) have outlined a Cerebellar Deficit Theory (CDT), believing that inadequate development of the cerebellum is implicated in such learning problems as dyslexia, dyspraxia and ADHD/ADD, because of the inability of those children affected to make their learned skills 'automatic'. They believe that Cerebellar Developmental Delay (CDD) is at the heart of much avoidable educational failure.

The thesis is controversial, and indeed our work showing considerable achievement gains from an exercise-based intervention designed to potentiate the cerebellum (the famed 'balancing on a wobble board' and the 'throwing of bean bags from one hand to the other') has been criticised by some for small sample sizes, and for inappropriate statistics (see Reynolds and Nicolson, 2006, and Reynolds, Nicolson and Hambly, 2003, for the original studies, and Nicolson and Reynolds, 2003, for a defence). Nevertheless, it remains possible that the educational system of the future needs to give as much attention to finding processes that can potentiate the cerebellum as to those which are aimed, more conventionally, at the 'thinking brain'.

The second set of insights is concerned with how to potentiate skill development for the brain as a whole. We have known for a long time that 'distributed' practice is more effective than 'massed' practice – i.e. it is better to learn a skill in six ten-minute sessions rather than in a one-hour time slot. This is probably because there are different stages in skill acquisition – from the storing in an easily alterable EEG form, to, in a few more hours, a more stable form (that can still be influenced) and then to a more concrete form, often produced with sleep. In the longer term, the neural pathways get further established. In these processes, sleep is of major importance. These stages need time to operate as the brain is stimulated. Simply, the brain needs space.

However, it is massed learning and non-distributed practice that remains the conventional educational method. Subjects are taught for an hour or longer, meaning merely that the information presented later in a long lesson interferes with that presented earlier. Then – compounding error upon error – nothing is done for a day or two in the same subject so that there is no developmental 'fine tuning'.

This conclusion contrasts with evidence from neuroscience and in particular the long-term potentiation (LTP) paradigm. LTP provides the theoretical basis for spaced learning (Eichenbaum and Otto, 1993; McGaugh, 2000), but in LTP the optimum spaces (intervals) between bursts of stimuli are of the order of minutes to hours. Early experiments found that the expression of key proteins required for the strengthening of synapses was optimised when the interval was ten minutes (Itoh et al., 1995; Frey and Morris, 1998).

Fields arrived at the same temporal pattern of activity when investigating the intracellular switches for DNA synthesis during development (Fields, 2005). His studies suggested that the activation of CREB, a key transcription factor involved in memory, was optimised by three pulses of stimulation separated by ten-minute intervals. (This material is taken from Kelley (2007), who reviews this literature extensively.)

The highly publicised 'spaced learning' experiments conducted at Monkseaton High School (Barkham, 2009), in which a pure spaced learning teaching session of only 90 minutes generated equivalent results to four months' conventional teaching, show the potential for radical redesign of teaching and learning in the Twenty-first Century School. Admittedly, the 'spaced learning' material was taught by an outstanding teacher, it was 'new' and therefore interest was high, the PowerPoints were multicoloured and of high quality, and the cerebellum may also have been potentiated by the fact that the ten-minute gaps between teaching were filled with sessions involving the dribbling of a football between cones in the school gymnasium. Nevertheless, there is nothing in the existing literature that could even partially explain gains of this size as due to these factors alone. One must begin to ask very serious questions of 'mass education' if these results are shown elsewhere.

The third insight from contemporary cognitive neuroscience concerns optimising brain function through appropriate resourcing. There are the hints about the positive effects of fish oil supplements – the major dietary change of the British population since the 1950s has been the decline in per capita fish consumption of approximately two-thirds, and the argument is that neural connectivity can be enhanced artificially by these supplements replacing what would have been naturally occurring through diet. Water is another important supplement argued to be implicated in improving learning outcomes.

The fourth insight from contemporary neuroscience comes in the work looking at sleeping patterns and the effects of the different patterns of circadian rhythms that are evidenced by children of different ages (Foster, 2007). Teenagers are heavily sleep deprived – they show delayed sleep and fewer hours of sleep once in bed. Sustained periods of reduced sleep generate poor performance in terms of increased errors, impaired vigilance, poor memory, reduced mental/physical reaction times, reduced motivation, reduced risk taking and increased depression. The practice of starting school early and of putting more demanding subjects in the morning timetable is disliked by teenagers and generates lower performance, which improves for this group later in the day.

Unfortunately, adult performance – of the teachers – is likely to be *higher* in the morning, which is why of course schools start early and the 'difficult' subjects are timetabled for the mornings. Ways of squaring this circle need to be found!

The dramatic gains shown by approaches influenced by cognitive neuroscience – from exercise to fish oils to spaced learning – may be because they are from enthusiasts, on often small samples in atypical situations. Too often they appear in *Bad Science*! Alternatively, it may be that they are, simply, more powerful interventions than our conventional educational 'weak' levers. Further large-scale research in these areas is clearly urgently necessary.

The need to encourage greater variation in provision

The final need for the Twenty-first Century School is that it inhabits a world of Twenty-first Century Educational Policies and that in particular it is freer than at present to vary its organisational processes, ethos and culture in accordance with its context – nationally, locally and in terms of the characteristics of its student group.

Current education policies are born of a belief that there is 'one right way' – born of the influence of school effectiveness and improvement – to achieve our goals, which is reflected in process checklists, lists of personal attributes/characteristics and indeed in the use of the 'exemplary' individuals and institutions as the model for others. Left unchecked, such practices will generate a relative uniformity of ineffectiveness in Twenty-first Century provision as they did in historical provision.

However, as research in school effectiveness and school improvement (SESI) has accumulated, there is more and more evidence that to be effective, processes may need to vary according to the:

*   cultural context of the nation (Alexander, 2000; Reynolds *et al.*, 2002);
*   the socio-economic composition of the school classrooms (Wimpelberg, Teddlie and Stringfield, 1989);
*   the effectiveness level of the school (Hopkins and Reynolds, 2001);
*   the trajectory of improvement that the school is on (Hopkins, 2001).

Additionally, recent evidence is that a wide variety of programmes may be equally effective, but that the key to effectiveness is to do something – indeed, probably anything – reliably, as shown in the interesting work of Stringfield *et al.* (1997) that evaluated the American government's 'Special Strategies' improvement schemes. The programme chosen by a school didn't matter – what did matter was co-constructing it and doing it reliably. Interestingly, our own High Reliability Schools Project (Stringfield, Reynolds and Schaffer, 2008) was based not upon trying to encourage schools to use 'right ways of doing things' but upon getting schools to use the right *concepts* and *systems* that enabled them to be intelligent organisations.

Our schools were therefore somewhat different in *what* they did, but the same in *how* they had worked out what to do.

The insights from SESI are in marked contrast to policies which still – even with the current OFSTED emphasis upon assessment of school capacity to review itself – believe in 'one right way'. The Twenty-first Century School needs to be resourced with the data systems, the time for training and reflection, the resources for personal and collective development and the attitudes that support education as a co-constructed process between teachers and learners. But this needs to be in an educational context that permits and encourages the very high levels of institutional variation appropriate to an increasingly heterogeneous, and varied, population. Certainly, there are universals that need to be acknowledged – about the importance of leadership for example (Harris, 2006), or effective formative assessment practices. But the precise ways in which these things are brought into practice, and to an extent the things themselves, are likely to be highly context-dependent.

The advantage of encouraging greater variation in the Twenty-first Century School is that it is likely that greater development of our teachers and educators will occur when they are left relatively free to determine which educational process should be in existence, rather than if they are instructed by others in what these characteristics should be.

Conclusions

The Twenty-first Century School, therefore, may well need to be close to the vision of the future in the Consultation document, with the addition of considerably more concern/competence in the area of IT literacy and sustainability, as both philosophies and practices.

However, one must have real doubts about whether current policy paradigms are adequate in terms of the conceptualisation and measurement of a broader range of outcomes, the neglect of much focus upon teaching and learning, and the neglect of the possibilities to be offered by a focus upon disaggregating the school.

There is also little recognition currently of the importance of emerging cognitive neuroscience, where advances have interestingly been made possible by a change in methodology (through MRI scanning) in the same way as SESI was transformed by multilevel modelling in the mid 1980s. There is also no recognition of the importance – indeed, the need – of avoiding invalid 'one right way' solutions.

But, ultimately, the Twenty-first Century School requires a rejection of the 'apprenticeship' mentality that now pervades educational policies, and its replacement with an 'empirical, rational' problem solving approach that sees education as research orientated at its heart, not merely in its superficial rhetoric. Entire programmes – National Challenge is an example – are built upon educational leaders being encouraged to pick up good practices from those deemed to possess them. But in times of rapid educational change, the educational 'master' or 'mistress' cannot have practised what is necessary to be effective in the emerging situation – they bring to their 'apprentices' only what worked historically in the past. As an example, they will not have knowledge of the emerging cognitive neuroscience paradigm.

The only model that is appropriate for the educational professionals of the Twenty-first Century Schools is the empirical–rational problem solving one, where professionals take an enquiry orientation, try out solutions to problems and measure the effects, changing provision as necessary. Some of the international surveys are picking up the importance of high quality, research-based CPD focused upon classroom practice as the explanation for the Finnish and the Pacific Rim success. And of course, one of the world's most rapidly improving systems – Cuba – teaches research methods within teacher education, gives teachers time and encouragement to research, and ensures the feedback of the research that teachers do within their schools and within groups of schools.

It is possible to believe that the Twenty-first Century School will need largely an intensification of present policy paradigms – that we have *validity* and merely need more *reliability* in implementation for policies to work. Or it is possible to believe that what we see currently is the exhaustion of a paradigm, and the need to replace it with one that will work better. All the evidence to me suggests the latter.

Source

This was originally presented at an invitational seminar on the White Paper *Twenty-first Century Schools* at the Department for Children, Schools and Families, London, March 2009. It was written with Paul Clarke and Tony Kelly.

References

Acton, T. A. (1980). Educational criteria of success: some problems in the work of Rutter, Maughan, Mortimore and Ouston, *Educational Researcher*, 22(3), 163–173.

Aiken, W. M. (1942). *The Story of the Eight Year Study*. New York: Harper.

Ainscow, M., Hopkins, D., Southworth, G. and West, M. (1994). *Creating the Conditions for School Improvement*. London: David Fulton.

Aitkin, M. and Longford, N. (1986). Statistical modelling issues in school effectiveness studies, *Journal of the Royal Statistical Society, Series A*, 149(1), 1–43.

Alexander, R. (1996). *Other Primary Schools and Ours*. Coventry: University of Warwick Press.

Alexander, R. (2000). *Culture and Pedagogy*. Oxford: Basil Blackwell.

Anghileri, J. (Ed.) (1995). *Children's Mathematical Thinking in the Primary Years: Perspectives on Children's Learning*. London: Cassell.

Asher, S. R. and Dodge, K. A. (1986). Identifying children who are rejected by their peers, *Developmental Psychology*, 22(4), 444–449.

Askew, M. and William, D. (1995). *Recent Research in Mathematics Education 5–16*. London: Office for Standards in Education.

Askew, M., Rhodes, V., Brown, M., William, D. and Johnson, D. (1997). *Effective Teachers of Numeracy: Report of a Study Carried Out for the Teacher Training Agency*. London: King's College London, School of Education.

Barber, M. (1995). Shedding light on the dark side of the moon, *Times Educational Supplement*, 12 May, 3–4.

Barber, M. and Dann, R. (Eds) (1996). *Raising Educational Standards in the Inner Cities*. London: Cassell.

Barkham, P. (2009). Can you really do a GCSE in just three days?, *Guardian, G2 Section*, 13 February, 4–7.

Basic Skills Agency (1997). *International Numeracy Survey: A Comparison of the Basic Numeracy Skills of Adults 16–60 in Seven Countries*. London: Basic Skills Agency.

Berg, L. (1968). *Risinghill*. Harmondsworth: Penguin.

Berman, P. and McLaughlin, M. (1977). *Federal Programs Supporting Educational Change*, Vol. VII: *Factors Affecting Implementation and Continuation*. Santa Monica, CA: Rand.

Bernstein, B. (1968). Education cannot compensate for society, *New Society*, 387, 344–347,

Bodilly, S. (1996). Lessons learned: RAND's formative assessment of NAS's Phase 2 demonstration effort. In S. Stringfield, S. Ross and L. Smith (Eds), *Bold Plans for School Restructuring: The New American Schools Designs*. Mahwah, NJ: Erlbaum.

Boocock, S. (1972). *An Introduction to the Sociology of Learning*. Boston: Houghton Mifflin.

Borg, M. and Gall, W. (1989). *Educational Research*. (5th ed.). New York: Longman.

Borich, G. (1996). *Effective Teaching Methods* (3rd ed.). New York: Macmillan.

Bosker, R. and Scheerens, J. (1997). *The Foundations of School Effectiveness*. Oxford: Pergamon Press.

Brophy, J. (1986). Teaching and learning mathematics: Where research should be going, *Journal for Research in Mathematics Education*, 17(5), 323–346.

Brophy, J. E. and Good, T. L. (1986). Teacher behaviour and student achievement. In M. C. Wittrock (Ed.), *Handbook of Research on Teaching*. New York: Macmillan.

Bynner, J. and Parsons, S. (1997). *Does Numeracy Matter?* London: Basic Skills Agency.

Byrne, D. and Williamson, B. (1975). *The Poverty of Education*. London: Martin Robertson.

Cabinet Office (2008). *Excellence and Fairness: Achieving World-Class Public Services*. London: Cabinet Office.

Central Advisory Council for Education (1959). *15 to 18* (Crowther Report). London: HMSO.

Chanan, G. and Delamont, S. (1975). *Frontiers of Classroom Research*. Slough: NFER Publishing.

Cicourel, A. V. (1968). *The Social Organization of Juvenile Justice*. New York: Wiley.

Cicourel, A. V. and Kitsuse, J. I. (1963). *The Educational Decision-Makers*. New York: Bobbs Merrill.

Clarke, P. (2009). Sustainability and improvement: A problem 'of' education and 'for' education, *Improving Schools*, 12(1), 11–17.

Clegg, A. and Megson, B. (1968). *Children in Distress*. Harmondsworth: Penguin.

Cloward, R. A. and Ohlin, L. E. (1961). *Delinquency and Opportunity*. London: Routledge & Kegan Paul.

Cohen, A. K. (1955). *Delinquent Boys*. Chicago: Free Press.

Coleman, J. S., Campbell, E., Hobson, C., McPartland, J., Mood, A., Weinfeld, F. and York, R. (1966). *Equality of Educational Opportunity*. Washington, DC: US Government Printing Office.

Cook, T. D. and Campbell, D. T. (1979). *Quasi-experimentation: Design and Analysis Issues for Field Settings*. Boston: Houghton Mifflin.

Cooney, T. J. (1994). Research and teacher education: In search of common ground. *Journal for Research in Mathematics Education*, 25(6), 608–636.

Corwin, R. G. (1974). *Education in Crisis*. London: Wiley.

Crandall, D. P., Loucks-Horsley, S., Bauchner, J. E., Schmidt, W. B., Eiseman, J. W., Cox, P. L., Miles, M. B., Huberman, A. M., Taylor, B. L., Goldberg, J. A., Shive, G., Thompson, C. L. and Taylor, J. A. (1982). *People, Policies and Practices: Examining the Chain of School Improvement* (Vols 1–10). Andover, MA: The NETWORK.

Creemers, B. P. M. (1994). *The Effective Classroom*. London: Cassell.

Creemers, B. P. M. and Reezigt, G. J. (1996). School-level conditions affecting the effectiveness of instruction, *School Effectiveness and School Improvement*, 7, 197–228.

Creemers, B. P. M. and Reynolds, D. (1996). Issues and implications of international effectiveness research, *International Journal of Educational Research*, 25(3), 257–266

Creemers, B. P. M., Reynolds, D., Stringfield, S. and Teddlie, C. (1996). World-Class Schools: Some Further Findings. Paper presented at the annual meeting of the American Educational Research Association, New York, NY.

Creemers, B. P. M. and Scheerens, J. (1994). Developments in the educational effectiveness research programme. In R. J. Bosker, B. P. M. Creemers and J. Scheerens (Eds), *Conceptual and Methodological Advances in Educational Effectiveness Research*. Special issue of *International Journal of Educational Research*, 21(2), 125–140.

Croll, P. (1996). Teacher–pupil interaction in the classroom. In P. Croll and N. Hastings (Eds), *Effective Primary Teaching*. London: David Fulton.

Crone, L. J., Lang, M. H., Teddlie, C. and Franklin, B. (1995). Achievement measures of school effectiveness: Comparison of model stability across years, *Applied Measurement in Education*, 8(4), 365–377.

Crone, L. J. and Teddlie, C. (1995). Further examination of teacher behavior in differentially effective schools: Selection and socialisation processes, *Journal of Classroom Interaction*, 30(1), 1–9.

Cuban, L. (1993). Foreword. In C. Teddlie and S. Stringfield, *Schools Make a Difference*. New York: Teachers College.

Cuttance, P. (1982). Reflections on the Rutter ethos: The professional researchers' response to 'Fifteen Thousand Hours: Secondary Schools and Their Effects on Children', *Urban Education*, 16(4), 483–492.

Daly, P. (1991). How large are secondary school effects in Northern Ireland? *School Effectiveness and School Improvement*, 2(4), 305–323.

Datnow, A., Hubbard, L. and Mehan, H. (1998). *Educational Reform Implementation: A Coconstructed Process*. Santa Cruz, CA: University of California, Center for Research on Education, Diversity, and Excellence.

Datnow, A. and Stringfield, S. (2000). Working together for reliable school reform, *Journal of Education for Students Placed at Risk*, 5(1), 183–204.

Davie, R. et al. (1972). *From Birth to Seven*. London: Longman.

Department for Education and Employment (1998). *Numeracy Matters: The Preliminary Report of the Numeracy Task Force*. London: DfEE.

Department of Education and Science (1967). *Children and Their Primary Schools (Plowden Report)*. London: HMSO.

Department of Education and Science (1983) *School Standards and Spending: Statistical Analysis*. London: DES.

Department of Education and Science (1984) *School Standards and Spending: A Further Appreciation*. London: DES.

Durland, M. M. (1996). The Application of Network Analysis to the Study of Differentially Effective Schools. Unpublished doctoral dissertation, Louisiana State University, Baton Rouge, LA.

Durland, M. and Teddlie, C. (1996). A Network Analysis of the Structural Dimensions of Principal Leadership in Differentially Effective Schools. Paper presented at the annual meeting of the American Educational Research Association, New York, NY.

Dyer, H. S. (1968). School factors and equal educational opportunity, *Harvard Educational Review*, 38(1), 38–56.

Edmonds, R. (1979). Effective schools for the urban poor, *Educational Leadership*, 37, 15–27.

Eichenbaum, H. and Otto, T. (1993). LTP and memory: Can we enhance the connection?, *Trends in Neurosciences*, 16(5), 163–164.

Elliott, J. (1996). School effectiveness research and its critics: Alternative visions of schooling, *Cambridge Journal of Education*, 26(2), 199–223.

Evertson, C. M., Anderson, C. W., Anderson, L. M. and Brophy, J. E. (1980). Relationships between classroom behaviors and student outcomes in junior high mathematics and English classes, *American Educational Research Journal*, 17(1), 43–60.

Farrington, D. (1980) Truancy, delinquency, the home and the school. In L. Hersov and I. Berg (Eds), *Out of School*. Chichester: John Wiley.

Fielding, M., Bragg, S., Craig, J., Cunningham, I., Eraut, M., Gillinson, S., Horne, M., Robinson, C. and Thorp, J. (2005). *Factors Influencing the Transfer of Good Practice*. DfES Research Paper 615.

Fields, R. D. (2005). Making memories stick, *Scientific American*, 292, 58–65.

Fitz-Gibbon, C. (1985) A-level results in comprehensive schools: The Coombes Project, year one, *Oxford Review of Education*, 11(1), 43–58.

Fitz-Gibbon, C. (1991). Multilevel modelling in an indicator system. In S. Raudenbush and J. D. Willms (Eds), *Schools, Pupils and Classrooms: International Studies of Schooling from a Multilevel Perspective*. London and New York: Academic Press.

Fitz-Gibbon, C. (1992) School effects at A-level: Genesis of an information system. In D. Reynolds and P. Cuttance (Eds), *School Effectiveness: Research, Policy and Practice*. London: Cassell.

Fitz-Gibbon, C. (1996). *Monitoring Education: Indicators, Quality and Effectiveness*. London, New York: Cassell.

Fitz-Gibbon, C., Tymms, P. B. and Hazlewood, R. D. (1989) Performance indicators and information systems. In D. Reynolds, B. P. M. Creemers and T. Peters (Eds), *School Effectiveness and Improvement: Selected Proceedings of the First ICSEI*. Groningen: RION

Foster, R. G. (2007). The young and wise are late to rise, *The Times Higher Educational Supplement*, 5 January, pp. 16–17.

Frey, U. and Morris, R. G. M. (1998). Weak before strong: Dissociating synaptic tagging and plasticity-factor accounts of late-LTP, *Neuropharmacology*, 37, 545–552.

Fullan, M. G. (1991). *The New Meaning of Educational Change*, London: Cassell.

Fullan, M. G. (1992). *Successful School Improvement*. Ballmoor, Bucks: Open University Press.

Galton, M. (1987). An ORACLE chronicle: A decade of classroom research, *Teaching and Teacher Education*, 3(4), 299–313.

Galton, M. and Croll, P. (1980). Pupil progress in the basic skills. In M. Gallon and B. Simon (Eds), *Progress and Performance in the Primary Classroom*. London: Routledge.

Gath, D. (1972). Child guidance and delinquency in a London borough, *Psychological Medicine*, 2, 185–191.

Goldstein, H. (1980). Critical notice – *Fifteen Thousand Hours* by Rutter et al., *Journal of Child Psychology and Psychiatry*, 21(4), 364–366.

Goldstein, H. (1995). *Multilevel Models in Educational and Social Research: A Revised Edition*. London: Edward Arnold.

Goldstein, H., Rasbash, J., Yang, M., Woodhouse, G., Pan, H., Nuttall, D. and Thomas, S. (1993). A multilevel analysis of school examination results, *Oxford Review of Education*, 19(4), 425–433

Good, T. (1983). Classroom research: A decade of progress, *Educational Psychologist*, 18, 127–144.

Good, T. L. and Brophy, J. E. (1986). School effects. In M. Wittrock (Ed.), *Third Handbook of Research on Teaching*. New York: Macmillan.

Good, T.L., Grouws, D.A., et al. (1983). Active Mathematics Teaching. New York: Longman.

Gray, J. (1981). A competitive edge: Examination results and the probable limits of secondary school effectiveness, Educational Review, 33(1), 25–35.

Gray, J. (1982). Towards effective schools: Problems and progress in British research, British Educational Research Journal, 7(1), 59–79.

Gray, J. (1990). The quality of schooling: Frameworks for judgement, Bristol Journal of Educational Studies, 38(3), 204–233.

Gray, J. and Jesson, D. (1987). Exam results and local authority league tables. In A. Harrison and J. Gretton (Eds), Education and Training UK 1987, 33–41.

Gray, J., Jesson, D., Goldstein, H., Hedger, K. and Nasbash, J. (1995). A multilevel analysis of school improvement: Changes in schools' performance over time, School Effectiveness and Improvement, 6(2), 97–114.

Gray, J., Jesson, D. and Jones, B. (1984). Predicting differences in examination results between local education authorities: Does school organisation matter? Oxford Review of Education, 10(1), 45–68.

Gray, J., Jesson, D. and Jones, B. (1986). The search for a fairer way of comparing schools' examination results, Research Reports in Education, 1(2), 91–122.

Gray, J., Jesson, D. and Sime, N. (1990). Estimating differences in the examination performance of secondary schools in six LEAs: A multilevel approach to school effectiveness, Oxford Review of Education, 16(2), 137–158.

Gray, J., Hopkins, D., Reynolds, D., Wilcox, B., Farrell, S. and Jesson, D. (1999). Improving Schools: Performance and Potential. Buckingham: Open University Press.

Gray, J., McPherson, A.F. and Raffe, D. (1983). Reconstructions of Secondary Education: Theory, Myth and Practice since the War. London: Routledge & Kegan Paul.

Gray, J., Reynolds, D., Fitz-Gibbon, C. and Jesson, D. (1996). Merging Traditions: The Future of Research on School Effectiveness and School Improvement. London: Cassell.

Griffin, G. A. and Barnes, S. (1986). Using research findings to change school and classroom practice: Results of an experimental study, American Educational Research Journal, 23(4), 572–586.

Grosin, L. (1993). School effectiveness research as a point of departure for school evaluation, Scandinavian Journal of Educational Research, 37, 317–330.

Hafner, A. L. (1993). Teaching-method scales and mathematics-class achievement: What works with different outcomes?, American Educational Research Journal, 30(1), 71–94.

Hallinger, P. and Heck, R. H. (1996). Reassessing the principal's role in school effectiveness: A review of the empirical research, 1980–1995, Educational Administration Quarterly, 32(1), 5–44.

Hallinger, P. and Murphy, J. (1986). The social context of effective schools, American Journal of Education, 94, 328–355.

Hannaway, J. and Talbert, J. E. (1993). Bringing context into effective schools research: Urban–suburban differences, Educational Administration Quarterly, 29(2), 164–186.

Hargreaves, D. (1997). Paper presented to the symposium on 'Ineffective Schools', Annual Meeting of the International Congress for School Effectiveness and Improvement, Memphis, TN.

Hargreaves, D. (2004). Working Laterally: How Innovation Networks Make an Education Epidemic. London: DfES Innovation Unit.

Hargreaves, D. H. (1967). Social Relations in a Secondary School. London: Routledge & Kegan Paul.

Hargreaves, D. H. (1972). Interpersonal Relations and Education. London: Routledge & Kegan Paul.

Harris, A. (2006). *Distributed Leadership*. London: Routledge.

Harris, S., Keys, W. and Fernandes, C. (1997). *Third International Mathematics and Science Study (TIMSS), Second National Report, Part 1*. Slough: National Foundation for Educational Research.

High Reliability Schools website: www.highreliabilityschools.co.uk.

Hopkins, D. (Ed.) (1987). *Improving the Quality of Schooling*. London: Falmer Press.

Hopkins, D. (1996). Towards a theory for school improvement. In J. Gray, D. Reynolds and C. Fitz-Gibbon (Eds), *Merging Traditions: The Future of Research on School Effectiveness and School Improvement*. London: Cassell.

Hopkins, D. (2001). *School Improvement for Real*. London: RoutledgeFalmer.

Hopkins, D., Ainscow, M. and West, M. (1994). *School Improvement in an Era of Change*. London: Cassell.

Hopkins, D. and Harris, A. (1997). Understanding the school's capacity for development: Growth states and strategies, *School Leadership and Management*, 17(3), 401–411.

Hopkins, D. and Reynolds, D. (2001). The past, present and future of school improvement: Towards the Third Age, *British Educational Research Journal*, 27(4), 459–475.

Itoh, K., Stevens, B., Schachner, M. and Fields, R. D. (1995). Regulation of expression of the neural cell adhesion molecule L1 by specific patterns of neural impulses, *Science*, 270, 1369–1372.

Jencks, C. S., Smith, M., Ackland, H., Bane, M. J., Cohen, D., Gintis, H., Heyns, B. and Michelson, S. (1972). *Inequality: A Reassessment of the Effect of the Family and Schooling in America*. New York: Basic Books.

Jesson, D. and Gray, J. (1991). Slants and slopes: Using multi-level models to investigate differential school effectiveness and its impact on pupils' examination results, *School Effectiveness and School Improvement*, 2(3), 230–247.

Joyce, B. and Weil, M. (1996). *Models of teaching* (5th ed.). Boston: Allyn & Bacon.

Kelley, P. (2007). *Making Minds*. London: Routledge.

Kelly, A. (2009). Education Choice and Schooling Theory: Adapting Sen's Early Work on 'Capability' to Choice and Sustainability. Unpublished paper.

King, R. (1983). *The Sociology of School Organisation*. London: Methuen.

Kitsuse, J. I. and Cicourel, A. V. (1963). A note on the use of official statistics, *Social Problems*, 11, 131.

Kochan, S. E., Tashakkori, A. and Teddlie, C. (1996). You can't judge a high school by test data alone: Constructing an alternative indicator of secondary school effectiveness. Paper presented at the annual meeting of the American Educational Research Association, New York, NY.

Lampert, M. (1988). What can research on teacher education tell us about improving quality in mathematics education?, *Teaching and Teacher Education*, 4(2), 157–170.

Lang, M. H. (1991). Effective School Status: A Methodological Study of Classification Consistency. Unpublished doctoral dissertation, Louisiana State University, Baton Rouge.

Lang, M. H., Teddlie, C. and Oescher, J. (1992). The effect that varying the test mode had on school effectiveness ratings. Paper presented at the annual meeting of the American Educational Research Association, San Francisco.

LaPorte, T. and Consolini, P. (1991). Working in practice but not in theory: Theoretical challenges of high-reliability organizations, *Journal of Public Administration Research and Theory*, 1(1), 19–48.

Launder, H. (2000). The dilemmas of comparative research and policy importation, *British Journal of Sociology of Education*, 21 (3), 465–475.

Leadbetter, C. (2008). *What's Next? 21 Ideas for 21st Century Learning*. London: The Innovation Unit.

Levine, D. U. and Lezotte, L. W. (1990). *Unusually Effective Schools: A Review and Analysis of Research and Practice*. Madison, WI: National Center for Effective Schools Research and Development.

Little, A. *et al.* (1971). Do small classes help a pupil?, *New Society*, 18(473), 769–771.

McDill, E. L. and Rigsby, L. C. (1973). *Structure and Process in Secondary Schools*. Baltimore. MD: Johns Hopkins Press.

McGaugh, J. L. (2000). Memory: A century of consolidation, *Science*, 287(5451), 248–252.

McLaughlin, M. (1991). The Rand Change Agent Study revisited: Macro perspectives and micro realities, *Educational Researcher*, 19(9), 11–16.

Maden, M. and Hillman, J. (1996). *Success against the Odds*. London: Routledge.

Mintzberg, H. (1979). *The Structuring of Organizations*. Englewood Cliffs, NJ: Prentice Hall.

Moreno, J. L. (1953). *Who Will Survive?* New York: Beacon.

Mortimore, P. (1986). *The Junior School Project: A Summary of the Main Report*. London: Inner London Education Authority.

Mortimore, P. (1991). School effectiveness research: Which way at the crossroads?, *School Effectiveness and School Improvement*, 2(3), 213–229.

Mortimore, P. and Byford, D. (1981). Monitoring examination results within an LEA. In I. Plewis, J. Gray, K. Fogelman, P. Mortimore and D. Byford (Eds), *Publishing School Examination Results: A Discussion*. London: Institute of Education.

Mortimore, P., Sammons, P., Stoll, L., Lewis, D. and Ecob, R. (1988). *School Matters: The Junior Years*. Somerset: Open Books. (Reprinted in 1995 by Paul Chapman, London.)

Muijs, D. and Reynolds, D. (2000a). School effectiveness and teacher effectiveness: Some preliminary findings from the evaluation of the Mathematics Enhancement Programme, *School Effectiveness and School Improvement*, 11(2), 323–327.

Muijs, D. and Reynolds, D. (2000b). Effective Mathematics Teaching: Year 2 of a Research Project. Paper presented at the International Conference on School Effectiveness and School Improvement, Hong Kong, 8 January.

Muijs, R. D. and Reynolds, D. (2001). *Effective Teaching*. London: Sage Publishing.

Muijs, D. and Reynolds, D. (2003). Student background and teacher effects on achievement and attainment in mathematics, *Educational Research and Evaluation*, 9(1), 289–313.

Muijs, D. and Reynolds, D. (2005). *Effective Teaching: Research and Practice*. London: Paul Chapman.

Murphy, J. (1992). School effectiveness and school restructuring: Contributions to educational improvement, *School Effectiveness and School Improvement*, 3(2), 90–109.

Musgrove, F. (1981). *School and the Social Order*. Chichester: Wiley.

Myers, K. (1994). Why schools in difficulty may find the research on school effectiveness and school improvement inappropriate for their needs. Unpublished EdD assignment, University of Bristol.

Myers, K. (1996). *School Improvement in Practice: Schools Make a Difference Project*. London: Falmer Press.

National College for School Leadership (NCSL) (2006). *Narrowing the Gap: Reducing Within School Variation in Pupil Outcomes*. Nottingham: NCSL.

Nicolson, R., Fawcett, A. and Dean, P. (2001). Developmental dyslexia: The cerebellar deficit hypothesis, *Trends in Neuroscience*, 24(9), 508–511.

Nicolson, R. and Reynolds, D. (2003). Science, sense and synergy: Response to commentators, *Dyslexia*, 9(2), 167–176.

Numeracy Task Force (1998). *Numeracy Matters: The Preliminary Report of the Numeracy Task Force*. London: DfEE.

Nunes, T. and Bryant, P. (1996). *Children Doing Mathematics*. Oxford: Blackwell.

Nuttall, D. L., Goldstein, H., Prosser, R. and Rasbash, J. (1989). Differential school effectiveness. In B. P. M. Creemers and J. Scheerens (Eds), *Developments in School Effectiveness Research. Special Issue of International Journal of Educational, Research*, 13(7), 769–776.

O'Connor, M., Hales, E., Davies, G. and Tomlinson, S. (1999). *Hackney Downs*. London: Cassell.

Owens, R. G. (1987). *Organisational Behaviour in Education* (3rd ed.). Englewood Cliffs, NJ: Prentice Hall.

Phillipson, C. M. (1971). Juvenile delinquency and the school. In W. G. Carson and P. Wiles (Eds), *Crime and Delinquency in Britain*. London: Martin Robertson.

Pinnell, G. (1989). Reading Recovery: Helping at-risk children learn to read, *Elementary School Journal*, 90, 161–182.

Plowden Report (Central Advisory Committee for Education) (1967). *Children and Their Primary Schools*. London: HMSO.

Power, M. J. (1967). Delinquent schools, *New Society*, 19 October, 542–543.

Power, M. J. (1972). Neighbourhood, school and juveniles before the courts, *British Journal of Criminology*, 12, 111–132.

Ralph, J. H. and Fennessey, J. (1983). Science or reform: Some questions about the effective schools model, *Phi Delta Kappan*, 64(10), 689–694.

Raven, J. C. (1960). *Guide to the Standard Progressive Matrices*. London: H. K. Lewis.

Resnick, L. B. and Resnick, D. P. (1992). Assessing the thinking curriculum. In B. R. Gifford and M. C. O'Connor (Eds), *Changing Assessment: Alternative Views of Aptitude, Achievement and Instruction*. Boston: Kluwer Academic Publishers.

Reynolds, D. (1976a). The delinquent school. In M. Hammersley and P. Woods (Eds), *The Process of Schooling*. London: Routledge & Kegan Paul.

Reynolds, D. (1976b). When teachers and pupils refuse a truce. In G. Mungham and G. Pearson (Eds), *Working-Class Youth Culture*. London: Routledge & Kegan Paul.

Reynolds, D. (1991). Changing ineffective schools. In M. Ainscow (Ed.), *Effective Schools for All*. London: David Fulton.

Reynolds, D. (1994). School effectiveness and quality in education. In P. Ribbins and E. Burridge (Eds), *Improving Education*. London: Cassell.

Reynolds, D. (1996a). Turning around ineffective schools: Some evidence and some speculations. In J. Gray, D. Reynolds, C. Fitz-Gibbon and D. Jesson (Eds.), *Merging Traditions: The Future of Research on School Effectiveness and School Improvement*. London: Cassell.

Reynolds, D. (1996b). The effective school: An inaugural lecture, *Evaluation and Research in Education*, 9(2), 57–73.

Reynolds, D. (1996c). The truth, the whole-class truth, *Times Educational Supplement*, 7 June, 2.

Reynolds, D. (1999). School effectiveness, school improvement and contemporary educational policies. In J. Demaine (Ed.), *Contemporary Educational Policy and Politics*. London: Macmillan.

Reynolds, D. (2004) Within-school variation: Its extent and causes. A background paper for DfES, presented to the National Within School Variation Conference, July 2004.

Reynolds, D. (2007). *Schools Learning from Their Best: The Within School Variation Project*. Nottingham: NCSL.

Reynolds, D., Bollen, R., Creemers, B., Hopkins, D., Stoll, L. and Lagerweij, N. (1996). *Making Good Schools: Linking School Effectiveness and School Improvement*. London: Routledge.

Reynolds, D., Creemers, B. P. M., Stringfield, S. and Teddlie, C. (1991). *International School Effects Research*. Taiwan: Kaohsiung Normal University.

Reynolds, D., Creemers, B. P. M., Stringfield, S., Teddlie, C. and Schaffer, G. (2002). *World-Class Schools: International Perspectives in School Effectiveness*. London: RoutledgeFalmer.

Reynolds, D., Creemers, B. P. M., Stringfield, S., Teddlie, C., Schaffer, E. and Nesselrodt, P. S. (1994). *Advances in School Effectiveness Research and Practice*. Oxford: Pergamon Press.

Reynolds, D. and Cuttance, P. (1992). *School Effectiveness: Research, Policy and Practice*. London: Cassell.

Reynolds, D., Davie, R. and Phillips, D. (1989). The Cardiff programme: An effective school improvement programme based on school effectiveness research, *International Journal of Educational Research*, 13(7), 800–814.

Reynolds, D. and Farrell, S. (1996). *Worlds Apart? A Review of International Studies of Educational Achievement Involving England*. London: HMSO for OFSTED.

Reynolds, D., Hopkins, D. and Stoll, L. (1993). Linking school effectiveness knowledge and school improvement practice: Towards synergy, *School Effectiveness and School Improvement*, 4(1), 37–58.

Reynolds, D. and Muijs, D. (1999a). *Numeracy: An Annotated Bibliography for Schools and Colleges*. London: DfEE.

Reynolds, D. and Muijs, R. D. (1999b). The effective teaching of mathematics: A review of research, *School Leadership and Management*, 19(3), 273–288.

Reynolds, D. and Muijs, R. D. (1999c). Numeracy matters: Contemporary policy issues in the teaching of mathematics. In I. Thompson (Ed.), *Issues in Teaching Numeracy in Primary Schools*. Ballmoor, Bucks: Open University Press.

Reynolds, D. and Murgatroyd, S. (1974). Being absent from school, *British Journal of Law and Society*, 1(1), 78–81.

Reynolds, D. and Nicolson, R. (2006). Follow-up of an exercise-based treatment for children with reading difficulties, *Dyslexia*, 13, 78–96.

Reynolds, D., Nicolson, R. and Hambly, H. (2003) Evaluation of an exercise-based treatment for children with reading difficulties, *Dyslexia*, 9, 48–71.

Reynolds, D. and Packer, A. (1992). School effectiveness and school improvement in the 1990s. In D. Reynolds and P. Cuttance (Eds), *School Effectiveness: Research, Policy and Practice*. London: Cassell.

Reynolds, D., Sammons, P., Stoll, L., Barber, B. and Hillman, J. (1996). School effectiveness and school improvement in the United Kingdom, *School Effectiveness and School Improvement*, 7(2), 133–158.

Reynolds, D. and Sullivan, M. (1981). The effects of school: A radical faith re-stated. In B. Gilham (Ed.), *Problem Behaviour in the Secondary School*. London: Croom Helm.

Reynolds, D., Sullivan, M. and Murgatroyd, S. J. (1987). *The Comprehensive Experiment*. Lewes: Falmer Press.

Reynolds, D. and Teddlie, C. (1996). World-class schools: Some further findings. Paper presented to the Annual Meeting of the American Educational Research Association, New York.

Roberts, K. (1993). *New Challenges to Understanding Organizations*. New York: Macmillan.

Rogers, E. M. and Kincaid, D. L. (1980). *Communication Networks: Toward a New Paradigm for Research*. New York: Macmillan.

Rosenholtz, S. (1989). *Teachers' Workplace: The Social Organization of Schools*. New York: Longman.

Rowan, B. (1984). Shamanistic rituals in effective schools, *Issues in Education*, 2, 76–87.

Rowan, B., Bossert, S. T. and Dwyer, D. C. (1983). Research on effective schools: A cautionary note, *Educational Researcher*, 12(4), 24–31.

Rutter, M. (1973). Why are London children so disturbed?, *Proceedings of the Royal Society of Medicine*, 66, 1221–1225.

Rutter, M. (1983). School effects on pupil progress: Findings and policy implications, *Child Development*, 54(1), 1–29.

Rutter, M., Maughan, B., Mortimore, P. and Ouston, J. with Smith, A. (1979). *Fifteen Thousand Hours: Secondary Schools and Their Effects on Children*. London: Open Books and Cambridge, MA: Harvard University Press.

Sammons, P., Hillman, J. and Mortimore, P. (1995). *Key Characteristics of Effective Schools: A Review of School Effectiveness Research*. London: OFSTED.

Sammons, P., Mortimore, P. and Thomas, S. (1996). Do schools perform consistently across outcomes and areas? In J. Gray, D. Reynolds, C. Fitz-Gibbon and D. Jesson (Eds), *Merging Traditions: The Future of Research on School Effectiveness and School Improvement*. London: Cassell.

Sammons, P., Nuttall, D. and Cuttance, P. (1993). Differential school effectiveness: Results from a re-analysis of the Inner London Education Authority's junior school project data, *British Educational Research Journal*, 19(4), 381–405.

Sammons, P., Thomas, S. and Mortimore, P. (1996). Differential school effectiveness: Departmental variations in GCSE attainment. Paper presented at the School Effectiveness and Improvement Symposium of the Annual Meeting of the American Educational Research Association, New York, 8 April.

Sammons, P., Thomas, S. and Mortimore, P. (1997). *Forging Links: Effective Schools and Effective Departments*. London: Paul Chapman.

Sarason, S. (1981). *The Culture of the School and the Problem of Educational Change*. Boston: Allyn & Bacon.

Schaffer, E. G., Muijs, R. D., Kitson, C. and Reynolds, D. (1998). *Mathematics Enhancement Classroom Observation Record*. Newcastle upon Tyne: Educational Effectiveness and Improvement Centre.

Scheerens, J. (1992). *Effective Schooling: Research, Theory and Practice*. London: Cassell.

Scheerens, J. (1993). Basic school effectiveness research: Items for a research agenda, *School Effectiveness and School Improvement*, 4(1), 17–36.

Scheerens, J. and Bosker, R. (1997). *The Foundations of School Effectiveness*. Oxford: Pergamon Press.

Scheerens, J. and Creemers, B. P. M. (1989). Towards a more comprehensive conceptualisation of school effectiveness. In B. P. M. Creemers, T. Peters and D. Reynolds (Eds), *School Effectiveness and School Improvement: Proceedings of the Second International Congress*. Amsterdam: Swets & Zeitlinger.

Scheerens, J., and Creemers, B. P. M. (1996). School effectiveness in the Netherlands: The modest influence of a research programme, *School Effectiveness and School Improvement*, 7, 181–195.

School Effectiveness and School Improvement. *Special Issue on Criticisms of School Effectiveness Research*, 12(1).

Secada, W. G. (1992). Race, ethnicity, social class, language, and achievement in mathematics. In D. A. Grouws (Ed.), *Handbook of Research on Mathematics Teaching and Learning*. New York: Macmillan.

Senge, P. (2006). *Presence: Human Purpose as the Field of the Future.* Cambridge, MA: Society for Organizational Learning

Shrivastava, P. (1986). *Bhopal.* New York: Basic Books.

Silver, E. A. (1987). Foundations of cognitive theory and research for mathematics problem-solving instruction. In A. H. Schoenfeld (Ed.), *Cognitive Science and Mathematics Education.* Hillsdale, NJ: Lawrence Erlbaum.

Sizer, T. R. (1984). *Horace's Compromise: The Dilemma of the American High School.* Boston: Houghton Mifflin.

Slater, R. O. and Teddlie, C. (1992). Toward a theory of school effectiveness and leadership, *School Effectiveness and School Improvement,* 3(4), 247–257.

Slavin, R. (1996). *Education for All.* Lisse: Swets & Zeitlinger.

Slavin, R. E., Madden, N. A., Dolan, L. J., Wasik, B. A., Ross, S., Smith, L. and Dianda, M. (1996). Success for All: A summary of research, *Journal of Education for Students Placed at Risk,* 1(1), 41–76.

Slavin, R., Madden, N., Karweit, N., Livermon, B. and Dolan, L. (1990). Success for All: First-year outcomes of a comprehensive plan for reforming urban education, *American Education Research Journal,* 27(2), 255–278.

Smith, D. J. and Tomlinson, S. (1989). *The School Effect: A Study of Multi-racial Comprehensives.* London: Policy Studies Institute.

Southworth, G. (2000). How primary schools learn, *Education,* 15(3), 275–291.

Stallings, J., and Kaskowitz, D. (1974). *Follow-through Classroom Observation Evaluation, 1972–1973.* Menlo Park, CA: Stanford Research Institute.

Stallings, N. A., Weisler, S. W., Chase, C. H., Feinstein, M. H., Garfield, J. L. and Risland, E. L. (1995). *Cognitive Psychology.* Cambridge, MA: MIT Press.

Steedman, J. (1980). *Progress in Secondary Schools.* London: National Children's Bureau.

Steedman, J. (1983). *Examination Results in Selective and Non-Selective Schools.* London: National Children's Bureau.

Stigler, J. and Hiebert, J. (1999). *The Teaching Gap.* New York: Free Press.

Stoll, L. (1995). The Complexity and Challenge of Ineffective Schools. Paper presented at the European Conference on Educational Research Association, Bath, UK.

Stoll, L. and Fink, D. (1996). *Changing Our Schools.* Buckingham: Open University Press.

Stoll, L. and Myers, K. (Eds) (1998). *No Quick Fixes: Perspectives on Schools in Difficulty.* Lewes: Falmer Press.

Stoll, L., Myers, K. and Reynolds, D. (1996). Understanding Ineffectiveness. Paper presented at the annual meeting of the American Educational Research Association, New York.

Stringfield, S. (1994). A model of elementary school effects. In D. Reynolds, B. P. M. Creemers, P. S. Nesselrodt, E. C. Schaffer, S. Stringfield and C. Teddlie (Eds), *Advances in School Effectiveness Research and Practice.* Oxford: Pergamon.

Stringfield, S. (1995). Attempts to enhance students' learning: A search for valid programs and highly reliable implementation techniques, *School Effectiveness and School Improvement,* 6(1), 67–96.

Stringfield, S. (1998). An anatomy of ineffectiveness. In L. Stoll and K. Myers (Eds), *No Quick Fixes: Perspectives on Schools in Difficulties.* London: Falmer.

Stringfield, S., Millsap, M. A., Herman, R., Yoder, N., Brigham, N., Nesselrodt, P., Schaffer, E., Karweit, N., Levin, M. and Stevens, R. (with Gamse, B., Puma, M., Rosenblum, S., Beaumont, J., Randall, B. and Smith, L.) (1997). *Urban and Suburban/Rural Special Strategies for Educating Disadvantaged Children. Final Report.* Washington, DC: US Department of Education.

Stringfield, S., Reynolds, D. and Schaffer, E. (2008). Improving secondary schools' academic achievement through a focus on reform reliability: Four- and nine-year finding from the High Reliability Schools Project, *School Effectiveness and School Improvement*, 19(4), 409–428.

Stringfield, S. and Teddlie, C. (1991). Observers as predictors of schools' multi-year outlier status, *Elementary School Journal*, 91(4), 357–376.

Teddlie, C. (1996). *School Effectiveness Indices: East Baton Rouge Parish Public Schools, Academic Years 1991–92, 1992–93, 1993–94*. Baton Rouge, LA: Louisiana State University, College of Education.

Teddlie, C. and Kochan, S. (1991). Evaluation of a troubled high school: Methods, results, and implications. Paper presented at the annual meeting of the American Education Research Association, Chicago.

Teddlie, C., Lang, M. H. and Oescher, J. (1995). The masking of the delivery of educational services to lower achieving students, *Urban Education*, 30(2), 125–149.

Teddlie, C. and Reynolds, D. (2000). *The International Handbook of School Effectiveness Research*. London: Falmer Press.

Teddlie, C. and Reynolds, D. (2001). Countering the critics: Responses to recent criticism of school effectiveness research, *School Effectiveness and School Improvement*, 12(1), 41–82.

Teddlie, C. and Stringfield, S. (1993). *Schools Make a Difference: Lessons Learned from a Ten-Year Study of School Effects*. New York: Teachers College Press.

Thrupp, M. (2002). Why 'meddling' is necessary: A response to Teddlie, Reynolds, Townsend, Scheerens, Bosker and Creemers, *School Effectiveness and School Improvement*, 13(1), 1–14.

Tyerman, H. J. (1958). A research into truancy, *British Journal of Educational Psychology*, 28, 217–225.

Tymms, P., Merrill, C. and Henderson, B. (1997). The first year at school: a quantitative investigation of the attainment and progress of pupils, *Educational Research and Evaluation*, 3(3), 101–118.

Tyne, T. F. and Geary, W. (1980). Patterns of acceptance–rejection among male–female elementary school students, *Child Study Journal*, 10, 179–190.

van de Grift, W. (1989). Self perceptions of educational leadership and mean pupil achievements. In D. Reynolds, B. P. M. Creemers and T. Peters (Eds), *School Effectiveness and School Improvement: Selected Proceedings of the First International Congress for School Effectiveness*. Groningen, Netherlands: RION.

van de Grift, W. (1990). Educational leadership and academic achievement in secondary education, *School Effectiveness and School Improvement*, 1(1), 26–40.

Walberg, H. J. (1986). Syntheses of research on teaching. In M. C. Wittrock (Ed.), *Handbook of Research on Teaching*. New York: Macmillan.

Webb, E. J., Campbell, D. T., Schwartz, R. D., Sechrest, L. and Grove, J. B. (1981). *Nonreactive Measures in the Social Sciences*. Boston: Houghton Mifflin.

Werthman, C. (1967). The function of social definitions in the development of delinquent careers. In *Juvenile Delinquency and Youth Crime*. Washington, DC: US Government Printing Office.

Westerhof, K. J. (1992). On the effectiveness of teaching: Direct versus indirect instruction, *School Effectiveness and School Improvement*, 3, 204–215.

Willms, J. D. (1985). The balance thesis: Contextual effects of ability on pupils' 'O' grade examination results, *Oxford Review of Education*, 11(1), 33–41.

Willms, J. D. (1986). Social class segregation and its relationship to pupils' examination results in Scotland, *American Sociological Review*, 51(2), 224–241.

Willms, J. D. (1987). Differences between Scottish Education Authorities in their examination attainments, *Oxford Review of Education*, 13, 211–237.

Willms, J. D. and Cuttance, P. (1985). School effects in Scottish secondary schools, *British Journal of Sociology of Education*, 6(3), 289–305.

Wimpelberg, R., Teddlie, C. and Stringfield, S. (1989). Sensitivity to context: The past and future of effective schools research, *Educational Administration Quarterly*, 25(1), 82–107.

Woodhouse, G. and Goldstein, H. (1988). Educational performance indicators and LEA league tables, *Oxford Review of Education*, 14(3), 301–320.

Index

Lightning Source UK Ltd.
Milton Keynes UK
UKOW032345250313

208156UK00003B/96/P